CONTEMPORARY
I·S·M·S

CONTEMPORARY
I·S·M·S
a political economy perspective

CHARLES ALLAN McCOY

Lehigh University
in collaboration with
ELAINE McCOY
Lafayette College

Franklin Watts
New York   London   Toronto   Sydney

To Allan, Graeme, Ian, and Sarah

Library of Congress Cataloging in Publication Data

McCoy, Charles Allan, 1920–
        Contemporary isms :
    a political economy perspective.

  Bibliography: p.
  Includes index.
        1. Comparative government.
        2. Comparative economics.
        I. McCoy, Elaine. II. Title.
JF51.M446   320.3   81-16274
ISBN 0-531-05639-2   AACR2

Franklin Watts
730 Fifth Avenue
New York, New York 10019

PREFACE

Our hope for this work is twofold. First, we hope that it may lead to a better understanding both of Marxism and the Soviet Union and of Liberalism and the United States and, thereby, mitigate against the emerging revival of the cold war with its all too real possibility of nuclear destruction.

Second, we hope that this work may contribute to the maintenance of the struggle for justice and equality in which all humanity is engaged, whether knowingly or not. While we are not optimistic about the short-run future, particularly with respect to the human misery with which the most vulnerable and innocent people will be burdened in the decades ahead, we insist upon a recognition of the certain knowledge that people shape their own history and that, in the long run, humanity renews its struggle to become ever more truly emancipated, ever more truly human.

Charles Allan McCoy
Elaine McCoy

CONTENTS

2

COMMUNISM: THE CASE OF THE SOVIET UNION
51

3

LIBERALISM
107

4

LIBERALISM: THE CASE OF THE UNITED STATES
155

5

MARKET SOCIALISM
209

TABLES

FIGURES

INTRODUCTION

The underlying power struggle in the contemporary industrial world is the struggle for control of the productive forces of the nation. Politics is economics, and economics is politics.

Ideology refers to the significance of ideas in directing and justifying the manner in which the economy is managed and in rationalizing social organization. In the contemporary world the economies of large industrial nations are managed primarily in one of two ways. On one side is capitalism, which utilizes *markets* as the essential technique of organization. A competing system, that of communism, organizes the economy through *authority* or command systems. It needs to be recognized that all market systems utilize authority, indeed could not exist without authority, and that authoritative systems use markets, either overtly or covertly. The fact that both systems use markets and authority should not blur the basic distinction between developed industrial nations, i.e., fundamental difference in the organization of economic production and distribution.

The ideology that justifies, defends, and prescribes the *authoritative* mode is communism. It is the ideology that throughout the world is the chief challenger to capitalism. Liberalism, as an ideology, has served a similar function in the justification, defense, and prescription of a *market* mode of organization, or capitalism.

The great support and success of the liberal ideology

stemmed from the rationalization it provided the bourgeoisie in their extended struggle with the landed aristocracy during the period when capitalism was established as the dominant mode of economic organization throughout the world. Liberalism's period of ascendancy lasted from the decline of feudalism to the middle of the nineteenth century. Since that time liberalism has been engaged in a rearguard action, and appears to be particularly hard-pressed at present in its attempt to defend and justify capitalism.

It is extremely important that these monumental ideological forces be understood. Analysis must focus on the impact of ideologies in the real world. That ideologies influence human behavior is beyond doubt. They are of extreme importance in determining such vital questions as war or peace, growth or stagnation, harmony or discord, even justice or injustice. What is needed is an examination and analysis of these ideologies, not in terms of moralistic judgment, but in terms of their consequences in the real world of politics and economics.

This volume undertakes such an analysis, an analysis which, while certainly not disinterested, is committed to exploring ideologies not as abstractions but, without favor, in terms of their concrete impact in the real world.

The book is organized in six chapters. Chapter 1, the Theoretical Origins of Communism, develops the intellectual and theoretical foundation of communism. We draw extensively upon the writings of Karl Marx and Lenin. Contemporary and neo-Marxian analyses are used when they seem appropriate to a clearer understanding of communism. It seems axiomatic that an ideology remains only an abstraction until it is observed in a concrete situation. It is impossible to understand communism or liberalism until the practice of these ideologies is analyzed.

The second chapter, Communism: The Case of the Soviet Union, continues the analysis of communism through an examination of the Soviet Union, which is taken as the prototype of communism. The central focus of this chapter is the examination of the extent to which communist ideology has been realized in the Soviet Union. It is, of course, recognized that in no case does a theory, an intellectual abstraction, correspond totally to the real world. There are no "perfect fits." The correspondence of the ideology of communism and the reality of the Soviet Union as a system based on authoritative organization does, however, enable us to understand more fully both the abstract theory of communism and the reality of the Soviet Union.

The third chapter, Liberalism, describes and analyzes the lengthy development of liberal ideology. It traces that development from the writings of Thomas Hobbes in the seventeenth century to such recent contributors as John Maynard Keynes. It is not surprising that liberalism, having developed over such a long period of time and having been shaped by so many thinkers, is a less coherent and unified ideology than communism. Nevertheless, liberalism has served to justify and direct capitalist development with great vigor in the real world of capitalist nations.

The fourth chapter, Liberalism: The Case of the United States, provides an analysis of the United States as the hegemonic model of capitalist nations. The United States occupies a distinctive place among capitalist nations. It has compromised less than others with socialist and other forms of social organization. More important, the United States' influence among capitalist nations is so pervasive and powerful that capitalism, at least in its present form, could not continue if the hegemonic stature of the United States were to cease. An analogous relationship could be drawn between the situation of Britain and the development of capitalism during the nineteenth century and the relationship of the United States to mature capitalism during the comtemporary era. It will be seen that in the United States liberalism has shaped the history, politics, and economics of this leader of the capitalist world. Developed in earlier centuries to serve the interests of a newly emerging capitalist class, liberalism has continued to shape and preserve the interests of that same class to the present day. The early success of liberalism was partly due to providing the capitalist elite with its élan and legitimating their power through authority, but liberalism seems in the current scene to be losing this prime functional characteristic.

Chapters 5 and 6 examine two additional ideologies, market socialism and fascism. These ideologies are treated as derivative from the two main ideologies and from the circumstances of economic performance, described in the earlier chapters. Chapter 5 does not provide a case study of socialist ideology, for there exists no state system which can serve as a complete model. Our model is, therefore, one that examines a series of socialist practices found in such countries as Sweden and Yugoslavia, which taken together form a composite of socialist policies and structures. Moreover, this composite melds a number of "communist" and "liberal" prerequisites. Market socialism is treated as a mixed and derivative system.

The final chapter examines a system which is similarly derivative but, in contrast to market socialism, retrogressive. Fascism is presented not as an unfortunate or aberrant circumstance of past history, but as a potential development in any class society faced with an economic crisis that is deep and extensive enough to threaten the class rule of an economic and political elite.

CONTEMPORARY
I·S·M·S

.1.
THE THEORETICAL ORIGINS OF COMMUNISM

The term *communism* has been deliberately selected for this chapter in order to distinguish this ideology from other variants of socialism. By selecting this term it is our intention to underscore the militant, noncompromising character of the ideology—an ideology which proudly asserts its scientific and rational base. It most directly traces its lineage to Karl Marx and nearly as directly to Vladimir Ilyich Ulyanov, better known as Lenin. Its prototype in the contemporary world is the USSR, with its commitment to rational economic planning and authoritative allocation of goods and services by the state.

In any discussion of communism or socialism, one person stands out as the most dominant figure. That person is, of course, Karl Marx. Of the three giants of the nineteenth century—Darwin, Marx, and John Stuart Mill—it seems safe to say that Marx has been the most significant in shaping world history. Regardless of the nature of one's political sympathies, a recognition of Marx's contribution to politics is imperative for an understanding of communism and, indeed, of the contemporary world. His contribution remains unchallenged. Psychologists drawing from his early writings view him as a great humanist. Economists have come to recognize Marx's genius in the development of a macromodel of economics long before John Maynard Keynes or the development of current national accounts. Philosophers and historical and political theorists under-

1

stand the explanatory power of Marx's method for delineating the operation of capitalism and for comprehending the nature of social change. While there has been what almost amounts to a conspiracy to denigrate Marx's contribution to intellectual history, it has increasingly failed as the study of Marx's ideas and method has gained a wider audience and a fairer hearing. We hope that this present volume can contribute to that development.

Although there is only one Marx, for the purpose of analysis this work will concentrate on three aspects of Marx's ideas. First, Marx's views on the nature of humanity and his concern for humankind's alienation from their work and themselves will be examined. Emphasis will be on the early writings of Marx, sometimes referred to as the "humanistic Marx." Second, there is the scientific and economic Marx of *Capital*. Third, there is the historic and philosophic Marx. The present work will be less an exegesis of the writings of Marx, however, than an interpretive essay.

THE HUMANISTIC MARX

In Marx's early writings (which were not discovered until nearly fifty years after his death), Marx developed in a rather abstract manner his views on humanity and the ends of human life. During this period, the influence of Hegel was notable.

During Marx's formative years Georg Wilhelm Friedrich Hegel (1770–1831) dominated German philosophy. Hegel's most lasting influence on the development of philosophy lies in his concept of the dialectic. In Hegel's search for the true nature of reality he focused his attention on the nature of change. He observed that nothing is as it appears to be but is always in a state of unrest, of becoming something different from what it was. He regarded this process of change as occurring not in a linear fashion but in a dialectical one, that is, by a process of negating what exists and then arriving at a new synthesis that is both more real and more rational than what preceded it. Hegel's *Philosophy of History,* in which he stated his view of historical change, had a profound influence on Marx, though Marx came to reject Hegel's idealism as too abstract, with its use of such concepts as the Absolute Spirit as the guiding force of history.

Marx joined other young scholars in what was to become a diffuse group known as the "left Hegelians." Their critique of Hegel, whose ideas they considered too remote from real-life experience, in turn shaped Marx's early thinking. Among those students of Hegel, one who greatly influenced Marx was Ludwig Feuerbach, and it was in Marx's reply to Feuerbach, the *Theses on Feuerbach,* that Marx's early ideas took their most definitive form.

Marx regarded humanity as a species-being. By that he meant that people, as distinct from animals, focus their consciousness on the entire species, and through the species-activity, labor, society "humanizes" itself. The human activity of labor is, indeed, the way in which people realize their human, as distinct from animal, nature. People are not, according to Marx, passive beings seeking only happiness, as they were thought to be by utilitarian writers of the nineteenth century. Rather, people are "makers"—achievers who realize their humanity through their labor. Not only does humankind change the material world through its labor, but people also change themselves. Labor, for Marx, plays the same significant role that will does for Kant and reason for Plato.

As Marx states in the 1844 manuscripts:

Thus it is in the working over the objective world that man first really affirms himself as species-being. This production is his active species-life. Through it nature appears as his work and his reality. The object of work is therefore the objectification of the species-life of man; for he duplicates himself not only intellectually, in his mind, but also actively in reality and thus can look at his image in a world he has created.[1]

That Marx never abandoned this central belief in the absolute essential quality of labor for people remains evident when two decades later Marx expressed the same idea in even more concrete terms:

Labor is, in the first place, a process in which both man and Nature participate, and in which man of his own accord starts, regulates, and controls the material reactions between himself and Nature. He opposes himself to Nature as one of her own forces, setting in motion arms and legs, head and hands, the natural forces of his body, in order to appropriate Nature's productions in a form adapted to his own wants. By thus acting on the external world and changing it, he at the same time changes his own nature.[2]

Marx's concern for people's humanity and its relation to their work remained always his central concern. It was Marx's understanding of the creative nature of human labor that led him to reject capitalism, for, in Marx's view, human labor under capitalism is alienated labor, and therefore people's humanity—their very existence as human beings rather than as beasts—is threatened, if not destroyed.

It is important to consider how capitalism is alienating. The truly human character of labor is that a product exists first as an idea before it is made by humans. Under capitalism this union between the idea and the object is broken. This idea-object unity is peculiarly human. In clarifying this distinctive human quality, Marx relies on the fact that human work is conscious and purposive whereas the work of other animals is merely instinctual. Thus labor, in its human form, was called intelligent action by Aristotle, who states: "Art indeed consists in the conception of the result to be produced before its realization in the material."[3]

The separation of the idea of what is to be made from the process of making it has resulted in an alienation which is widespread in the modern industrial world. Within the capitalist world, this alienation is, according to a Marxian perspective, at the root of most of the social ills that plague society. Although the assembly-line worker is, in recent commentary, the archetype of the alienated worker, the lot of the typist in the insurance company pool is not much better. In fact, Harry Braverman in his *Labor and Monopoly Capital* argues persuasively that almost all modern work, even that employing workers with professional training, is repetitive, boring, and alienating in character.[4] This alienation takes four distinct forms. First, the worker is alienated from the product of his or her work. The craftsmen of old may sell their products but, in a sense, they are always the craftsmen's. For example, to this day, regardless of who owns them, Paul Revere's silver candlesticks are renowned as the product of his work. They remain expressions of his creativity, of his unique human qualities. But who can tell one Pinto from another? How can the worker on the Pinto assembly line take pride in a product that is indistinguishable from a thousand other products and to which the worker's contribution is the tightening of a few bolts on a chrome bumper? An identical situation exists for the typist who arrives in the morning and takes a place as part of the typing pool in a large room, types letters from a prerecorded tape dictated by someone never seen about a product the typist never uses and whose purpose is unknown, and finally sends the completed letter to a firm she or he has no contact with to be received by people who are never met. Such jobs, with slight variations, are endemic to the modern bureaucratic world.

The second form of alienation is even more severe than the first. In this sense, the worker is alienated from the work process itself. A worker is required to work at the speed and rhythm of a machine—a pace not determined by the worker, whose safety and comfort is little regarded. The machine dictates that it must be run night and day for the sake of a production schedule, and the shift-worker is required to follow those dictates. The effects upon the worker's family and health, and the quality of life endured by the worker, are of secondary importance to the requisite functions of the machine.

The worker is related to the product of his labour as to an alien object. The object he produces does not belong to him, dominates him, and only serves in the long run to increase his poverty. Alienation appears not only in the result, but also in the process of production and productive activity itself. The worker is not at home in his work which he views as only a means of satisfying other needs. It is an activity directed against himself, that is independent of him and does not belong to him. Thirdly, alienated labour succeeds in alienating man from his species. Species-life, productive life, life creating life, turns into a mere means of sustaining the worker's individual existence, and man is alienated from his fellow men. Finally, nature itself is alienated from man, who thus loses his own inorganic body.[5]

As the above quotation from Marx indicates, there are two further types of alienation. People are alienated in a modern capitalist society from their fellow workers. Labor is no longer either an individual or a cooperative enterprise; rather, the division of labor makes the tasks simple and mindless. Skill is increasingly minimized and the competitive character of work is dominant and ever-increasing. Workers can no longer look upon their fellow or sister workers as colleagues and comrades but must see every other worker as a competitor, as someone to be feared, as someone who threatens their own livelihood. Anyone who has observed how comparisons of productivity rates can be carried out to many decimal places can appreciate the extremes to which this competitiveness is driven. What one does not see without reflection is how the worker becomes alienated from other workers—how the worker becomes isolated and alone.

Finally, one becomes alienated from oneself. This is the extreme form of alienation. Marx rejects the Hegelian view that alienation is part of the human condition in that no person can be at one with the Absolute Spirit. Rather, Marx understands alienation as rooted fundamentally in the alienation of labor caused by the brutal appropriation of both labor and humanity by the capitalist system. In this system people themselves become objects, things, and indeed not highly regarded things but devalued things which are bought and sold on the market like any other piece of undifferentiated machinery. The ultimate alienation occurs when people accept the definition of themselves imposed by the system and come to regard their own worth and the worth of others by their value in the marketplace. Neither the character nor the contribution of the individual is regarded, only the wage. People are alienated when, because their wages are lower than their neighbors', they judge themselves failures. They are alienated when they accept as just and real the capitalist appraisal of their worth.

Marx expresses this type of self-alienation and the pain it produces as follows:

The less you eat and read books; the less you go to the theatre, the dance-hall, the public house; the less you think, love, theorize, sing, paint, fence, etc., the more you *save*—the *greater* becomes your treasure which neither moths nor rust will devour—your capital. The less you *are*, the *more* you *have;* the less you express of your own life, the greater is your *externalized* life—the greater is the store of your alienated being. Everything that the political economist takes from you in life and in humanity, he replaces for you in money and wealth; and all the things that you cannot do, your money can do.... All passions and all activity must therefore be submerged in greed.[6]

The social costs of alienation are truly staggering, for from a Marxist perspective almost all social disintegration has its roots in either poverty or the alienating character of work. For example, Marxists would view child abuse or wife-beating as the result of the pent-up frustrations of the worker. This anger and frustration not only cannot be released at the workplace but, on the contrary, must be masked with smiles and civility, whether to the foreman or the patron. When the anguish of an alienated life does find its release, as it must, the all-too-frequent result is antisocial behavior. Perhaps one of the more benign releases is to watch professional athletes beat each other's brains out in a ring or on a field which the viewer listlessly watches on television while downing a quota of beer.

It has been suggested by some, including a few Marxists, that although Marx has rightly focused on the destructive nature of alienation, he has erred in defining the capitalist system as the root cause of alienation. Rather, it has been suggested, alienation lies in the nature of the industrial process itself, that is, in the processes of modern technology and the concomitant requirements of extreme divisions of labor. Contemporary "new leftists" who accept this view tend to advocate a return to a simpler life and call into question the benefits of the modern age. For example, denying the benefits of the automobile, these critics stress not only the harm done to workers who produce the machine but its environmental and life-style liabilities as well. Others recognize both alienation and environmental harm but tend to consider these as being within acceptable margins, by-products of an indispensable modern technology. The "cost of progress" is worth paying, in their view, considering the benefits; and, in any case, the tendency of "progress" is "irreversible." The preponderant view of Marxism is antithetical to both of these revisions. It is not technology, itself, which is at fault but the way in which technology is managed by the capitalist class. Contemporary Marxists therefore argue in favor of four strategies for overcoming alienation—strategies which would be available to a socialist economy and denied to a capitalist economy.

First, socialists argue that under capitalism, with its superordinate profit motive, no incentive exists for the development of technology which is nonalienating. If, on the contrary, research and development efforts focused more upon the creation of specifically nonalienating machinery and diverse modes of production, a great deal could be done to alleviate the primitive features of industrial life. As long as dollar profit and expanding markets remain the chief aims and measures of economic success, experimental methods of production for the sake of elevating the quality of human labor will not be seriously attempted. We can get some idea of the possibilities for the success of such efforts when we witness the steps a few capitalists took when they became aware of the high cost of alienation in terms of reduced productivity, high absenteeism, and poor quality control. Perhaps the best example of the movement toward nonalienating modes of production is the change from assembly-line work to team construction of entire automobiles made by Volvo, the Swedish auto company. Both teamwork and the rotation of job tasks were used to alleviate assembly-line fatigue and alienation. Overcoming alienation was viewed as cost-effective in the production of superior quality as well as the enhancement of process efficiency. It has been suggested that if management in a greater number of industries were further freed from calculating the profitability of experimental modes of production, a great deal could be done to redesign the industrial process in a more humane fashion and still maintain or improve production efficiency. Given the remarkable advances in technology, it is difficult not to accept the view that human labor and the work process itself can be shaped by human ingenuity for the sake of humanity itself.

Second, socialists argue that even if the alienating effects of industrial technology cannot be altogether eliminated, socialism is capable of providing the worker with commensurate compensation rather than hardship and exploitation. While this aspect of socialist reform will be more fully explained later, in the section on the labor theory of value, we will only briefly touch here upon the idea of equitable distribution of surplus. Simply stated, the surplus that the worker creates would be the worker's, either directly (as increased income) or indirectly (as public goods for the worker's benefit, for example, in an increased abundance of recreation facilities, cultural opportunities, and educational facilities). These compensating benefits could be especially designed to overcome or reduce the residual effects of an alienating work process. Furthermore, there is reason to assume, within the framework of this second argument, that if the unproductive workers (e.g., Madison Avenue advertising executives) of the capitalist mode of production were put to work the labor time of all workers would be reduced and the burden of the yet-unrealized progress borne more equitably.

A third and promising reform argument among socialists is the movement for worker-control over the production process itself. The socialist contention is that the separation of control over what is to be produced (and how it is to be produced) from the persons who labor to produce the object is perhaps the most alienating factor of the capitalist mode of production. Therefore, some socialists view worker control as a prerequisite and essential feature of a socialist economy.

Last, socialists acknowledge that even if all these steps were taken, there would remain disagreeable tasks which must be performed. The performance and organization of these tasks, however, would be very different within socialism. For example, under socialism, which stresses both egalitarian enjoyment of the fruits of a cooperative society and egalitarian obligation and duties for the maintenance of that society, tasks would be fairly shared and organized by all members. They would cease to be the exclusive burden of the weak and minority members of society as they are under capitalism. The performance of these tasks need not remain a badge of "failure" or function as punitive and disciplinary measures. In short, they would cease to be the stigma of an underclass.

THE LATER MARX

As Marx noted, the task of philosophy is not to understand history but to change it. In the evolution of his own thought, Marx shifted away from, although he certainly did not abandon, his investigation of alienation and turned to the more difficult task of simultaneously understanding and changing history. To see the depth and scope of Marx's own comprehension of history, a reading of the original work is mandatory. Marx's command of language, ideas, the course of history, and a critical intellectual method, his humor, certainly his compassion, his astonishing sharpness of mind and habit of integrity, his accessibility and relevance—these are all characteristic of Marx's writing and can only be discovered by reading the original work. What will be attempted here will be a brief discussion and organization of the vast material of the later writings under the following topics: dialectical materialism and the historical dialectic;

class and revolution; the party and the state; and finally, the Marxian vision of communism.

Dialectical Materialism

Marx, like all students of his time in Germany, engaged in a dialogue with Hegel, who had come to dominate German intellectual thought. But for Marx, as well as for other young Hegelians such as Feuerbach, Hegel was too abstract and idealistic, too much involved in examining the role of the spirit and the will in the shaping of human destiny. These young Hegelians accepted the premise that history moved in a dialectical manner, that change was an ever-present reality, and that in order to understand reality one had to understand the process of change. Furthermore, they agreed with Hegel that the process of change was progressive—progressive not linearly but dialectically, as Hegel had understood it. This is to say that nothing is as it appears to be but rather that all things are constantly in the process of becoming something different. They are always in the process of "negating" themselves, of changing into their opposite. Conflict between opposing forces was seen to be the "midwife" of history. The human condition was comprehended as one of constant unrest, a constant striving to be what is not yet—to deny what now is. This abstract Germanic idea so central to the philosophies of both Kant and Hegel was taken over by Marx and given vitality and life. In lifting these ideas from the sterile atmosphere of academic halls and academic abstractions and placing them in the midst of everyday life and the struggle of humanity, Marx changed the ideas and the history of the world.

This transformation was accomplished by changing the Hegelian dialectic, which maintained that the causal forces in the world were Ideas, the Will, and the Spirit. Hegel thought these were the forces that moved humanity. *But this is certainly not so, replied Marx.* It is not ideas that shape humanity's destiny, according to Marx, but the material conditions of life. More than this, it is the material condition of life that shapes people's ideas. Once again, Marx himself expresses better than others his disagreement with Hegel on the nature of the dialectic:

My dialectical method is not only different from the Hegelian, but its direct opposite. To Hegel, the life process of thinking, which under the name of the 'Idea', he even transforms into an independent subject, is the demiurgos (creator) of the real world, and the real world is only the external, phenomenal form of the 'idea'. With me on the contrary the idea is nothing else than the material world reflected by the human mind, and translated into forms of thought....With Hegel [the dialectic]...is standing on its head. It must be turned rightside up again....[7]

At the core of Marx's writing is his understanding of the dialectical method. Marx never used the term *historical dialectic,* and might well have resisted the term *dialectical materialism* because of its deterministic connotation. Marx spoke instead of the "materialistic conception of history" or the "materialist conditions of production." Nevertheless, Marx's benefactor and collaborator Friedrich Engels used the term *dialectical materialism,* which seems to be an apt expression for Marx's dialectical method if one is careful not to assume an overly deterministic character for the concept. It is the conviction that the material conditions of our lives determine the nature of our existence, that there exists a definite relationship, in particular, between the technology and organization of the material world and the character of the social, political, and spiritual life of the community.

At a certain level this seems elementary and obvious. The changes, for example, brought about when nomadic tribes settled down to farming along the Nile introduced a mode of production which profoundly affected the social (i.e., family), political (authority patterns), and spiritual life of the people. While Karl Marx was interested in the development of primitive modes and ancient peoples, he was most interested in the relationships between industrial modes of production and society in his time—between the substructure and superstructure of modern society. One modern technological innovation, the power jenny, for example, fundamentally changed the society of England. The most obvious ramifications of the development of the jenny include the demise of cottage industries and the development of factory production which, in turn, changed the nature of familial relationships, introduced the need for formal education and "freed up" the labor power of women and children. Increased social differentiation and the requisite needs for social organization and regulation both prompted and followed the emergence of the contemporary state. For example, the role of the state in education, in the authoritative allocation of social and political values, rules of conduct, credentialing, and licensing functions follows from and interacts with basic changes in material conditions.[8]

Marx was particularly interested in how the mode of production, and the social relations which are a part of that mode, conditioned and determined the superstructure of society. It is the systemic relationship between the mode of production and the entire social system that is the core of Marx's contribution. He used a variety of terms to describe these systemic relationships; terms such as *capitalism* and *feudalism* best capture his intention. In a preface to *A Contribution to the Critique of Political Economy*, Marx describes most succinctly the relationship between an economic substructure and superstructure of society:

My investigation led to the result that legal relations as well as forms of state are to be grasped neither from themselves nor from the so-called general development of the human mind, but rather have their roots in the material conditions of life....In the social production of their life men enter into definite relations that are indispensable and independent of their will, relations of production which correspond to a definite stage of development of their material productive forces. The sum total of these relations of production constitutes the economic structure of society, the real foundation, on which rises a legal and political superstructure and to which correspond definite forms of social consciousness. The mode of production of material life conditions the social, political and intellectual life processes in general. It is not the consciousness of men that determines their being, but, on the contrary, their social being that determines their consciousness.[9]

The following diagram provides a schematic representation of primary relationships:[10]

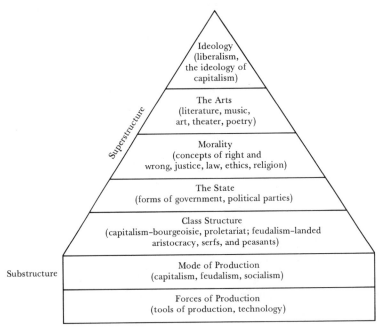

Figure 1.1 The Structure of Society

Historical Materialism

While it is the substructure which provides the base and orientation of overall social organization and development, and indeed this base which must be the target for a radical transformation of society, it is important to avoid conceptualizing the relationship between the substructure and superstructure as one of crude determinism. Marx, himself, clearly recognized an existing interplay between the substructure and superstructure. In contemporary language one might think of these structural determinants as interdependent variables rather than either dependent or independent variables. The interdependence of formal economic, social, and political structures is effectuated by the presence of living human beings who themselves are subject to, factors within, and shapers of material production. The dialectic is a human dialectic. As such, it is conscious, historical, and concrete.

Without major exception, all of Marx's writings need to be understood in terms of the operation of the dialectical process. Nothing discussed by Marx is static, and his method of observation is an attempt to comprehend the transformation of all that is becoming without losing the essence of what is:

It seems to be correct to begin with the real and the concrete ...[however]....The concrete is concrete because it is the concentration of many determinations, hence unity of the diverse.[11]

Marx's antagonism toward crass empiricism is clear in his definition of the "concrete." To name or describe a simple idea, a subset (such as population), or an event without examining it within the context in which it occurs (namely, history) is, for Marx, useless metaphysics—the construction of abstractions which pretend to describe and explain but in actuality isolate and abstract. Only an examination of the totality can disclose the *reality* of any given idea, subset, or event. And only the real is concrete. To discover reality, one must start with a particular idea, subset, or event (for example, population) and proceed to find the elements upon which it rests and the functions it performs. In other words, one must discover what is real by overcoming chaotic conceptions and establishing concrete characteristics and fixed determinations within a greater totality. Population, without a concept of class, is a chaotic idea. With a concept of class, one can then examine population with regard to wage labor, the division of labor, economic exchange, and so on. Marx regarded his method as scientific because it overcame abstraction.

The remaining element of primary structural determination which requires examination is class. It is Marx's contention that in every society since the time of written history there have been class conflicts. In every society there has existed a ruling class, which rules because it controls the mode of production of the epoch, *and* the ruled class, which has no control over the means of production. For example, in feudal times the ruled class included the serfs and peasants, and the ruling class was the landed aristocracy. In modern times the ruling class is the bourgeoisie who control the capital of contemporary industrial society, while the workers, the proletariat, are the ruled class. Although this two-class division is paramount, there are subdivisions within each class.

A contemporary approximation of class stratification in contemporary capitalist societies is as follows.[12] The largest subgrouping within the working class, or the proletariat, is the "commodity-producing" class. This stratum is designated the *working class proper.* This is the traditional blue-collar working class, which, according to Charles H. Anderson, comprises about 40 percent of the total workforce. Added to this is the "new working class," which is distinguished from the former stratum by such characteristics as higher education and increasingly sophisticated skill requirements for their jobs. These are the white-collar personnel working in production-related scientific and technological jobs. If one adds the entire professional and technological segment of the workforce, an additional 13 percent would be added to the 40 percent proper. Moreover, there are the service, sales, and clerical workers who, from the standpoint of income and status, may be added to the working class and who comprise an additional 35 percent.

Two other subgroups ought to be accounted for. There are at one extreme the *lumpenproletariat* about whom Marx spoke. These unfortunate people have no legitimate place within the social order—the pimps, prostitutes, and thieves. Though it may be true that some of these people have become rich living off the fat underbelly of capitalism, most, numbering into the tens and hundreds of thousands, are the dregs of society—more victim than victimizer. At the other end of the scale are the equally difficult to classify "humanistic intellectuals," in many ways as exceptional and as parasitic as their counterparts in the underworld. Perhaps they are best left outside of the class structure which is determined by the mode of production in modern capitalist society. Peasants and the landed aristocracy are excluded from existing class analysis because they are remnants of another era; the "humanistic intellectuals" are excluded because, as "free floating" intellectuals, they seem to be outside class analysis. This is in striking contrast to most intellectuals who are skilled and willing to serve the interests of elites.

Adding together the various groups within the working class we can recapitulate as follows: blue-collar production workers, 40 to 45 percent; technical and scientific workers employed either directly or indirectly in production, 13 percent; service, sales, and clerical workers, 35 percent. Together these add up to approximately 88 percent of the total workforce. This leaves only about 12 percent of the population which composes the bourgeoisie or capitalist class.

The capitalist class itself may be subdivided. The major sectors within this class are the old middle class, the private entrepreneurs, and the small, independent businessmen (whom Marx called the petite bourgeoisie). The prime function of this class is to maintain the myth of competitive capitalism. According to U.S. Labor Department statistics the number of self-employed people had declined from 22 percent in 1940 to 9 percent in 1969.[13] A larger, and immensely more significant subdivision is the professional intellectual class. The legal and medical profession who serve capitalism, a large segment of the bureaucracy, and members of the academic profession who act as apologists for capitalism make up an increasing proportion of a subcapitalist class. Finally, there remains the most significant segment, the capitalist class *per se*. Comprising perhaps not more than 1 or 2 percent of the population, this class includes the relatively few who control the major industrial and banking firms either through ownership or managerial position.

In sum, the Marxian position focuses upon two basic classes which, while not undifferentiated, are related to each other in an antagonistic power relationship. The real significance of the classes is the power which lies between them rather than stylistic differences among the various strata within each class.

In order for classes to play their historic role there must be more between them than the mere existence of class distinctions. That is, each class must develop its own class consciousness; each must become a class *for itself* as well as a class *in itself*. Until this occurs a class cannot play its proper role as an agent of change. In *The Eighteenth Brumaire of Louis Bonaparte* Marx states:

In so far as millions of families live under economic conditions of existence that separate their mode of life, their interests and their culture from those of other classes, and put them in hostile opposition to the latter, they form a class. In so far as there is merely a local interconnection among...[them] and the identity of their interests begets no community, no national bond and no political organization among them, they do not form a class. They are consequently incapable of enforcing their class interest in their own name, whether through a parliament or through a convention. They cannot represent themselves, they must be represented. Their representative must at the same time appear as the master, as an authority over them, as an unlimited governmental power that protects them against the other classes and sends them rain and sunshine from above.[14]

So, then, to be a class merely in itself is to be vulnerable to particular servitude. While this passage describes the situation of the peasant class in France during the Revolution of 1848–51, and their servitude of "willing" subjugation, the bourgeoisie as a class seem capable of exhibiting a no-less illusory class consciousness. The idea of the "people," for example, functions primarily as illusion but in the interest of the petty bourgeoisie. The following describes the bourgeoisie's illusion:

[T]he democrat, because he represents the petty bourgeoisie, that is a *transition class* in which the interests of two classes are simultaneously mutually blunted, imagines himself elevated above class antagonisms generally. The democrats concede a privileged class confronts them, but they along with the rest of the nation, form the *people.*[15]

Isolation, illusion, and alienation reflect material and social conditions and mitigate against the development of class consciousness. But in times of conflict and crisis, the material conditions of the proletariat change, and instead of preventing class consciousness become agents that form and inform class consciousness.

Political, social, and, indeed, class relations in the Marxian view are thus not static and immutable sets of behavioral patterns. Rather they are fluid, and sometimes volatile, expressions of an historical dialectic which has substance at the level of both material economic production and concrete social-political organization. The transformation of society follows the various interplays within dialectical materialism sketched above. We now turn to a closer examination of social transformation.

SOCIAL TRANSFORMATION

The two primary objectives of social transformation in the Marxian view are freedom and the rational use of the material conditions of human life. As explained above, these objectives are conceived to exist in a dialectical relationship through, by, and for the sake of human life. A simple way of saying this is to say that history should be the expression of human dignity. While the objectives of social transformation are important, one must ask a further question to fully understand the import of Marxism: *Freedom and ma-*

terial well-being for whom? The very distinctive answer of Marxism is *for the masses,* the workers whose labor has already transformed the mode of production from a feudal order to a capitalist order and who yet remain excluded from decisions regarding either development of the mode of production or the organization of economic, social, and political life—in short, from decisions regarding their own destiny and the destiny of their children and their nation. Social transformation under Marxism is thus both a historical and a mass concept. Praxis and egalitarianism, respectively, are the chief characteristics of a Marxist idea of social transformation.

At the outset of this chapter on the theoretical origins of Marxism, you will recall, we distinguished Marxism from other variants of socialism in that it has a militant, uncompromising character. This characteristic is in part attributable to the realism of Marxism; that is, Marxism sees itself as having great explanatory value in delineating power relations in a capitalist order. It is also a recognition of the tenacity of class relations within both capitalism and socialism.

How can we more explicitly distinguish the uncompromising character of Marxism? Perhaps in contrast to the compromised character of social democracy:

The peculiar character of the Social-Democracy is epitomized in the fact that the democratic-republican institutions are demanded as a means not of doing away with two extremes, capital and wage labour, but of weakening their antagonism and transforming it into harmony. However different the means proposed for the attainment of this end may be, however much it may be trimmed with more or less revolutionary notions, the content remains the same. This content is the transformation of society in a democractic way but a transformation within the bounds of the petty bourgeoisie. Only one must not form the narrow-minded notion that the petty bourgeoisie on principle wishes to enforce an egoistic class interest. *Rather* it believes that the *special* conditions of its emancipation are the *general* conditions within the frame of which alone modern society can be saved and the class struggle avoided.[16]

The object of social democracy, reform, is not so much transformational as restorative; the "restoration" of social harmony, the avoidance of heightened class conflict and the brutality of terrorism, and especially the orderly progress of civilization which its liberal ideology assumes is the natural path of all human organization. Society is rather more managed than transformed. When management fails and crisis ensues, revolution may occur, but this, too, can be distinguished from the Marxian idea of a successful proletarian revolution:

Bourgeois revolutions, like those of the eighteenth century, storm swiftly from success to success; their dramatic effects outdo each other; men and things seem set in sparkling brilliants; ecstacy is the everyday spirit; but they are short-lived; soon they have attained their zenith, and a long crapulent depression lays hold of society before it learns soberly to assimilate the results of its storm-and-stress period.[17]

Although there is a great body of literature regarding social transformation within Marxism and neo-Marxism, we will deal here only with the notion of revolution.[18] It must be stated in passing, however, that the People's Republic of China, under Mao Tse-tung, provided a rich historical laboratory of experimentation in social transformation. Both the modern history of the People's Republic and Mao's own philosophical and theoretical writings will profoundly affect future attempts at socialist transformation. It is, however, beyond the scope of this book to explore Mao's use of Marxism.

In considering revolution and social transformation, Marxian theoreticians have increasingly been drawn to an analysis of the state. The idea of the state as a set of relations informing a macroanalysis and as a particular apparatus whose structures and functions must be understood in order to mold effective strategies of rebuttal will be examined here.

Revolution

There are two questions to be considered in dealing with revolution: what causes a revolution, and what brings it about? These are not the same question. The former involves the underlying and motivating conditions contributing to revolutionary situations, whereas the latter involves immediate questions of tactics and rule. In considering the first of these questions we look primarily to Marx and secondarily to Lenin. The second question requires a primary focus on Lenin.

Marx explained perhaps three primary causes for revolution which will be briefly described in descending order of significance.[19] First, as the following quotations indicate, Marx understood that the continued exploitation of the workers by the capitalist class would, in a sense, *force* the workers to revolt. Exploitation both impoverishes the working class (productive laborers *and* the reserved army of the unemployed) and creates a condition of awareness among the people of the working class regarding their impoverishment along with an acute need to alleviate those conditions:

...in the fully developed proletariat, everything human is taken away, even the *appearance* of humanity. In the conditions of existence of the proletariat are condensed, in the most inhuman form, all the conditions of existence of present-day society. Man has lost himself, but he has not only acquired, at the same time, a theoretical consciousness of his loss, he has been forced, by an ineluctable, irremediable and imperious *distress*—by practical *necessity*—to revolt against this inhumanity. It is for these reasons that the proletariat can and must emancipate itself. But it can only emancipate itself by destroying its own conditions of existence. It can only destroy its own conditions of existence by destroying *all* the inhuman conditions of existence of present-day society, conditions which are epitomized in its situation.[20]

It will be recalled here that the proletariat as a class is itself the product of capitalist development—a product of capitalist development "achieved against its will" (i.e., the "will" of the private propertied class):

...proletariat *as* proletariat, poverty conscious of its moral and physical poverty, degradation conscious of its degradation, and for this reason trying to abolish itself.[21]

An awareness by the proletariat of the conditions of its own impoverishment is, of course, part of the general development from a class-in-itself to a class-for-itself. But the revolutionary potential of this development goes beyond the subjective enhancement of a class ideology to the development of objective material contradictions or antagonisms. For example:

Large-scale industry assembles in one place a crowd of people who are unknown to each other. Competition divides their interests. But the maintenance of their wages, this common interest which they have against their employer, brings them together in the same idea of resistance—*combination*. ... If the original aim of resistance was that of maintaining wages, to the extent that the capitalists, in their turn, unite with the aim of repressive measures, the combinations, at first isolated, become organized into groups, and in the face of the unity of the capitalists, the maintenance becomes more important than the level of wages. ...

   Economic conditions had in the first place transformed the mass of people into workers. The domination of capital created the common situation and common interests of this class. Thus this mass is already a class in relation to capital, but not yet a class for itself. In the struggle ... this mass unites and forms itself into a class for itself. The interests which it defends become class interests. But the struggle between classes is a political struggle.[22]

This process of "ripening" is, as always, a dialectical process involving an interaction between the objective material conditions of production and the class struggle *and* the proletariat's subjective appropriation of its own historic role in the continuing struggle.

Of all the instruments of production, the greatest productive force is the revolutionary class itself. The organization of the revolutionary elements as a class presupposes that all the productive forces that could develop within the old society are in existence.[23]

This interaction occurs along with an increased awareness on the part of the bourgeoisie of the rising "stakes" of
the struggle. In a sense, the triad composed of two polar
classes and a particular stage of economic development represents an historic conjuncture at the moment of revolution.
The struggle is as much a struggle over the direction of
human history as it is a struggle for control over a particular
mode of production. "Merely political"[24] revolutions can
become social transformations depending on the outcome,
which is simply to say depending upon which class is vic-
torious. Marx defines revolutionary genius as "that revolutionary daring which throws at its adversary the defiant
phrase, *I am nothing, and I should be everything.*"[25]

The importance of the proletariat, both as a carrier of
this revolutionary genius and as a potential victor in the
class struggle, is due to the distinct and complete form of
the proletariat's alienation. Marx conceived of the transformation of society following a true proletarian victory as fundamental and irrevocable. The downfall of existing society
through a working-class victory is described as follows:

Does this mean that the downfall of the old society will be followed
by a new class domination? No. The condition for the emancipation of the working class is the abolition of all classes, just as
the condition for the emancipation of the third estate, of the
bourgeoisie, was the abolition of all estates and orders.

The working class, in the course of its development, will sub-
stitute for the old civil society an association which will exclude
classes and their antagonism, and there will be no longer any
political power, properly so-called, since political power is precisely the official expression of the antagonism in civil society.[26]

For Marx, the explicit aim of all revolution, indeed of
all politics, is human emancipation. Human freedom, for
Marx, requires first and foremost a conscious appreciation
of one's own humanity and a means of "practicing humanity" in daily life. The material conditions of human work
and social organization, and the knowledge of that material
basis provide the necessary conditions for freedom. The
idealized institutions of a class society and the myths which

support class domination through those institutions will be replaced. The harshness of working-class exploitation and a class awareness of that brutality are the first step toward a revolutionary impulse and the "transformational" knowledge which accompanies a proletarian victory:

> Human emancipation will only be complete when the real, individual man has absorbed in himself the abstract citizen, when as an individual man, in his everyday life, in his work, and in his relationships, he has become a *social being,* and when he has recognized and organized his own powers (*forces propres*) as *social* powers, and consequently no longer separates this social power from himself as *political* power.[27]

Of course, neither the brutality of working-class oppression nor the startling realism of true revolution can be captured in literary exegeses or "explanations" of revolution. We tend to forget, if we were ever aware of it, how harshly workers were treated in the middle of the nineteenth century:

> The boys and girls—they were all about ten years old—were whipped day and night, not only for the slightest fault, but to stimulate their flagging industry. And compared with a factory at Litton where Blincoe was subsequently transferred, conditions at Lowdham were rather humane. At Litton the children scrambled with the pigs for the slops in the trough; they were kicked and punched and sexually abused; and their employer, one Ellice Needham, had the chilling habit of pinching the children's ears until his nails met through the flesh. The foreman of the plant was even worse. He hung Blincoe up by his wrists over a machine so that his knees were bent and then he piled heavy weights on his shoulders. The child and his co-workers were almost naked in the cold of winter and (seemingly as a purely gratuitous sadistic flourish) their teeth were filed down! (From an 1828 publication in England, *The Lion,* telling the history of Robert Blincoe, a pauper-child who worked in the factories, as reported by Robert Heilbroner.)[28]

The second underlying cause of revolution as seen by Marx is the economic collapse of capitalism. This is a condition obviously not unrelated to a growing class antagonism.[29]

Marx's economic analysis of the collapse of capitalism is based on his understanding that there exists an internal contradiction within the capitalist mode of production. This contradiction is the need for expanding profit which is confronted by a consistent tendency within capitalism for the rate of profit to decline. It should be said, at the outset, following a recent analysis by Manuel Castells that this decline in the rate of profit is understood by Marx to be a *tendency* which, while constant, may be vitiated by countermeasures taken by capital. This struggle around a falling rate of profit is one of the major dialectical movements within capitalism to which Marx paid particular attention. Economic determinism is so little a part of the dialectical economics of Marx that charges of that nature can only be taken as a superficial understanding of either the method or explanatory analysis of Marx.

The manner through which Marx arrived at this method of analysis was itself very remarkable because it was the first attempt to develop a macroeconomics similar to the national income accounts with which we are now so familiar. It should be remembered that national income data such as gross national product (GNP) and disposable income were unavailable—even the concepts were unknown in Marx's time. Marx started from the basic notion that all value comes from labor. Capitalists would not employ laborers unless they produced more value for the capitalist than the cost of the wages to employ them. This is quintessentially a "reasonable assumption" within capitalism. Marx refrained from converting value into dollar amounts, preferring instead to write in terms of hours of labor. For example, workers might produce enough goods in six hours to cover their wages; however, they would be required to work twelve hours to actually earn a wage. What the workers produced in the later six hours would belong not to the workers who produced the commodity but to the capitalist.

The following formula expresses the concept above as follows: $e = \frac{s}{v}$; where e is the rate of exploitation, s is surplus or the unpaid portion of labor, and v is variable capital or the paid portion of labor—the wage bill.

A second formula developed by Marx explains the organic composition of capital which is the measure of the degree of labor or capital intensiveness which an economy exhibits. The expressed formula is as follows: $g = \frac{c}{v}$; where g is the organic composition of capital, c is constant capital (i.e., the depreciation of machinery, buildings, and the consumption of raw materials in the production process), and v is variable capital.

The rate of profit is then expressed in a third formula as follows: $p = \frac{s}{c+v}$; where p is the rate of profit, s is the surplus, and c is constant capital, while v is variable capital—the "wage bill." There is a tendency for the rate of profit to decline as c is constantly rising because past realized surplus is constantly being reinvested in more and more fixed capital. Profits will not decline as long as the increased investment in capital results in greater exploitation of the worker. That is to say, where the increased investment in capital provides a situation in which the worker can produce the same amount of goods in a shorter time than he or she could before the investment. This is so because more of the workers' hours of labor are being devoted not to covering their own costs but to enhancing surplus for their employer. If, for a variety of reasons, the workers' productivity does not increase or the wage bill increases faster than productivity (due, for example, to union demands or political accommodations), then the increased c becomes a basic cause of a decreasing rate of profit. This tendency is increased when machinery and other capital goods become obsolete and the depreciation allowances are inadequate to cover their replacement, in which case they have to be replaced before they have earned back their initial investment. (For example, obsolescence of American steel production in a market which demands competition with modern Japanese steel production exacerbates the structural contradiction.) Another factor that increases the tendency toward a falling rate of profit is the need for expanding taxes supporting a concomitantly growing state apparatus to administer capitalist society. The state, in a sense, must also be "paid" out of the surplus created by the worker, thus leaving less surplus for the capitalist.

A variety of steps have been taken to mitigate the falling rate of profit. The growth of foreign investment and multinational corporations; the movement of companies within the United States to the South where unions are weak or or nonexistent and right-to-work laws are "freeing up" the labor supply; and the seeking of government subsidy in the form of research and development funds and tax exemptions have all acted to buoy up American enterprise.[30]

The third and last underlying cause which we might consider, and which is perhaps the most pervasive Marxian argument for the failure of capitalism, runs as follows: In the eighteenth and early nineteenth centuries capitalism represented a profoundly progressive force. It grew to be a vehicle which released and channeled imagination and creativity while freeing human enterprise from the dead weight of feudal institutions and practices. The entrepreneurial capitalists were men of daring and vision.[31] The period from 1750 to 1850 represents one of the great advances of humankind. What began with such promise, however, has run its course and today the key institutions of private property and private profit (and with them virtually the entire scheme of capitalist society) have become the greatest hindrances to the solution of human problems—obstacles to overcome rather than inducements for change. In Marx's prescient words, they have become "fetters" upon human progress.

This moribundity can be seen in a host of contemporary problems. It has become increasingly clear, for example, that energy should be conserved, yet capitalism, through its reliance on the profit motive, functions naturally to promote consumption—even irrational consumption—through contradictory consumer inducements. The persistence of urban decay, including increased crime rates, the emergence of vigilante "neighborhood protection" gangs, the rise in hoodlumism—both official and unofficial—and a general array of social disintegration have all taken a terrible toll on people's lives.

These examples point to a more subtle argument, however. There are conceivable remedies, even within capitalism, for problems such as the two mentioned above. Indeed, state and local legislators in the United States and other beleaguered countries endlessly debate the virtues of competing solutions. Public interest groups have sprung up like mushrooms in the last decade and a half, each promoting a set of particular remedial plans, with some even achieving limited success. The point is that capitalism serves not as a facilitator of these remedies but rather as an obstacle to be overcome. It is a mode of production that obstructs human development rather than promotes the betterment of human life. Thus, at the core of Marxism is the idea that as social problems mount and capitalism becomes increasingly obstructive to the solution of these problems, a pattern of stress within the system will become more and more evident. Just as feudalism had eventually to give way to the regenerative forces of capitalism, so will a moribund capitalism face its own demise.

History is the judge—its executioner, the proletariat.[32]

Revolutionary Tactics

The causes for revolution, that historical "judgment" which moribund systems face, must be understood in order to execute a plan for revolt. Yet the mere comprehension of those conditions is insufficient to the task of revolution. Vladmir Ilyich Ulyanov, better known as Lenin, conceived of a unified political party as both a vehicle and a mechanism best suited for the performance of the task of revolution. His notion of a vanguard party well-equipped for the task was the Communist party of Russia. Lenin's view contrasted with that of Marx, whose views on a political party are summarized by a contemporary author:

...Marx's concept of the party was never some ideal institution, but always based on what political organization was already in existence. However, he did insist that this party should have a completely democratic internal organization; that it should be the independent creation of the workers themselves; that it was distinguished by a theoretical understanding of working-class goals; and that (usually) its organization was not to be a part of, or dependent on, any other political party.[33]

The utility of a party for the purpose of capturing a state apparatus and wresting power from the capitalist class was not unknown to Marx. But, for Marx, the type of emancipation achieved, the extent of social transformation following revolution, was of a fundamental and profound nature:

Both for the production on a mass scale of this Communist consciousness, and for the success of the cause itself, the alteration of men on a mass scale is necessary, an alteration which can only take place in a practical movement, in a revolution; this revolution is necessary, therefore, *not only* because the ruling class cannot be overthrown in any other way, but also because the class overthrowing it can only in a revolution succeed in ridding itself of all the muck of ages and become fitted to found society anew.[34] (italics added)

The exigency of revolutionary activity and the profundity of an imminent and hostile class confrontation were decisive elements in Lenin's theory of class and party. For the party to be an agent of and *for* revolution, Lenin saw the necessity for a small number of dedicated, disciplined adherents of Marxism who were willing to undergo hardship and make extreme sacrifices for the ultimate success of the revolution. In a word, Lenin saw the need for "professional revolutionaries." For Lenin, the vulnerability of large organizations to manipulation required the concept of a vanguard party:

We all complain, and cannot but complain of the ease with which the *organizations* can be caught, with the result that it is impossible to maintain continuity in the movement. I assert that it is far more difficult to catch ten wise men than it is to catch a hundred fools. And this premise I shall defend no matter how much you instigate the crowd against me for my 'anti-democratic' views, etc. As I have already said, by 'wise men', in connection with organization I mean *professional revolutionists* irrespective of whether they are students or working men. I assert: 1. That no movement can be durable without a stable organization of leaders to maintain continuity; 2. that the more widely the masses are drawn into the struggle and form the basis of the movement, the more necessary it is to have such an organization and the more stable must it be (for it is much easier then for demagogues to side-track the more backward sections of the masses); 3. that the organization must consist chiefly of persons engaged in revolutionary activity; 4. that in an autocratic state, the more we *confine* the membership of such an organization to people who are professionally engaged in revolutionary activity and who have been professionally trained in the art of combating the political police, the more difficult it will be to unearth the organization; and 5. the *wider* will be the circle of men and women of the working class or of other classes of society able to join the movement and perform active work in it....[35]

Moreover it is not only revolutionary tactics which persuade Lenin of the necessity of elite Party rule. An equally fundamental problem for Lenin is involved in his view that alienated workers are unable to develop class consciousness unless aided by a vanguard of party members who have knowledge of the dialectical method and use it to appraise immediate circumstances—who are thus competent to provide direction and shape the goals which are essential to developing a socialist movement. Proletarian life in and of itself was simply an inadequate preparation for class rule or revolutionary activity. Lenin succinctly states his opinion on this matter in a 1902 pamphlet entitled, *What Is To Be Done?*

The history of all countries shows that the working class, exclusively by its own effort, is able to develop only trade union consciousness.[36]

The economic relationship of worker to exploiter within the workplace could prompt a spontaneous but unschooled rebuttal to capital. The concentration of the economic struggle *within* the *political* struggle required an instrument capable of *authoritative* rebuttal:

When I say that the Party should be the *sum* (and not the mere arithmetical sum, but a complex) of *organisations,* does that mean I "confuse" the concepts of Party and organisation? Of course not. I thereby express clearly and precisely my wish, my demand, that the Party, as the vanguard of the class, should be as organised as possible.

and further:

...*previously* our Party was not a formally organised whole, but merely a sum of separate groups, and therefore no other relations except those of ideological influence were possible between these groups. *Now* we have become an organised Party, and this implies the establishment of authority, the transformation of the power of ideas into the power of authority, the subordination of lower Party bodies into higher ones.[37]

This has become formally promulgated in the *Rules of the Communist Party,* as the definition of democratic centralism of the Communist party:

19. The guiding principle of the organizational structure of the Party is democratic centralism, which signifies:
    a) Election of all leading Party bodies, from the lowest to the highest;
    b) Periodic reports of Party bodies to their Party organizations and to higher bodies;
    c) Strict Party discipline and subordination of the minority to the majority;
    d) That the decisions of the higher bodies are obligatory for the lower bodies.[38]

A variety of views stemming from this core view have divided Marxists as much as any other issue in Marxist theory.

However, as contemporary events such as those in Chile and El Salvador seem to signal an increasingly aggressive and brutal resistance to popular socialist movements, the validity of Lenin's disciplined vanguard-type party, rather than such vehicles as internally democratic workers' movements, is becoming increasingly apparent to Central American revolutionaries. The goal of transformation is as political and "politicized" as the particular conditions of particular societies dictate. Theories regarding the role of the party both follow and inform political developments. Since Lenin, the strategic and tactical dimensions of theory-building as a specifically revolutionary activity has informed virtually all Marxian discussions of politics.

The State

A central theoretical issue which remains to be examined is the Marxian idea of the state. We will consider this concept in two ways: the state in a capitalist society and the state remaining after a proletarian revolution.

The crudest view which Marxists take of the state draws its inspiration from the *Manifesto* in which Marx, after having traced the development of the bourgeoisie and the corresponding *political* development of that class, says of the bourgeoisie's final period of domination and entrenchment:

...the bourgeoisie has at last, since the establishment of Modern Industry and of the world market, conquered for itself, in the modern representative State, exclusive political sway. *The executive of the modern State is but a committee for managing the common affairs of the whole bourgeoisie.*[39] (italics added)

While the simplistic reduction which some Marxists use to exploit this passage has resulted in a gross overstatement of state repression and in caricature rather than analysis, the essential notion of exclusivity of control remains valid. Indeed the efficient organization of state control is a highly cherished goal of contemporary bourgeoisie analysts and politicians. The managerial presidency, bureaucratic reorganization, "cutting the fat out of government," close liaison among the various branches of government and business—these are a few of the "reforms" which strive for efficient control. The "other governments"—those private policy-making bodies such as the Trilateral Commission (see pp. 168, 201, and 252), as well as informal modes of control and interaction such as the network of interlocking corporate directorates, strive for an equally efficient and monolithic control. The state, then, as a set of class relations rather than as a particular type of governmental apparatus, does indeed exist to further the interests of the bourgeoisie.

Recent developments in Marxian theories of the state have gone beyond examining the "committee" of the bourgeoisie, and a rather more sophisticated analysis is underway. Two schools of thought have emerged from this analytical trend, namely, the structuralist and the instrumentalist schools.

The latter view is in some ways the simpler one and stresses the ties of culture, education, status, wealth, and class interaction between the leaders of the capitalist economy and the leaders of government in capitalist societies. C. Wright Mills popularized this view in his seminal work, *The Power Elite*[40] which followed previous studies by Floyd Hunter.[41] The Hunter-Mills tradition in the United States has been carried on with skill and energy by writers such as Gabriel Kolko [42] and G. William Domhoff.[43] At least one president, Dwight D. Eisenhower, concurred with the analysis in part, and warned of the threat of the emerging military-industrial complex.[44]

A rather more intricate view of the state has developed in Europe regarding the role of the state, namely, the structuralist position. Briefly, this view affirms that, although the state does indeed always act in the best long-term interests of the capitalist class, to be successful in fulfilling that role the state must have autonomy from specific capitalist powers. This autonomy, both developmental and institutional phenomena, conditions the power relations among various actors within the bourgeoisie *as well as* between the classes.

Without a notion of state autonomy, structuralists maintain, the continued existence of the state as the overseer of class struggle and the course of its demise in the form of a "crisis" of the state cannot be properly understood.

Structural analysis recognizes the necessity for the state to act against the express wishes and even the short-term interests of any particular capitalist, such as U.S. Steel, or against the steel industry as a whole. The most prominent writers expressing a structural view of the role of the state in a capitalist society are Louis Althusser[45] and Claus Offe.[46] James O'Connor, an American scholar, has contributed to an American analysis of the role of the state.[47]

Certainly the instrumentalist and structuralist approaches are not as neatly separable as the above outline suggests. Whichever interpretation or focus one uses, it is clear that the main elements of class domination and the use of the state as an instrument for domination compose the Marxian core of the analysis. The use of history promises to be the chief synthesizing method in developing an analysis of the state. Alan Wolfe's recent work in this area anticipates both the direction and the degree of increased sophistication which future analysis will perhaps take.[48]

Even after a successful proletarian revolution, it is the Marxist view that the state will, as long as it exists, remain an instrument of control. As Marx stated in his *Critique of the Gotha Program*:

Between capitalist and communist society lies the period of the revolutionary transformation of the one into the other. There corresponds to this also *a political transition period* in which the state can be nothing but *the revolutionary dictatorship of the proletariat.*[49]

The period of transition remains a period of *political* activity precisely because it is a period of continued class struggle. In a manner of speaking, it is simply the odds which are changed. Marx expands his explanation in a letter to Bakunin predating the *Critique*:

...as long as the other classes, and in particular the capitalist class, still exist, as long as the proletariat is still struggling with it (because, with the proletariat's conquest of governmental power its enemies and the old organisation of society have not yet disappeared), it must use coercive means, hence governmental means; it is still a class and the economic conditions on which the class struggle and the existence of classes depend, have not yet disappeared and must be removed by force, or transformed and their process of transformation speeded up by force.[50]

Lenin seized upon Marx's fragmentary writings on the dictatorship of the proletariat and developed a theory of state power and rebuttal by rigid party rule. Lenin's idea of democratic centralism is in a sense the subordination of "politics" to party for the sake of both speeding up the transition which the party must face during proletarian rule and maintaining a rebuttal to remaining elements of old class domination. As long as the class struggle remains, the direction and speed of transition toward socialism is contingent upon the continuing struggle, that is, transition remains "political" and uncertain. The discipline provided by party rule, with its own inner discipline provided by professional cadres and democratic centralism, is regarded by Lenin as essential to the progress toward socialism during transition. Remember, also, that both Marx and Lenin understood that the context of transition is global, and that the particular forms the state took would vary from one society to another. Lenin summarized Marx as follows:

...the substance of the teachings of Marx about the state is assimilated only by one who understands that the dictatorship of a *single* class is necessary not only for any class society generally, not only for the *proletariat* which has overthrown the bourgeoisie, but for the entire *historic period* which separates capitalism from "classless society," from Communism. The forms of bourgeois states are exceedingly variegated, but their essence is the same: in one way or another, all these states are in the last analysis inevitably a *dictatorship of the bourgeoisie*. The transition from capitalism to Communism will certainly bring a great variety and abundance of political forms, but the essence will inevitably be one: the *dictatorship of the proletariat*.[51]

COMMUNISM: THE GOAL

It has been frequently noted that Marx refused to provide a blueprint for the future, nor did he attempt prediction, which he regarded as part and parcel of the idealism of utopian socialists. But his theoretical work as well as his empirical inquiry involved the discovery of scientific laws of development, especially development within capitalist society. The developmental theory is a theory of historical materialism and involves both prospective and retrospective analysis. Marx's notions regarding communism are thus definitions of historical *progress* which are derived from *materialist* assumptions regarding the changing world. Marx, in eschewing "recipes for the cook-shops of the future,"[52] nevertheless offered a fairly clear picture of a communist "future":

Communism differs from all previous movements in that it overturns the basis of all earlier relations of production and intercourse, and for the first time consciously treats all natural premises as the creatures of men, strips them all of their natural character and subjugates them to the power of individuals united. Its organization is, therefore, essentially economic, the material production of the conditions of this unity; it turns existing conditions into conditions of unity. The reality which communism is creating, is precisely the real basis for rendering it impossible that anything should exist independently of individuals, in so far as things are only a product of the preceding intercourse of individuals themselves....

Only in community with others has each individual the means of cultivating his gifts in all directions; only in community, therefore, is personal freedom possible. In the previous substitutes for the community, in the State, etc., personal freedom has existed only for the individuals who developed within the relationships of the ruling class. The illusory community, in which individuals up to now have been combined, always took on an independent existence in relation to them, and was at the same time, since it was the combination of one class over against another, not only a completely illusory community, but a new fetter as well. In the real community the individuals obtain their freedom in and through their association.[53]

The establishment of real community existence requires the overcoming of that illusory existence which, as we have seen, Marxists regard as both alienating to individuals and irrational as a system of material production. As the chief instrument for perpetuating the "unreal" and moribund existence of the mass of people under capitalism is seen to be the state, it is this which must be transformed and eventually wither away. Much has been written about the disappearance of the state under communism. While it is true that Marx did envision the disappearance of the state, that goal must be taken in the context in which the state existed in the nineteenth century. The functions of the state at that time were severely restricted; they were limited to those of an oppressive physical character. The state apparatus was most visible in the police, the military, penal institutions, and the authoritarian rule of rather clearly defined class actors. The state could not at that time have been conceived of as a "service" state—the kind of state which today we call a "welfare state"—whose primary functions include the provision of the health and safety of the greater mass of people who reside as citizens within the national borders. In fact the state, at that time, was only beginning to take an interest in organizing the educational function for society, and only because of the recognition that an increasingly manufacturing-oriented society required a higher degree of education than did the older agricultural society, as a stimulus to efficient production by the workers and as a means of disciplining and molding civil society.[54] In a sense there was a great deal less to "wither away" than there is now, in terms of apparatus and reach of the state, although the set of class relations which define the state as much as its apparatus remain intact as it was at the origin of the modern state, discussions about the "permeability" of the contemporary state notwithstanding. There is little reason to suppose, given the limited definition of state functions in the nineteenth century that the purely administrative functions of the state would ever necessarily disappear. In the *Manifesto* Marx sums up his position as follows:

When, in the course of development, class distinctions have disappeared, and all production has been concentrated in the hands of a vast association of the whole nation, the public power will lose its political character. Political power, properly so called, is merely the organized power of one class for oppressing another. If the proletariat during its contest with the bourgeoisie is compelled, by the force of circumstances, to organize itself as a class, and as such, sweeps away by force the old conditions of production then it will, along with those conditions, have swept away the conditions for the existence of class antagonisms and of classes generally, and will thereby have abolished its own supremacy as a class.

In place of the old bourgeois society, with its classes and class antagonisms, we shall have an association, in which the free development of each is the condition for the free development of all.[55] (italics added)

It is clear that the ultimate communist society will not come immediately after the overthrow of capitalism. The defects of capitalist society, the inequity and injustices, will remain for some time along with the residual state, wage differentials, and even a money economy. Twenty-seven years after the *Communist Manifesto,* Marx stated the situation as follows:

But these defects are inevitable in the first phase of communist society as it is when it has just emerged after prolonged birth pangs from capitalist society. Right can never be higher than the economic structure of society and its cultural development thereby.

In a higher phase of communist society, after the enslaving subordination of the individual to the division of labor, and therewith also the antithesis between mental and physical labor, has vanished; after labor has become not only a means of life but life's prime want; after the productive forces have also increased with the all-round development of the individual, and all the springs of co-operative wealth flow more abundantly—only then can the narrow horizon of bourgeois right be crossed in its entirety and society inscribe on its banners: From each according to his ability, to each according to his needs![56]

NOTES

1. Karl Marx, *1844 Manuscripts: Early Texts*, ed. David McLellan (London: Oxford University Press, 1971), p. 139. First published in German in Karl Marx and Frederick Engels, *Historisch-Gesamtausgabe*, edited by D. Riazanov and D. Adoratsky, Vol. 3. 1932.
2. Karl Marx, *Capital* (New York: International Publishers, 1967), Vol. 1, p. 177. Originally published in Hamburg in 1867. First English translation by Samuel Moore and Edward Aveling, edited by Frederick Engels in 1887.
3. Aristotle, *De Partibus Animalium*, i.1.640^{a}32, as quoted in Harry Braverman, *Labor and Monopoly Capital* (New York: Monthly Review Press, 1974), note p. 46.
4. Ibid., see especially pp. 139–52.
5. Karl Marx, *1844 Manuscripts*, p. 137.
6. Karl Marx, *Historisch-Kritische Gesamtausgabe*, Vol. 3, as quoted in Lee Cameron McDonald, *Western Political Theory from Its Origins to the Present* (New York: Harcourt, Brace & World, 1968), p. 494.
7. Karl Marx, Afterword to the Second German Edition, *Capital*, Original Second German Edition, 1873.
8. See, for example, Richard C. Edwards, Michael Reich, and Thomas Weisskopf, eds., *The Capitalist System: A Radical Analysis of American Society*, 2d ed. (Englewood Cliffs, N.J.: Prentice-Hall, 1978), for a discussion in numerous articles of these developing interactions in capitalist society.
9. Karl Marx, *Preface to a Contribution to the Critique of Political Economy* (New York: International Publishers, 1968), p. 182. Originally published in German in 1859.
10. Alan Wolfe and Charles A. McCoy, *Political Analysis, An Unorthodox Approach* (New York: Thomas Y. Crowell Company, 1968), p. 182.
11. Karl Marx, *The Grundrisse: Foundations of the Critique of Political Economy*, trans. by Martin Nicolaus (New York: Vintage Books, 1973), pp. 100–101. Written in 1858 and originally published in Moscow in 1939–41 as *Grundrisse der Kritik de Polischen Okonomie*.
12. Charles H. Anderson, *The Political Economy of Social Class* (Englewood Cliffs, N.J.: Prentice-Hall, 1974), pp. 124–34.
13. U.S. Census, 1940, *Special Reports: The Labor Force*, Table All, p. 228; *Manpower Report of the President*, 1970, Table 19, pp. 36–37, as reported in Manuel Castells, *The Economic Crisis and American Society* (Princeton, N.J.: Princeton University Press, 1980), p. 156.
14. Karl Marx, *The Eighteenth Brumaire of Louis Bonaparte* (New York: International Publishers, 1963), p. 124. Originally published in the magazine *Die Revolution* in German (New York, 1852).
15. Ibid., p. 54.
16. Ibid., p. 50.
17. Ibid., p. 19.

18. See, for example, Maurice Dobb et al., *The Transition from Feudalism to Capitalism* (New York: Schocken Books, 1978).

19. These categories are, of course, not mutually exclusive nor do they occur in linear progression, one after another; rather they are interacting causes and primary in the sense of their formative influences.

20. Karl Marx and Frederick Engels, *Die Heilige Familie* as found in the original *Marx-Engels Gesamtausgabe* (Moscow, 1927), Vol. 1/3, pp. 205–07, and translated by T. B. Bottomore: *Karl Marx, Selected Writings in Sociology and Social Philosophy* (New York: McGraw-Hill Book Company, 1956), p. 232. Written in 1844, and considered the first jointly written work of Marx and Engels.

21. Ibid.

22. Karl Marx, *Poverty of Philosophy*, as found in the original *Marx-Engels Gesamtausgabe* (Moscow, 1927), Vol. 1/6, pp. 226–27, in ibid., pp. 187–88. Written in 1847.

23. Karl Marx, *Poverty of Philosophy* in ibid., p. 239.

24. "Merely political" refers to a simple exchange or sharing of power, as occurs in coalitional governments. In revolutionary periods coalitions can be either progressive or retrogressive. Marx, in the *Eighteenth Brumaire*, uses the Revolution of 1848 in France as an example of the latter type and indicates the weakness of "merely political" revolutions:

> ...with the Revolution of 1848. The proletarian party appears as an appendage of the petit bourgeois-democratic party. It is betrayed and dropped by the latter.... The democratic party, in its turn, leans on the shoulders of the bourgeois-republican party. The bourgeois republicans no sooner believe themselves well established than they shake off their troublesome comrades and support themselves on the shoulders of the party of the order. The party of the order hunches its shoulders, lets the bourgeois republicans tumble and throws itself on the shoulders of the armed forces. It fancies it is still sitting on its shoulders when, one fine morning, it perceives that the shoulders have transformed themselves into bayonets. Each party kicks from behind at that driving forward and in front leans over towards the party which presses backwards. No wonder that in this ridiculous posture it loses its balance, and having made the inevitable grimaces, collapses with curious capers. The revolution thus moves in a descending line.

25. Karl Marx, *Critique of Hegel's Philosophy of Right* as found in the original *Marx-Engels Gesamtausgabe* (Moscow, 1927), Vol. I/1/1/, pp. 617–21, in *Selected Writings*, trans. Bottomore, *op. cit.*, p. 180. Written in 1844.

26. Karl Marx, *Poverty of Philosophy*, in ibid., p. 239.

27. Karl Marx, *The Jewish Question* as found in the original *Marx-Engels Gesamtausgabe* (Moscow, 1927), Vol. I/1/1/, pp. 596–99, and translated and ed. by T. B. Bottomore: *Karl Marx, Early Writings* (New

York: McGraw-Hill Book Company, 1963), p. 31. Written in 1844.

28. As reported in Robert L. Heilbroner, *The Worldly Philosophers*, 4th ed. (New York: Simon and Schuster/Touchstone, 1972), pp. 102–3.

29. For further discussion of this interaction, see Manuel Castells, *The Economic Crisis and American Society* (Princeton, N.J.: Princeton University Press, 1980), and John G. Gurley, *Challengers to Capitalism*, 2d ed. (New York: W. W. Norton & Company, 1979).

30. See especially, Castells, *The Economic Crisis*, pp. 102–23.

31. For one version of the demise of entrepreneurial vision, see Joseph A. Schumpeter, *Capitalism, Socialism and Democracy*, 3d ed. (New York: Harper & Row, 1962), Chapter XII, "Crumbling Walls," pp. 131–43.

32. Karl Marx, *Speech on the Anniversary of the People's Paper* from K. Marx and F. Engels, *Selected Works* (Moscow, 1962), p. 360, as found in David McLellan, *The Thought of Karl Marx* (New York: Harper & Row, 1971), p. 208. Written in 1856.

33. Ibid., p. 171.

34. Karl Marx and Frederick Engels, *The German Ideology*, Parts I and III, ed. and introduction by R. Pascal (New York: International Publishers, 1947), p. 69. Written in 1846 and published in its entirety in the *Gesamtausgabe* in 1932.

35. V. I. Lenin, *What Is To Be Done?* (New York: International Publishers, 1929), pp. 117–18. Originally written and published in 1902 in Stuttgart.

36. Ibid., p. 33.

37. V. I. Lenin, "One Step Forward, Two Steps Back," in *Lenin, Collected Works*, 2d ed., trans. Abraham Fineberg and Naomi Jochel, ed. Emil Dutt (Moscow: Progress Publishers, 1965), Vol. 7, September 1903-December 1904, pp. 258 and 368, respectively. Originally written and published in Geneva in 1904.

38. *Rules of the Communist Party*, Adopted by the Twenty-second Party Congress, October 31, 1961 and amended through the Twenty-fifth Party Congress, March 1976.

39. Karl Marx and Frederick Engels, *The Communist Manifesto* (New York: International Publishers, 1948), p. 11. Written and originally published in London in 1848.

40. C. Wright Mills, *The Power Elite* (New York: Oxford University Press, 1959).

41. Floyd Hunter, *Community Power Structure* (New York: Anchor Books, 1963).

42. Gabriel Kolko, *Wealth and Power in America* (New York: Praeger, 1962).

43. G. William Domhoff, *Who Rules America?* (Englewood Cliffs, N.J.: Prentice-Hall, 1967), and *The Higher Circles* (New York: Vintage Press, 1970).

44. Dwight D. Eisenhower. "Farewell Address," as reported in Ira Katz-

nelson and Mark Kesselman, *The Politics of Power* (New York: Harcourt, Brace, Jovanovich, 1975), pp. 183–84.

45. Louis Althusser and Etienne Balibar, *For Marx*, trans. Ben Brewster (New York: Vintage Press, 1970); *Reading Capital*, trans. Ben Brewster (London: New Left Books, 1970); *Politics and History*, trans. Ben Brewster (London: New Left Books, 1972).

46. For a clear defense of the structuralist view, see Nico Poulantzas, debating with Ralph Miliband in *New Left Review*, vol. 58 (Nov.-Dec. 1969); vol. 59 (Jan.-Feb. 1970); vol. 82 (Nov.-Dec. 1973); vol. 95 (Jan.-Feb. 1976), also *Political Power and Social Classes*, trans. Timothy O'Hagan (New York: Schocken Books, 1978).

47. James O'Connor, *The Fiscal Crisis of the State* (New York: St. Martin's Press, 1973).

48. Alan Wolfe, *The Limits of Legitimacy* (New York: Free Press, 1977).

49. Karl Marx, *Critique of the Gotha Program* (1875), as found in the original *Marx-Engels Gesamtausgabe*, (Moscow, 1927), in *Selected Writings*, trans. Bottomore, op. cit., p. 256.

50. Karl Marx, "Letter to Bakunin" as found in the original, K. Marx and F. Engels, *Werke* (Berlin: 1956), pp. xviii, 630, quoted in McLellan, *The Thought of Karl Marx*, p. 210.

51. V. I. Lenin, *State and Revolution* (New York: International Publishers, 1932), p. 31.

52. Karl Marx, *Capital*, Vol. 1 (New York: International Publishers, 1974), p. 17.

53. Karl Marx, *The German Ideology*, pp. 70, 74–75.

54. For an extensive analysis, see Perry Anderson, *Lineages of the Absolutist State* (London: New Left Books, 1974). For the debate which ensued following the publication of this book, see Rodney Hilton et al., *The Transition from Feudalism to Capitalism* (London: New Left Books, 1976).

55. Karl Marx and Frederick Engels, *The Communist Manifesto*, p. 31.

56. Karl Marx, *Critique of the Gotha Program*, in McLellan, *The Thought of Karl Marx*, p. 224.

BIBLIOGRAPHIC NOTE

The literature on communism and theoretical Marxism is immense. It is international in scope and engages nearly every form of academic and intellectual inquiry. In the United States in recent years, Marxian scholarship has been active in roughly four areas of interest, all of which seek to understand the historical movement of capitalism and the struggle between socialism and capitalism.

The first area of interest mirrors the concern of Marxists, and indeed of Karl Marx, regarding the emancipatory possibilities of socialism in terms of the release of human creative potential and a guarantee of individual well-being. Drawing from the early writings of Marx and the real-world experimentation in communist countries with communal and socialist organization, these scholars concentrate on socio-pyschological and cultural aspects of capitalist and socialist organization of society. From a left perspective, Erich Fromm represents an early investigation into the psychology of freedom. Later investigations into specific areas such as alienation may be represented by the work of Bertell Ollman. Herbert Marcuse, from the perspective of the Frankurt School, provides an accessible statement of that school's attempt to consider Freudian and Marxian contributions to the understanding of social psychology.

Political culture and social organization are the focus of scholarly concerns similarly derived from the humanism of Marx. The place and construction of ideas within culture is a major concern of contemporary Marxian scholars. The seminal works of Antonio Gramsci, whose writings of the 1920s, were made available to English-speaking scholars in the 1960s, and the works of Georg Lukacs and Karl Korsch have spurred contemporary debate and research into political culture. One such debate—that between French structuralists, following the lead of Louis Althusser who asserts the primacy of structures as motivating history, and those who assert the primacy of the subject and human volition in history (E. P. Thompson's rebuttal to Althusser is particularly effective)—has been especially lengthy and labored.

Thirdly, an interest in theories of the state forms the locus for research and debate regarding the political response of the state to economic crisis; the transition of the state from feudalism to capitalism and the prospective transition from capitalism to socialism; and generally, the debate over who rules within capitalism. The flexibility and, thus, viability of the capitalist state in meeting both economic and political crises have prompted investigations into both the internal dynamics of state control and development of mature state systems. The nature of state control is a particularly lively subject in contemporary literature. The debate between Nicos Poulantzas and Ralph Miliband, for example, represents two antagonistic poles of thought. Poulantzas' defense of "structuralism" may be counterpointed with Miliband's "instrumentalist" view which posits elite control of the instruments of state power, including governmental legislative agendas and regulatory powers. Research into the nature of class is a matter of both political control and economic determination. Nicos Poulantzas, Eric Olin Wright, Harry Braverman, and Charles Anderson represent comtemporary authors who attempt to understand class within capitalism. Control, class, and crisis are the foci of literature on the state. James O'Connor's work stresses the political determinants of economic crisis in the United States within the context of the state's role in the fiscal administration of capitalism. Other works focus upon the economic determinants of crisis and the political attempts to rationalize the capitalist system. The development of the state apparatus to deal with both class challenges and economic crisis comprises much of the literature regarding development and transition from one epoch to another. The works of Perry Anderson, Maurice Dobb, Harry Magdoff, and Immanuel Wallerstein represent and address the historical rise of the modern state.

One of the truly remarkable developments in political economy and Marxist studies in recent years has been the renewed interest in Marx as an economist. This fourth area of concern involves both the method of Marxian inquiry, and the application of that method within empirical analysis. Data collection, the establishment of correct and fruitful units of analysis, and the predictive capacity of Marxist models have been strengthened due to this renewed interest. The explanatory and predictive validity of Marxian economic theory has been reasserted in a number of critical works investigating capitalist development. Ernest Mandel's work over the past fifteen years represents an excellence of exposition and analysis. Attempts to present empirical verifications of Marxian theory and application of the method may be represented by such diverse approaches as those of Manuel Castells, David Gordon, Michael Kalecki, and James O'Connor. Other studies of Marxian economics utilize intellectual history and analyze Marx's place in the development of economic thought. The work of Maurice Dobb, Robert Heilbroner, and Ronald Meek represent these efforts. Two valuable journals presenting quite different but useful approaches are the *Monthly Review* (New York) and *The Review of Radical Political Economics,* published quarterly by the Union For Radical Political Economy (New York).

The four areas of interest which we note are certainly not discrete categories of analysis. Scholars working in any one of the areas are informed to a very great extent by work in the other areas. Marxism seeks a unity of thought within analytical inquiry. The four areas which we note are intended to indicate merely the general foci of contemporary interests and concerns. Our delineation is, of course, intended to be in no way exhaustive.

BIBLIOGRAPHY

Adoratsky, V. *Dialectical Materialism.* New York: International Publishers, 1934.

Althusser, Louis. *For Marx.* Trans. Ben Brewster. New York: Vintage Press, 1970.

———— *Lenin and Other Essays.* Trans. Ben Brewster. London: New Left Books, 1971.

———— *Politics and History.* Trans. Ben Brewster. London: New Left Books, 1972.

———— and Balibar, Etienne. *Reading Capital.* Trans. Ben Brewster. London: New Left Books, 1970.

Amin, Samir. *Unequal Development: An Essay on the Social Foundations of Peripheral Capitalism.* New York: Monthly Review Press, 1976.

Anderson, Charles H. *The Political Economy of Social Class.* Englewood Cliffs, N.J.: Prentice-Hall, 1974.

Anderson, Perry. *Lineages of the Absolutist State.* London: New Left Books, 1974.

Applebaum, Richard and Chotiner, Harry. "Science, Critique and Praxis in Marxist Method." *Socialist Review,* Vol. 9, no. 4 (July-August 1979).

Avineri, Shlomo. *The Social And Political Thought of Karl Marx.* Cambridge, England: Cambridge University Press, 1968.

Bernstein, Eduard. *Evolutionary Socialism: A Criticism and Affirmation.* New York: Schocken Books, 1961.

Block, Fred. "The Ruling Class Does Not Rule: Notes on the Marxist Theory of the State." *Socialist Revolution,* Vol. 7, no. 3 (May-June 1977).

Bottomore, T. B., trans. and ed. *Karl Marx: Early Writings.* New York: McGraw-Hill, 1964.

———— and Rubul, Maximilien, eds. *Selected Writings in Sociology and Social Philosophy.* New York: McGraw-Hill, 1956.

Braverman, Harry. *Labor and Monopoly Capitalism.* New York: Monthly Review Press, 1974.

Bronfenbrenner, M. "Marxian Influences in Bourgeois Economics." *American Economic Review* 57 (May 1967).

Castells, Manuel. *The Economic Crisis and American Society.* Princeton, N.J.: Princeton University Press, 1980.

Colletti, Lucio. *From Rousseau to Lenin, Studies in Ideology and Society.* Trans. John Merrington and Judith White. New York: Monthly Review Press, 1974; first published as *Ideologia e Societa.* Rome, Italy: Editori Laterza, 1969.

Dobb, Maurice. "Marx's Capital and Its Place in Economic Thought." *Science and Society,* Vol. 32, no. 4 (1967).

———— *Theories of Value and Distribution Since Adam Smith.* Cambridge, England: Cambridge University Press, 1973.

Domhoff, G. William. *The Higher Circles.* New York: Vintage Press, 1970.

———— *Who Rules America?* Englewood Cliffs, N.J.: Prentice-Hall, 1967.

Ehrenberg, John R. "Lenin And The Politics of Organization!" *Science and Society,* Vol. 43, no. 1 (Spring 1979).

Fromm, Erich. *Marx's Concept of Man.* New York: Frederick Ungar, 1961.

Giddens, Anthony. *Capitalism and Modern Social Theory.* Cambridge, England: Cambridge University Press, 1971.

Gintis, Herbert. "On The Theory of Transitional Conjunctures." *The Review of Radical Political Economics*, Vol. 11, no. 3 (Fall 1979).

Gordon, David M. "Capital Vs. Labor: The Current Crisis in the Sphere of Production" in *Mainstream Reading and Radical Critiques*. David Mermelstein, ed. New York: Random House, 1976, pp. 362–72.

———"Up and Down the Long Roller Coaster" in *U.S. Capitalism in Crisis*. New York: URPE, 1978.

Gough, Ian. *The Political Economy of the Welfare State*. London: Macmillan, 1979.

Gramsci, Antonio. *Selections from the Prison Notebook*. Quinton Hoare and Geoffrey Nowell Smith, eds. London. Oxford University Press, 1971; New York: International Publishers, 1971.

Gurley, G. *Challengers to Capitalism*, 2nd ed. New York: W. W. Norton, 1979.

Habermas, Jürgen. *Legitimation Crisis*. Boston: Beacon Press, 1973.

Heilbroner, Robert L. *Marxism: For and Against*. New York: W. W. Norton, 1980.

——— *The Wordly Philosophers*, 4th ed. New York: Simon & Schuster/ Touchstone, 1972.

Hilton, Rodney, et al., eds. *The Transition from Feudalism to Capitalism*. London: New Left Books, 1976.

Hindess, B. and Hirst, P. *Pre-Capitalist Modes of Production*. London: Routledge & Kegan Paul, 1975.

Hirsch, Fred. *Social Limits to Growth*. Cambridge, Mass.: Harvard University Press, 1976.

Hoffman, John. *Marxism and the Theory of Praxis*. New York: International Publishers, 1975.

Hobsbawm, Eric, ed. *Pre-Capitalist Economic Formations*. New York: International Publishers, 1965.

Itoh, Makoto. "The Formation of Marx's Theory of Crisis." *Science and Society*, Vol. 42, no. 2 (Summer 1978).

——— "A Study of Marx's Theory of Value." *Science and Society*, Vol. 40, no. 3 (Fall 1976).

Kalecki, Michal. *Selected Essays on the Dynamics of Capitalist Societies*. New York: Cambridge University Press, 1971.

Kamenka, Eugene. *The Ethical Foundations of Marxism*. London: Routledge & Kegan Paul, 1962.

Kautsky, Karl. *The Dictatorship of the Proletariat*. Ann Arbor: University of Michigan Press, 1964. (Originally published in 1981 as *Die Diktaturdes Proletariats.)*

Kolko, Gabriel. *Wealth and Power in America*. New York: Praeger, 1962.

Korsch, Karl. *Marxism and Philosophy*. New York: Monthly Review Press, 1970 (Originally written and published in 1923.)

LaClau, Ernesto. *Politics and Ideology in Marxist Theory*. London: New Left Books, 1977.

Lenin, V. I. *Imperialism as the Highest Stage of Capitalism*, new ed. New

York: International Publishers, 1969. (Originally written and published in 1916.)

—— *Left-Wing Communism, An Infantile Disorder.* New York: International Publishers, 1940. (Originally written and published in 1920.)

—— *One Step Forward, Two Steps Back, The Crisis in our Party* in *V. I. Lenin, Collected Works,* Vol. 7, 2nd ed., trans. Abraham Fineberg and Naomi Jochel; ed. Clemens Dutt. Moscow: Progress Publishers, 1965, pp. 205–425. (Originally written and published in 1904.)

—— *The State and Revolution.* New York: International Publishers, 1968. (Originally written and published in 1917.)

—— *What Is To Be Done?* New York: International Publishers, 1929. (Originally written and published in 1902.)

Leontief, W. W. "The Significance of Marxian Economics for Present-day Economic Theory" *American Economic Review* 22 (March 1938.)

Lukacs, Georg. *History and Class Consciousness.* Cambridge, Mass.: M.I.T. Press, 1971. (Originally written and published in 1922.)

Magdoff, Harry. *The Age of Imperialism.* New York: Monthly Review Press, 1969.

Mandel, Ernest. *An Introduction to Marxian Economic Theory.* New York: Monthly Review Press, 1969.

—— *Late Capitalism.* London: New Left Books, 1978.

—— *The Long Waves of Capitalist Development.* Cambridge, England: Cambridge University Press, 1980.

Marcuse, Herbert. *Reason and Revolution: Hegel and the Rise of Social Theory.* Boston: The Beacon Press, 1954.

Marx, Karl. *Capital,* Vols. I, II, and III. New York: International Publishers, 1967. (Vol. I originally published in Hamburg, Germany, in 1867. First English translation by Samuel Moore and Edward Aveling, edited by Frederick Engels in 1887.)

—— *Critique of the Gotha Program.* Trans. T. B. Bottomore and found in his edition, *Karl Marx, Selected Writings in Sociology and Social Philosophy.* New York: McGraw-Hill Book Company, 1956. (Written in 1845 and originally published in Moscow in 1927 as Karl Marx and Frederick Engels, *Historisch-Gesamtausgabe,* Vol. 1.)

—— *Critique of Hegel's Philosophy of Right.* Trans. Bottomore, *Selected Writings.* (Written in 1844 and first published in the *Marx-Engels Gesamtausgabe,* 1927.)

—— *1844 Manuscripts: Early Texts.* Ed. David McLellan. London: Oxford University Press, 1971. First published in German as Karl Marx and Frederick Engels, *Historisch-Gesamtausgabe,* edited by D. Riazanov and V. Adoratsky, Vol. 3, 1932.)

—— *Grundrisse: Foundations of the Critique of Political Economy.* Trans. Martin Nicolaus. New York: Vintage Books, 1973. (A series of seven notebooks in rough draft written in 1858 and originally published in Berlin: Dietz, in 1953 as *Grundrisse der Kritik der Politischen Okonomie.)*

———— "Letter To Bakunin" cited in David McLellan, *The Thought of Karl Marx*. New York: Harper & Row, 1971. (Found originally in the 1956 Berlin: Dietz, K. Marx and F. Engels, *Werke*. xviii 630.)

———— *Poverty of Philosophy*. Trans. Bottomore, *Selected Writings*. (Written in 1847 and originally published in Vol. 1 of the *Marx-Engels Gesamtausgabe*, 1927.)

———— "Speech on the Anniversary of the People's Paper" found in McLellan, *The Thought of Karl Marx*. (Written in 1856 and published in K. Marx and F. Engels, *Selected Works*, Moscow, 1962.)

———— *The Eighteenth Brumaire of Louis Bonaparte*. New York: International Publishers, 1963. (Originally published in the magazine *Die Revolution* in German, in the city of New York, 1852.)

———— *The Jewish Question*. Trans. Bottomore, *Karl Marx, Early Writings*. New York: McGraw-Hill, 1963. (written in 1844 and found in the *Marx-Engels Gesamtausgabe*, Vol. 1, Moscow, 1927.)

———— and Engels, Frederick. *The Communist Manifesto* New York: International Publishers, 1948. (Originally written and published in London in 1848.)

———— *The German Ideology*. Parts I and III, ed. and introduction by R. Pascal. New York: International Publishers, 1967. (Written in 1846 and published in its entirety in Moscow by the Marx-Engels-Lenin Institute, in the *Marx-Engels Gesamtausgabe*, 1932.)

———— *The Holy Family*. Trans. Bottomore, *Selected Writings*. (Written in 1845 and published in the *Marx-Engels Gesamtausgabe*, 1927.)

Meek, Ronald L. *Smith, Marx, and After. Ten Essays in the Development of Economic Thought*. New York: John Wiley; London: Chapman & Hall, 1977.

———— *Studies in the Labor Theory of Value*. London: Lawrence & Wishart (first published in 1953), with a new introduction in 1973.

Miliband, Ralph. *The State in Capitalist Society*. London: Weidenfeld and Nicolson, 1969.

Murray, Martin. "Recent Views in the Transition from Feudalism to Capitalism." *Socialist Revolution*, Vol. 7, no. 4 (July-August 1977), pp. 64–89.

O'Connor, James. *The Fiscal Crisis of the State*. New York: St. Martin's, 1973.

Ollman, Bertell, *Alienation: Marx's Conception of Man in Capitalist Society*. New York: Cambridge University Press, 1971.

Parkin, Frank. *Class, Inequality, and Political Order*. New York: Praeger, 1971.

Plekhanov, G. *Selected Works*. Moscow: Foreign Languages Publishers, 1968.

Poulantzas, Nicos. *Classes in Contemporary Capitalism*. Trans. D. Fernbach. London: New Left Books; New York: Schocken, 1975.

———— *Political Power and Social Classes*. New York: Schocken 1978. (Originally published Paris: Maspero, 1968.)

50
CONTEMPORARY ISMS

———— see also a series of debates with Ralph Miliband in: *New Left Review*, Vol. 58 (Nov/Dec 1969); Vol. 59 (Jan/Feb 1970); Vol. 82 (Nov/Dec 1973); Vol. 95 (Jan/Feb 1976).

Resnick, Stephen and Wolff, Richard. "The Theory of Transitional Conjunctures from Feudalism to Capitalism." *The Review of Radical Political Economy*, Vol. 11, no. 3 (Fall 1979).

Robinson, Joan. *An Essay on Marxian Economics*, 2nd ed. New York: Macmillan, 1966.

Rules of the Communist Party 31 October, 1961. Adopted by the Twenty-second Party Congress and amended through the Twenty-fifth Party Congress, Moscow.

Samuelson, P. A. *Economics*, 4th ed. New York: McGraw-Hill, 1964.

———— "Marxian Economics as Economics." *American Economic Review* 57 (1964).

———— "The Economics of Marx: An Ecumenical Reply." *Journal of Economic Literature*, Vol. 10, no. 1 (1972).

Sartre, Jean-Paul. *Search for a Method.* Trans. Hazel E. Barnes. New York: Vintage Books, 1968. (Originally published in French as, "Question de Methode" and appearing as a prefatory essay to *Critique de la Raison Dialectique*, Vol. 1, © 1960, Librairie Gallimard.)

Tawney, R. H. *Religion and the Rise of Capitalism.* New York: Mentor, 1947.

Thompson, E. P. *The Poverty of Theory and Other Essays.* New York: Monthly Review Press, 1978.

Wallerstein, Immanuel. *The Modern World System: Capitalist Agriculture and the Origins of the European World-Economy in the Sixteenth Century.* London: New Left Books, 1974.

Weeks, John. "The Sphere of Production and the Analysis of Crisis in Capitalism." *Science and Society*, Vol. 41, no. 3 (Fall 1977).

Weintraub, Sidney. *Capitalism's Inflation and Unemployment Crisis.* Reading, Mass.: Addison-Wesley, 1978.

Williams, Raymond. *Culture and Society, Problems in Materialism and Culture: Selected Essays.* New York: Schocken, 1981.

Witfogel, K. *Oriental Despotism.* New Haven, Conn.: Yale University Press, 1957.

Wright, Eric Olin. *Class, Crisis and the State.* New York: New Left Books/Schocken, 1978.

2.
COMMUNISM: THE CASE OF THE SOVIET UNION

This chapter will consist of four parts. In the first part a description of the Soviet Union will be presented as a model of applied Marxist theory. As is the case with all models, this explanatory model will be rather abstract. It is required in order to set forth what we consider to be the primary and unique characteristics of the Soviet system. We stress those qualities which distinguish it from other societies.* The second part describes the role of the Communist party in the Soviet Union and, particularly, the manner in which that role both fulfills the Marxist-Leninist demands and plays a functional role vis-à-vis the model suggested in the first section. The third part concentrates upon the extent to which the Marxian goal of egalitarianism as a prerequisite to freedom has been achieved. In the final part of this chapter we speculate on the future of the Soviet Union and of communism as a world force.

THE SOVIET COMMUNIST MODEL

The Cold War, an era of "Super Powers," and decades of exchanges and recriminations between the bastions of cap-

*We acknowledge our indebtedness to the models developed by Charles Lindblom in his seminal work, *Politics and Markets, The World's Political-Economic System* (New York: Basic Books, 1977).

51

italism and the bastions of communism have cultivated an environment of cynicism among Western commentators on the Soviet Union and left a legacy of suspicion. It is necessary to clear these obstacles from our view if an attempt at understanding is to have any hope of success. At best, the "cautious reserve" which such obstacles prompt always borders on suspicion and a presumption of malintent on the part of the Soviets. We remain poised, not to understand, but to catch any act which might validate our suspicion. At worst, our cynicism and suspicion lead us to believe that the Soviet Union and its leaders are the incarnation of evil, and analysis becomes a crude preoccupation with red-baiting.

This is not to deny that widespread censorship exists in the Soviet Union, or that public trials and the quashing of dissent are similarly brutal denials of public expression. Neither is this to deny that alcoholism, hooliganism, and retrograde attitudes such as antisemitism are widespread. Nor do we wish to forget that during early periods of forced development, especially under Stalin, hundreds of thousands of people, citizens of the Soviet Union, were imprisoned, killed, or allowed to die unnecessarily. The litany of fault, even horrors, recall actual events, not imaginary tales. There are a number of apologies which have been offered for these events, and there are a number of harsh and bitter recollections and extrapolations. In all of this there has been little understanding.

If we recall our own past, our lengthy and incredibly primitive treatment of the native population in North America is a horrible history of genocide. Nor do our own sins belong to the distant past. There was the bombing of Dresden during World War II. The United States remains the only nation to have ever used the atomic bomb on fellow human beings and, later, in another part of Asia the Vietnam War once more demonstrated that we, too, are capable of barbaric behavior.

At home there are other and more contemporary problems, so serious that the most liberal of recent commentators can write the following:

In the United States...great wealth still leaves a segment of the population in a demoralizing welfare system. Its streets and homes are increasingly unsafe. Its expensive legal system is open to the rich, inaccessible to the poor for civil law, and hostile to the poor in criminal law. Its factories, automobiles, and indifferent citizens degrade the environment in countless ways. And many of its business leaders—among them not only a fringe of irresponsibles but executives of leading corporations—practice bribery of government officials.... This list too can be extended.[1]

This litany of fault and even horrors also reminds us of actual circumstances and events. And, with us, there are apologies and regrets and no little despair, and there is also a bitterness and harshness of judgment. Yet, here also, there seems to be little understanding.

If the systems of the United States and of the Soviet Union continue to compete for the status of worst offender, in the eyes of their respective "victims," and yet yield so little understanding, might it not behoove us to examine these systems with an eye to their competing potentials? We might measure the potential of these systems in terms of their own respective internal logic and values and of the more objective criteria of sustained economic growth and cultural vitality.[2]

We begin with the Soviet Union. Because of the irrational behavior which characterized the Soviet Union through much of Stalin's later years, and which Cold War attitudes reinforced, it is difficult for us to see that the most significant underlying character of the Soviet state is its commitment to a rational order. Charles Lindblom states, in explaining the difference between communist systems and polyarchical systems[3] (model 1 and model 2, respectively):

The key difference between the two visions—and it is not a difference that one would at first expect or appreciate as fundamental—is in the role of intellect in social organization. Model 1 might be called an intellectually guided society. It derives from a buoyant or optimistic view of man's intellectual capacities. Model 2 postulates other forms of guidance for society.

How societies weigh values and make calculated choices in various forms of politico-economic organization is a question we pursued in the analysis of how volitions are formed in the polyarchies. At this point in the book, we confront a watershed: on one side, a confident distinctive view of man using his intelligence in social organization; on the other side, a skeptical view of his capacity.[4]

The reliance on intellectual guidance which Lindblom stresses in this quotation certainly catches a key element of the Soviet model of social organization. And it is true that the faith in people's intellectual competence to meet the task of rational social organization derives from a profoundly optimistic view of human history. But this use of intellectual or rational bases of planning is also particularly forward-looking. In other words, rational planning is not used primarily to maintain a certain form of order or conserve certain national wealth or characteristics. Intellectual guidance here is guidance *toward the future,* in a world where, in Marxian thought, capitalism is the chief impediment of progress.

The question, then, about public policy and rational planning, has less to do with whether the "will of the people" or even the approval of the people molds public policy, but rather whether policy is "correct" or right with regard to the overall project of transformation. In this model there is no lack of concern about the needs of the people but rather a great distinction between what the people want and what they need. Contrary to what Lindblom seems to hold, it does not mean that leaders believe themselves infallible (though megalomania is as much a professional hazard among communist power holders as it is among capitalist leaders), but that their "correct" understanding of history and the scientific method enables them to exercise power in the service of history rather than as a prerogative of authority. In fact, this faith in the scientific method contains the same elements of skepticism which admit that today's evidence may be tomorrow's error. It nevertheless does follow that the intellectual elite is and, for communists, ought to be the political elite (remembering that politics itself is historically defined and does not represent, for communists, the end-all and be-all of human societies). The concept of plural and competing interests as a virtue is decidedly absent in both the theory and practice of communism.

Aside from the assumption about the efficacy of scientific socialism, there is a further assumption regarding the natural harmony of people's true needs. There is an assumption that people are essentially cooperative and nonaggressive creatures, and that competitiveness and aggression are behavioral patterns which reflect the material and social conditions within which people live.* The communist model therefore places little reliance on an interactive or pluralist method for arriving at solutions to social and political problems. At best, these methods are secondary and contained within institutional boundaries (e.g., democratic centralism is a way of insulating the process of pluralist interaction). There is a distrust and dislike for so-called open arenas of conflict resolution such as markets or public debates. While these arenas are not inimical to socialist state control and ownership, they are viewed as haphazard and likely to produce patterns of chaos.

Examples of public policy which explain the foregoing assumptions are those of income distribution and health care. Communists are unwilling to allow market forces to determine the distribution of these essential quantities. Instead, we see a preference for a distribution which is centrally planned and directed in terms of a holistic view of society—a view which seeks to mesh the substantive needs of people with the processual requirements of efficient distribution. This is not to say that there exists no recognition that great differences, for example cultural differences, exist within national borders. In a society as large and varied as the Soviet Union specific accommodations to different ethnic and racial groups are made. For example, the publication of newspapers in a variety of languages and ad-

---

*This commitment to a model of reason and science and the search for a correct if illusive right solution has an intellectual heritage which dates to antiquity. Plato, Rousseau, and Hegel are the chief proponents of this search.

TABLE 2·1
Scientists and Engineers Engaged in Research and Development (per 10,000 population)

1. Soviet Union	1973	44.4
2. United States	1973	25.0
3. West Germany	1972	16.2
4. Sweden	1971	12.2
5. France	1971	11.8
6. Great Britain	1969–70	7.9
7. Italy	1972	6.0

Source: UNESCO Statistical Yearbook, 1974 (Paris: UNESCO Press, 1975). pp. 642–47.

TABLE 2·2
Expenditures for Research and Development (as percentage of GNP)

1. Soviet Union	1973	5.0
2. United States	1973	2.5
3. West Germany	1972	2.3
4. Great Britain	1969–70	2.3
5. France	1971	1.8
6. Sweden	1971	1.5
7. Italy	1972	0.8

Source: UNESCO Statistical Yearbook, 1974 (Paris: UNESCO Press, 1975), pp. 642–47.

dressing a variety of cultural concerns is encouraged. The state's encouragement for minority republics to maintain language, dress, and cultural celebrations and holidays is strong. Formal participation of ethnic and racial groups is constitutionally mandated, within political institutions. In contrast to the "melting pot" of American society, there is, in the Soviet Union, a formal commitment to the maintenance of diversity and the reflection of that diversity in social and political institutions. The continued existence of Russian chauvinism and antisemitism are measures of the lack of progress which seriously degrades continued efforts at social transformation.

56

Even if one grants that the communist model places such emphasis upon intellectual, rational, planned, and centrally directed solutions, it might well be argued that in practice the model is so seriously marred by deviations such as the two mentioned above that the model is worthless either as a prototype or guiding mechanism or as an explanatory device. The remainder of this chapter will demonstrate that the model can be used as an explanatory vehicle and enhance our understanding of both communism, in general, and the Soviet Union, in particular.

Tables 2–1 and 2–2 should offer some convincing evidence that the Soviets themselves continue to place great faith in the capacity of the intellect to resolve problems.[5]

THE PARTY AS VANGUARD

Paragraph 19 of the Rules of the Communist Party of the Soviet Union clearly states that the principle of democratic centralism is to be a central principle of Party rule:*

19. The guiding principle of the organizational structure of the Party is democratic centralism, which signifies:
    a) Election of all leading Party bodies, from the lower to the higher;
    b) Periodic reports of Party bodies to their Party organization and to higher bodies;
    c) Strict Party discipline and subordination of the minority to the majority;
    d) That the decisions of higher bodies are obligatory for lower bodies.

The formal organizational structure of the Communist party includes the Primary Party Organization (PPO), the

*The Rules were adopted by the 22nd Party Congress, 31 October 1961 and amended through the 25th Party Congress, February 1976.

Party Congress, the Central Committee (CC), and the Politburo and Secretariat.

The PPO is the grass roots level of party organization. The units here are organized on the basis of the workplace, although some are organized on the basis of residence, such as in a large housing complex. The Rules state:

20. The Party is built on the territorial-and-production principle: primary organizations are established wherever Communists are employed, and are associated territorially in district, city, etc., organizations. An organization serving a given area is higher than any Party organization serving part of that area.

The ideal arrangement is for the PPO to be small enough that each member will have personal, face-to-face contact with all other members. Approximately half of all PPOs (totaling about 400,000) contain fewer than 15 members and most contain under 50 members. Total Party membership totals about 14 million full members and about 650,000 probationary or candidate members.[6] This figure is about 6 percent of the entire population or about 9 percent of the adult population. The concluding portion of section 59 of the Rules of the Communist Party captures the spirit desired in party members:

The Party organization must see to it that every Communist should observe in his own life and cultivate among working people the moral principles set forth in the Program of the CPSU—in the moral code of the builders of communism.

— loyalty to the communist cause, love of his own socialist country, and of other socialist countries;
— conscientious labor for the benefit of society: He who does not work, neither shall he eat;
— concern on everyone's part for the protection and increase of social wealth;
— a lofty sense of public duty, intolerance of violations of public interests;
— collectivism and comradely mutual assistance: one for all, and all for one;

— humane relations and mutual respect among people: man is to man a friend, comrade and brother;
— honesty and truthfulness, moral purity, unpretentiousness, and modesty in public and personal life;
— mutual respect in the family circle and concern for the upbringing of children;
— intolerance of injustice, parasitism, dishonesty, careerism, and greed;
— friendship and fraternity among all peoples of the U.S.S.R., intolerance of national and racial hostility;
— intolerance of the enemies of communism, the enemies of peace and those who oppose the freedom of the peoples;
— fraternal solidarity with the working people of all countries, with all peoples.

The Party has adhered to Lenin's original desire to keep a close watch on party membership and to reserve membership to those who are dedicated and willing to sacrifice for the Party. Nevertheless, with the growth of education, shifting demographic characteristics, and a greater social awareness, the Party has expanded its membership until today it is six times larger than during Lenin's period. By Western standards, however, membership is still very small, with approximately one out of nine of the adult population enjoying Party membership.

There are both advantages and disadvantages to Party membership for the individual. Undoubtedly, for some the motivation to join the Party is the personal advantage which Party membership brings. For example, certain key political, military, diplomatic, and security positions are open only to Party members. In many other occupations such as journalism, though Party membership is not required as an absolute condition, those with that status are clearly favored. Party members have been frequently favored in the receipt of objects which are in short supply, such as automobiles, housing, and a variety of commodities; and although special stores for Party members, where goods in short supply are sold, have been abolished, the problem of opportunism and the need for Party control over it remains.[7] But it would be a mistake to believe that it is only for the sake of personal gain that people seek Party membership. There exists among most Party members a feeling of pride in being a member of a core group committed to fulfilling the promise of a new society as envisioned by Marx and Lenin.

Certainly, politician for politician, the Soviet Party members are no less well motivated than their Western counterparts and perhaps more so, for along with advantages come many disadvantages for the Party member. He or she is expected to make almost unlimited sacrifice of personal free time for Party goals. The following, from the "Party Members, Their Duties and Rights," section 1 of the Rules:

b) To put Party decisions firmly and steadfastly into effect; to explain the policy of the Party to the masses; to help strengthen and multiply the Party's bonds with the people; to be considerate and attentive to the people; to respond promptly to the needs and requirements of the working people;

c) To take an active part in the political life of the country, in the administration of state affairs, and in economic and cultural development; to set an example in the fulfillment of his public duty; to assist in developing and strengthening communist social relations;

d) To master Marxist-Leninist theory, to improve his ideological knowledge, and to contribute to the molding and education of the man of communist society; to combat vigorously all manifestations of bourgeois ideology, remnants of private-property psychology, religious prejudices and other survivals of the past; to observe the principles of communist morality, and place public intentions above his own; . . .

f) To strengthen to the utmost the ideological and organizational unity of the Party; to safeguard the Party against the infiltration of people unworthy of the lofty name of Communist; to be truthful and honest with the Party and the people; to display vigilance; to guard Party and state secrets;

g) To develop criticism and self-criticism, boldly lay bare shortcomings and strive for their removal; to combat ostentation, conceit, complacency and parochial tendencies; to rebuff firmly all attempts at suppressing criticism; to resist all actions injurious to the Party and the state, and to give information about them to Party bodies, up to and including the CC CPSU;...

i) To observe Party and state discipline, which is equally binding on all Party members. The Party has one discipline, one law, for all Communists, irrespective of their past services or the positions they occupy....

Aside from these stipulated duties, the practical result of Party membership is spending many evenings attending Party meetings, listening to talks on Lenin and Marx, learning theory, volunteering to work with communist youth groups, and so on. In short, Party membership is very demanding. Many, if not most, Soviet citizens demur from the demands of Party membership.

Party membership is further limited by the requirement that the candidate be at least twenty-three years of age or have been a member of the Communist Youth League (Komsomol). More significant, the Party member must be nominated by three party members who have themselves been members for five years and who must vouch for the applicant's good character.

Furthermore, Rule 5 states:

5. Communists recommending applicants for Party membership are responsible to Party organizations for the impartiality of their description of the moral qualities and professional and political qualifications of those recommended.

In spite of these precautions, the Party is still faced with the problem of careerism and opportunism.

At times the regularly established procedures to weed out such individuals seem to have been inadequate and the Party has, from time to time, carried out a general review of the commitment made by Party members. This has resulted in "the exchange of Party Cards"—expulsion through the cancellation of membership in the party. To lose membership constitutes a serious loss of personal legitimacy. One observer indicates that it is far worse to have suffered expulsion than to have never joined at all.[8] The annual rate of expulsion is reported to be at about 50,000, although the rate is increasing among recent successful candidates (from approximately 0.04 percent to perhaps 1.5 percent.[9] It is reported that in 1976 approximately 437,000 members were dropped from the Party through the exchange of Party cards.[10] Duty requirements and the vigilance of the Party in attempting to combat "weak" members indicates the seriousness with which Party officials take the need for an active and dedicated Party, whose members provide a leadership elite to carry forward the goals of communism. The composition of the Party will be discussed under the sections dealing with equality as a primary Marxist goal, but it should be noted here that, while the Party in the Soviet Union is representative to a high degree (e.g., women make up one-fourth of the Party membership), it has not achieved a numerical equity of membership.[11]

The higher party organs, in ascending order of significance, are the Party Congress, the Central Committee, the Secretariat and the Politburo. It is unfortunate, for our purposes, that the highest organs of the Party are clouded in secrecy and that so little is known about their internal operation. Even the question of which has more power and prestige—the Politburo or the Secretariat—is difficult to answer or, more important, what specific roles each plays in the Soviet system, which differentiate them from each other. The general distinction seems to be that the Politburo is concerned with broad policy decisions for both the Party and the nation, while decisions regarding the internal control and direction of the Communist party would be directed by the ten or so Party secretaries who are named by the Central Committee and who make up the executive committee of the Secretariat. For example, a decision such as the invasion of Afghanistan or a major change in economic policy or internal security would be handled primarily, but not exclusively, within the Politburo. The most important people in the Soviet Union hold positions in both organs, and the general secretary of the Party is recognized as the chairman of each and the single most important political leader in the nation.

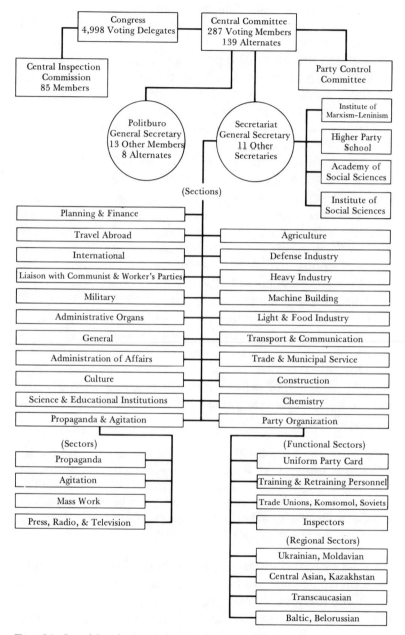

Figure 2.1 Central Organization of the Soviet Communist Party

The Secretariat and Politburo are the apex of the decision-making process and represent, in terms of our model, the rational application of Marxism-Leninism to governmental organization.[12] It is presumed that, through both the socialization and selection process, the individuals who make up these organizations are the best guardians of the dialectical process of historical materialism.

In a nation of approximately 250 million persons and with a GNP of approximately $1,200 billion,[13] it would be foolish to suppose that a general secretary, nine other secretaries of the Secretariat, plus fifteen members and seven alternate members of the Politburo run the USSR by themselves. There are approximately one-quarter million full-time Party workers in the country and a huge bureaucracy. However, through what amounts to an "interlocking leadership" among the Politburo and other government and Party organs[14] it is possible for the Party elite in the two top organizations to maintain a high degree of control and centralized power rivaling the most highly centralized nations of the world, and certainly out-administering any nonsocialist nation of comparable size.

One other device for control deserves special mention. It is the practice of *nomenklatura*, or a system of party and ideological security clearance. Recent authors describe *nomenklatura* as follows:

Each party unit has a list of positions, called the *nomenklatura*, for which it is responsible. It fills these positions by direct appointment or by nominating a single candidate if the post is filled by election. These leaders (who may or may not be party members) can generally be counted on to heed the party's guidance faithfully in the conduct of their jobs.[15]

All Party organizations, from the Secretariat to the PPO, have their *nomenklatura* list of positions. The higher the position, the higher the Party organ on whose list it will appear. High positions in the military, economy, press, television, Party apparatus, governmental bureaucracy, scientific and cultural organizations, in short, all forms of organized

TABLE 2•3
Social Background of the Soviet Political Elite, 1971

Nationality	Percentage of full members of the Central Committee	Percentage of all members of the Politburo
Great Russian (53.3%)*	59.8	52.4
Ukrainian Belorussian (20.5%)	25.0	28.5
Georgian, Armenian, Azer-baidzhanin (4.6%)	3.1	4.8
Lithuanian, Latvian, Estonian Moldavian, Jewish (4.1%)	3.1	4.8
Uzbek, Kazakh, Turkmen, Kir-giz, Tadzhik (8.1%)	5.4	9.5
Other minority (9.4%)	3.6	0
Occupational background		
Party apparatus	45.1	
State apparatus	26.4	
Military and police	10.2	
Symbol manipulators	2.1	
Mass organization apparatus (trade unions, etc.)	2.6	
Economic specialists	6.4	
Scientific-academic-intellectual	2.6	
Workers and peasants	4.7	

*Figures in parentheses are the percentage of the total population of the nationality groups.

Source: Robert H. Donaldson, "The 1971 Soviet Central Committee: An Assessment of the New Elite." World Politics XXIV (April 1972): 382–409.

activity come within the purview of the Party through *nomenklatura*. Moreover, not only do positions become nomenclatured but, in effect, the person holding the clearance for the position becomes nomenclatured. The status, as it is both conferred and controlled by the Party, provides a system of tight linkage and control.

Table 2–3 indicates the characteristics of the top echelon of Party leadership in the Soviet Union.[16]

One matter which should be of concern to the Party elite is the steady increase in average age among the top ranks of the Party. Although long-tenured leadership at the top levels certainly promotes stability, the problem of aging and entrenchment is a trade-off:

From other points of view...the Soviet Union pays a price for stability of elite membership. Since Central Committee members comprise most of the high officials who run all of the USSR's bureaucracies, the low rate of removal means that aging men are in charge at the intermediate level as well as in the inner core of the Politburo. Today only 10 per cent of the Central Committee voting members are under fifty years old; 35 per cent are in their fifties, 47 per cent in their sixties, and nearly 9 per cent in their seventies. Moreover the age level of the elite has been increasing....as recently as six years ago the center of gravity was an elite group in its fifties; now the median group is past sixty.[17]

Another author has computed that "in 1976, the average age of the Soviet Politburo member was 66, making it one of the 'oldest' national leadership bodies in the world."[18] In large part this characteristic may be understood as the result of the maturing of a system in which dismissal, disgrace, or worse has become less common as the mechanism for succession of leadership. Unfortunately, the practice of graceful retirement seems to have not yet become institutionalized.

Beneath the Politburo and Secretariat are two other Party organs which must be understood as functional parts of the Soviet model. These are the Central Committee and the Party Congress.

The formal powers of the Central Committee are quite impressive; they consist of the power to elect members of the Politburo and members of the Secretariat, and the authority to "direct" party activities between Party Congresses, the latter being held approximately every five years.[19] In practice, the Central Committee meets usually for only one day every six months. Nevertheless it would be wrong to assume that the Central Committee is an insignificant body. It is the only body to which the elite four hundred of the Communist party belong as a group. While that fact alone gives the Central Committee some significance, the potential for political combination or some sort of authoritative rebuttal to an existing policy is present. As always in the Soviet model, however, the potential for combination or counter-vailing power is not as serious an attribute of power as it may be elsewhere. Without autonomy, the potential for either power or fragmentation is checked by centralized control. In periods of leadership succession a competition between individuals and institutions may conceivably occur, as was the case with Khrushchev's struggle for power between 1955 and 1959, but it is certainly not a functional part of the Soviet model.[20] One should recognize that nearly half of the CC's four hundred members are members only because of their positions in other Party organs, such as the Politburo or Secretariat, the military, or the state apparatus. More accurately, the Central Committee performs a useful function for the Soviet system as a basis for recognition and leadership recruitment.

Finally, a brief discussion of the Party Congress is required. The Party Congress is referred to as the supreme organ of the Communist party of the Soviet Union. Currently, there are about five thousand delegates to a Congress, which is held about every five years. Although the Congresses today are a poor shadow of their former selves under Lenin, they are nevertheless more open and more frequent than during the Stalin years. The Party Congresses since Stalin have been noteworthy in that they have been used by the leadership to announce major changes in plans or policies. Perhaps the most remarkable of all was the Twentieth Party Congress during which Khrushchev gave his "secret speech" providing, in detail, a list of the crimes and terrorist acts of the Stalin years.[21] The Congresses have been perhaps most useful in mobilizing and inspiring the party membership to follow the lead set by Party leaders. The delegates to the Congress return to all parts of the Soviet Union with their own prestige enhanced and give personal witness to the Party's new positions, having heard it directly from the Party's most distinguished leaders, including the general secretary.

These pages outlining the functions, organization, and membership of the Party provide us with some idea of how the Party fits into the model of communism. We might speculate about the congruence of this model with the theoretical underpinnings of Marxism-Leninism. With regard to the Party-as-vanguard we would venture to say that the "fit" with Leninism is quite close. It is true that the Party is perhaps much larger than Lenin might have envisioned it, yet it remains still only about 6 percent of the population, which is somewhat typical of the developmental pattern of Communist party membership in other Communist countries.[22]

The Party still controls the commanding heights of the government, the military, and the social and educational organization of Soviet society. Its leadership has been adaptive, even succeeding eventually in overcoming the terror of the later Stalin years. Lenin would undoubtedly regret that the Party failed to heed his warning of Stalin's threat:

Comrade Stalin has unlimited authority concentrated in his hands, and I'm not sure whether he will always be capable of using that authority with sufficient caution... . Stalin is too rude and this defect, although quite tolerable in our midst...becomes intolerable in a Secretary-General. That is why I suggest that the comrades think about a way of removing Stalin from that post and appointing another man in his stead who in all other respects differs from Comrade Stalin in having only one advantage, namely that of being more tolerant, more loyal, more polite and more considerate to the comrades, less capricious, etc.[23]

As a whole, the operation of democratic centralism would be judged a close fit with the tenets of Leninism. Lenin himself would perhaps have wished to see an evolution of extended participation within the Party Congresses, that is, more debate and more vigorous interaction among comrades. The use of Party Congresses as sounding boards for the leadership would, perhaps, have elicited a warning opposing capriciousness and insulation, not unlike the tendency Lenin opposed in Stalin. In terms of development and evolution, Lenin would perhaps begin to believe that the Party and state were secure enough to extend membership to those who were ideologically qualified

TABLE 2·4
Communist Party Membership, 1975*

Country	Population	Total Communist Party Membership	Communist Party Membership as Percent of Population
China	942,012,000	28,000,000 (1973)	3.0
USSR	254,300,000	15,000,000 plus	5.9
Vietnam	45,166,000	1,080,000	2.4
Poland	34,022,000	2,453,000	7.2
Yugoslavia	21,352,000	1,192,446	5.6
Romania	21,100,000	2,500,000 (1974)	11.8
East Germany	17,050,000	1,900,000 plus	11.1
North Korea	16,507,000	2,000,000	12.1
Czechoslovakia	14,804,000	1,100,000 plus	7.4
Hungary	10,510,000	754,353	7.2
Cuba	9,252,000	200,000	2.2
Bulgaria	8,741,000	700,000 plus	8.0
Cambodia	7,634,000	10,000	.1
Laos	3,336,000	Unknown	–
Albania	2,378,000	100,000 plus	4.2
Mongolia	1,444,000	58,000 (1972)	4.0

Source: Richard F. Staar, ed., *Yearbook on International Communist Affairs* (Stanford, Calif.: Hoover Institution, 1976), pp. xv, xviii, xix.

*All figures are for 1975 unless otherwise indicated.

rather than as a reward for certain technical competencies. Reducing the personal cost of membership without risking the loss of professional Party commitment would be a means to extend the Party and maintain development and transformation of political class consciousness. A secure state should enhance rather than inhibit such a development under a proletarian rule.

The campaigns against careerism and opportunism and most likely the "exchange of cards" are in keeping with the ideological role of party-as-vanguard. However, the emphasis upon technical education at the expense of philosophical education and praxis is an unfortunate divergence from the Marxist-Leninist model. The use of *nomenklatura* as a device for rationalizing administrative control of the Party over the state is in keeping with the ideological and political supremacy of Party policy, but the potential of this mechanism to perform the retrograde function of political privilege is apparent.

The chief characteristics of the Communist party—its functions, organization, and membership—distinguish it greatly from the political parties of the West and seem to fit well within the model defined by the theoretical foundations of Marxism-Leninism. Its mission of transforming society from a proletarian regime to a classless society, however, is not well-known to the West. The degree of progress must be charted with supplementary information from other loci. We turn now to an examination of the Soviet economy in an attempt to more fully explain the veracity of the model.

THE ECONOMY

Economic Growth

If there was one hope which Marxism held out, it was the hope that the material condition of great masses of people, under the direction of the proletariat, would be improved.

Improvement was to come with a more rational mode of production and with a more equitable distribution than was possible under capitalism. The primitive forms of production and distribution in the economy would be surpassed or bypassed. In the Soviet Union, however, before the material condition of the proletariat could be improved the economy had to be industrialized and expanded. The industrial revolution through which the major Western nations had passed was initiated in the Soviet Union under the direction of the Communist party. State planning, rather than market exchange and private enterprise, incorporated economic decision making. Communists claimed that they could show better performance in economic growth than capitalists had during their industrial revolution. This section will examine those claims.

We will first look at the record of economic growth of the Soviet Union in both aggregate and specific terms. Second, we will examine the distribution of material and social benefits in a movement toward equality. Finally, we will look at the mechanism of state planning in the USSR.

Many in the United States believe that the Soviet economy is doomed to failure. Both academic and journalistic analyses of the Soviet economy have, for as long as we can remember, argued that the Soviet economy is headed for economic disaster. Our examination tells a different story. The facts which we present argue that, in gross terms as measured by increased GNP, the Soviet Union during its period of transition from an agricultural to an industrial economy has performed better than any of the capitalist nations during comparable periods of transition.

Table 2–5 permits a comparison of long-term growth rates of the USSR with those of capitalist countries during transition from agricultural to industrial economies.[24] It should first be noted, however, that the Soviet economy could not properly be termed "state-run" until after 1928. Between the period from, roughly, 1921 to 1928 the New Economic Policy (NEP), initiated by Lenin and adopted at the Tenth Party Congress, resulted in the application of commercial and market principles, first to agricultural

TABLE 2·5
Growth Rates of New Developed Countries

Developed country	Period	Percent Average Per Capita Growth Per Decade of National Product (in constant prices)
United Kingdom	1780–1881	13.4
	1855–1959	14.1
France	1840–1962	17.9
United States	1839–1962	17.2
Sweden	1861–1962	28.3
Japan	1879–1961	26.4
Russia/U.S.S.R.	1860–1913	14.4
	1913–1958	27.4
	1928–1958	43.9

production, next to small industry through the leasing of nominally nationalized industries to individuals and cooperatives, and eventually even to state-owned industries. The "seepage" of market principles to production, management, and finance was considered by Lenin a transitional phase which started out as an appeasement of the peasants but became a policy designed to exploit scarce managerial and production skills and allow an accumulation of capital (through world trade) as a prerequisite to heavy industrial growth. Political unification of peasant and proletarian and economic growth through initial capital accumulation were the twin goals of this transitional phase. Thus the condition of economic underdevelopment, so apparent to communist leaders following the 1917 Revolution, as well as the "incubation" of a socialist economy delayed the arrival of a full-blown state economy. The debate surrounding NEP and the strong theoretical objections to it in 1921–22 cannot be discussed here. Suffice it to say that the late twenties should properly mark the period of comparison. Table 2–5 presents aggregate growth rates.[25]

Furthermore, the superior rate for the Soviet economies has continued. Table 2–6 takes the growth rate from 1960 and permits a comparison of the USSR with other developed countries. It is noteworthy that only Japan with its phenom-

TABLE 2·6
Growth Rates of Total Product, 1960–73, in the Twenty-three Countries with the Largest 1974 Gross National Products

Country	1960–73 Average Annual Aggregate Output Growth Rate (percent)
Japan	10.6
Iran	9.8
Spain	7.0
Mexico	6.9
Brazil	6.6
France	5.7
China	5.6
U.S.S.R.	5.3
Netherlands	5.3
Australia	5.1
Italy	5.0
Austria	4.9
Poland	4.8
Belgium	4.8
Denmark	4.6
West Germany	4.6
United States	4.3
Switzerland	4.3
Argentina	4.2
India	3.5
East Germany	3.0
United Kingdom	2.9
Czechoslovakia	2.9

enal growth rate, and France, with its surge coinciding with the development of central planning, surpass that of the USSR, while other capitalist countries lag quite a way behind.[26]

A more direct comparison of the Soviet economy with the economy of the United States will provide a useful measurement of comparative economic performance.* A recent report begins:

*The following material is taken from a report submitted to the Joint Economic Committee of the Congress of the United States in 1979, entitled, "Soviet Economy in a Time of Change," by the Office of Economic Research, Central Intelligence Agency (hereafter cited as CIA *Compendium*).

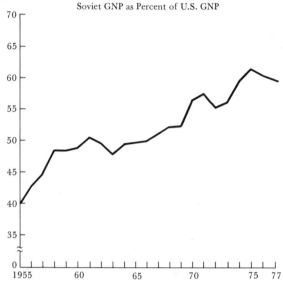

Figure 2.2 U.S. and U.S.S.R.: Trends in Relative Size of GNP

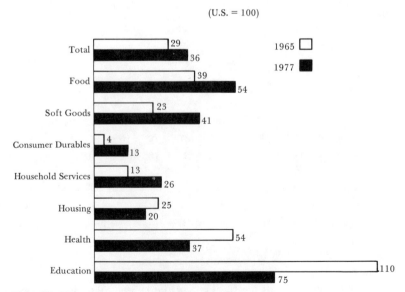

Figure 2.3 U.S. and U.S.S.R.: Relative Consumption per Capita—
U.S.S.R. Consumption as a Percentage of U.S. Consumption

TABLE 2·7
Trends in Soviet and U.S. GNP

Billion 1976 Dollars	1955 U.S.S.R.	1955 United States	1965 U.S.S.R.	1965 United States	1975 U.S.S.R.	1975 United States	1976 U.S.S.R.	1976 United States	1977 U.S.S.R.	1977 United States
GNP	464	880	793	1,252	1,202	1,607	1,253	1,700	1,294	1,782
Consumption	257	561	410	807	623	1,123	644	1,186	664	1,238
Food	84	160	121	200	172	230	175	242	179	251
Soft goods	23	68	45	98	81	136	85	140	89	145
Consumer durables	5	67	12	93	30	143	33	160	36	175
Household services	47	194	81	283	136	402	143	420	148	437
Health	45	38	69	70	94	111	96	118	97	122
Education	53	33	82	61	110	101	112	105	115	108
Investment	86	167	202	249	367	262	390	278	406	305
Machinery and equipment	27	51	80	83	150	111	164	116	173	129
Construction	50	116	102	167	175	151	181	162	185	176
Capital repair*	8		20		42		45		47	
Administration	41	44	49	64	75	122	77	128	80	137
Defense and space	NA	87	90	108	127	90	131	91	133	92
Other	80	20	42	24	11	10	11	17	11	10

*Capital repair is not an accounting category in U.S. national accounts.

TABLE 2·8
Percentage Distribution of GNP, 1976

	USSR	USA
Consumption	51.5	69.8
New fixed investment	31.1	16.4
Defense and space	10.4	5.4
Administration	6.1	7.5
Other	0.9	1.0

Since 1955 the Soviet economy has gained substantially on the American economy in relative terms although the absolute gap separating them is still increasing. In 1955, the post-war recovery completed, the USSR's gross national product (GNP) was 40 per cent of the U.S. GNP. Ten years later, the ratio had climbed to 50 per cent. After 1965, the USSR continued to close the gap, although at a slower rate. By 1977, Soviet GNP had reached 60 per cent of the U.S. level. Over the whole period 1956–77, the absolute difference between U.S. and Soviet GNP increased slightly.[27]

Figure 2.2 shows the aggregate changes in the relative size of the Soviet GNP.[28]

These aggregate data may conceal some important information. Table 2–7 breaks this aggregate data down into component parts and permits a more specific comparison of the GNPs of the United States and the USSR.[29]

These data make clear that the Soviet Union has held back on consumption expenditures in favor of a greater effort in investment and defense. The allocation, in 1976, of the total GNP is presented in the following table. These data go a long way to explain why the USSR is gaining ground on the United States in terms of total GNP.[30]

We now proceed to take a closer look at specific items of comparison: Consumption, New Fixed Investment, Defense and Space, and Administration.

Consumption

Data on relative consumption is presented in Table 2–9.[31]

TABLE 2·9
Expenditures on Consumption

	1955	1965	1977
Billion 1976 dollars:			
U.S.S.R.	257	410	664
United States	561	807	1,233
U.S.S.R. as percent of United States:			
Dollars	46	51	60

During the twenty-year period from 1955 to 1977, the Soviet Union gained in overall consumption but lost ground in comparison to the United States in two significant areas, namely health and education, according to the data presented above. The gains in food consumption and soft goods, two consumer items which were in high demand and short supply in 1955, indicate considerable progress. The Brezhnev livestock program also paid off very well as the per capita consumption of meat and dairy products rose from 27 per cent of the U.S. per capita consumption to 48 per cent in 1977.[32]

Taking a closer look at health services we can examine data provided by *World Health Statistics* and the World Health Organization.* Tables 2–10, 2–11, and 2–12 present the comparative data.[33]

As indicated by the tables, the USSR has made considerable progress in the area of health. In terms of infant mortality, the most frequently used measure of health care, the Soviet Union had reduced its rate from 75 deaths per 1,000 live born in 1950–54, to 24.7 deaths per 1,000 liveborn in 1972. However, a recent thirty-three-page study, published by the U.S. Census Bureau, asserts that there has been an alarming increase in USSR infant mortality rates since 1972. The authors of this report estimate an infant

*These tables are found in Richard L. Siegel and Leonard B. Weinberg, *Comparing Public Policies: United States, Soviet Union and Europe* (Homewood, Ill.: Dorsey Press, 1977).

TABLE 2·10
Infant Mortality per 1,000 Live-Born (ranked by 1972 ratios)

	1950–54	1955–59	1960–64	1965–69	1972
1. Sweden	20.0	17.0	15.4	12.9	13.3
2. France	46.2	33.9	25.5	20.2	16.0
3. England, Wales	27.9	23.2	21.2	18.6	17.2
4. East Germany	59.9	45.2	33.8	22.4	17.7
5. United States	28.1	26.4	25.3	22.7	18.5
6. West Germany	49.3	37.3	29.3	23.2	22.7
7. Soviet Union	75.0	–	–	26	24.7
8. Italy	61.0	48.7	40.7	33.3	27.0

Source: World Health Statistics Report 27, no. 10 (1974): 654–57, 678, 699.

TABLE 2·11
Physicians per 10,000
Population, 1971

Soviet Union	26.4
Italy	18.4
West Germany	17.8
East Germany	16.4
United States	16.1
Sweden	13.9
France	13.9
England, Wales	12.7

Source: World Health Statistics Annual, 1971, vol. 3, *Health Personnel and Hospital Establishments* (Geneva: World Health Organization, 1975), p. 49.

TABLE 2·12
Hospital Beds per 10,000
Population, 1971

Sweden	149.4
West Germany	112.6
Soviet Union	111.3
East Germany	110.2
Italy	105.8
France	103.9
England, Wales	91.2
United States	75.1

Source: World Health Statistics Annual, 1971, vol. 3, *Health Personnel and Hospital Establishments* (Geneva: World Health Organization, 1975), pp. 172–76.

mortality rate of 31.1 per 1,000 in 1976. Other comparable measures are the distribution of physicians per 10,000 population. Here the figures of comparison are 26.4 in the USSR compared to 16.1 in the United States. Not only the quantity of doctors available but quality, that is, the equity of the distribution of these physicians, is a factor which should be taken into account. A highly integrated and carefully planned service structure in the Soviet Union has allowed for a relatively low cost and percentage of GNP for the USSR. Hospital beds per 10,000 population indicate another measure of a greater extensiveness of service in the USSR; compare the rate of 111.3 in the USSR to a rate of 75.1 in the United States.[34]

Data provided by the Organization of Economic Cooperation and Development (OECD) and *UNESCO Statistical Yearbooks* provide a picture of Soviet effort in education.[35] We find that in this area the USSR spent more than twice the amount in 1977 than in 1955, but nevertheless lost the edge over the United States in per capita education consumption which it had established in 1955 (see Table 2–7, p. 75). In part, the United States gain reflects the tremendous rise in state expenditure on education following the launching of Sputnik and the entry of the federal government into the financing of education. During these years, 1955 to 1977, the Soviet Union has not slighted education, for in both 1965 and 1972 the USSR was spending a higher proportion of their GNP on education than was the United States.[36] However, in terms of gross enrollment at the age level 20 to 24, the Soviet Union ranks well below the United States in 1972 (although surprisingly, ahead of West Germany, the United Kingdom, and France and on a par with Sweden).[37]

Although the USSR has not maintained its edge in education and in its relative expenditures for health and housing that have declined, our overall judgement is that consumption during the past twenty years in the Soviet Union has improved considerably. Nevertheless, the Soviet leadership seems to have been careful to see to it that con-

TABLE 2·13
Public Expenditure on Education as Percentage of GNP (ranked by 1972 ratios)

	1972	1965	1955
1. Sweden	7.9*	6.2	4.14
2. Soviet Union†	7.6	7.3†	−
3. United States	6.5	5.3	3.35
4. United Kingdom	5.9	5.1	2.67
5. East Germany†	5.7	5.2	−
6. Italy	5.2	−	2.98
7. France	−	4.55	2.87
8. WestGermany	4.5 (1971)	3.4	2.17

*Percent of gross domestic product at market prices.
†Percent of net material product.

Sources: For 1955: *Reviews of National Policies for Education: France* (Paris: OECD, 1971), p. 48; all others: *UNESCO Statistical Yearbook, 1974* (Paris: UNESCO Press, 1975), pp. 466−90

TABLE 2·14
Median Educational Attainment of 25−34 Age Group

	Year	Median Years of Schooling
1. Sweden	1970	12.75
2. United States	1970	12.54
	1960	12.23
3. East Germany	1971	11.88
4. Soviet Union	1970	10.09 (age group 20−29)
	1959	7.52
5. West Germany	1970	6.98
6. France	1962	5.01
7. Italy	1961	4.05

Source: UNESCO Statistical Yearbook, 1974 (Paris: UNESCO Press, 1975), pp. 53−82.

TABLE 2·15
Gross Enrollment Ratios for Various Age Groups, All Students, and Females, 1972 (ranked by third-level ratios)

		Second Level (Age)	Third Level (20–24)
1. United States	M–F	96 (13–17)	51.48
	F	–	45.01
2. Sweden	M–F	74 (13–19)	22.39
	F	74	19.16
3. Soviet Union	M–F	67 (15–17)	22.25
	F	–	22.52
4. Italy	M–F	64 (11–18)	20.11
	F	59	15.68
5. West Germany	M–F	70 (11–18)	17.13
	F	66	–
6. France	M–F	81 (11–17)	16.99
	F	84	–
7. East Germany (1970)	M–F	61 (15–18)	15.04
	F	–	10.92
8. United Kingdom	M–F	76 (11–17)	15.00
	F	77	11.00

Sources: UNESCO Statistical Yearbook, 1974 (Paris: UNESCO Press, 1975), pp. 138–53; for East Germany: *UNESCO Statistical Yearbook, 1972,* p. 110.

sumption does not cut into a planned progress toward a continued expansion of capital investment and the military and space effort. Testimony to this determination is that only 51.5 percent of its total GNP is devoted to consumption compared to 69.8 percent in the United States, (see Table 2–8, p. 77). The Soviet decision is more dramatically illustrated by the manner in which the dollar amount of average annual increments in the GNP is put to use.[38]

Note that in the USSR 11.9 billion dollars of the increment was allocated to consumption in 1976–77, and 33.0 billion to new fixed investment, while in the United States, 57.5 billion dollars, more than 70 percent of the increase in GNP, was used for consumption and only 21.5 for new fixed investment.

TABLE 2·16
Average Annual Increments in GNP by End Use (in billions of 1976 dollars)

| | 1956–65 | | 1966–75 | | 1976–77 | |
	USSR	United States	USSR	United States	USSR	United States
Consumption	12.7	24.6	19.4	31.7	11.9	57.5
New fixed investment	9.7	8.2	11.4	1.3	33.0	21.5
Defense and space	NA	2.1	4.2	−1.8	3.5	1.0

TABLE 2·17
Expenditures on New Fixed Investment

	1955	1965	1977
Billion 1976 dollars			
U.S.S.R.	86	202	406
United States	167	249	305
U.S.S.R. as percent of United States			
Dollars	51	81	133
Geometric mean comparison	46	70	116

New Fixed Investment

Turning now to the specific area of new fixed investment, we find that during the past twenty years the USSR has continued their policy of investing heavily in increased productive capacity, although in the more recent past the USSR has pursued a policy of more intensive growth rather than extensive growth, that is, stressing increased productivity rather than an expanding labor force. The expenditure on new fixed investment doubled between 1955 and 1965 and then doubled again between 1966 and 1976. This tremendous increase in fixed investment is driven home by looking at the USSR expenditures as a percent of U.S. expenditures.[39]

In 1955, USSR expenditures stood at less than half of U.S. expenditures (46 percent). By 1965 these USSR expenditures reached nearly three-quarters of U.S. expenditures (70 percent). In 1977 the Soviet expenditure on new fixed investment surpassed the U.S. (116 percent). These years represent the latest available data on the USSR from reliable sources but, given the state of the U.S. economy since the mid-seventies, there is no reason to believe that the United States has narrowed the gap and many reasons to believe that indeed United States expenditures have declined even further in relation to expenditures of the USSR in this category.[40] It is the emphasis on increasing fixed investment at such a fast rate which has permitted total expansion of the Soviet GNP and shown such a remarkable performance in relation to most other capitalist countries, with Japan as the exception.

Further evidence of the effort made by the Soviet Union in this area is the number of scientists and engineers engaged in research and development per 10,000 population compared with the number in the United States. In 1973 the ratio was 44.4 scientists and engineers per 10,000 thus engaged in the USSR, and 25.0 in the United States.[41] Furthermore, expenditures on research and development as a percent of GNP in 1974 shows the USSR spending twice the percentage of its GNP than the United States spent: USSR, 5 percent and the United States, 2.5 percent.[42] The practical impact of these differences can be seen in the crucial area of energy policy:

An often overlooked factor in the current debate over energy policy is the relatively small amount of output which the United States obtains from its energy consumption. For each per capita unit of commercial energy used, the U.S. receives a return of only 50 cents' worth of per capita GNP, compared with 93 cents for West Germany and $1.10 for Sweden. The USSR manages to produce 66 cents for each unit of energy, and, furthermore, while the output per unit of energy consumed is declining in the U.S., it is increasing in the USSR....[43]

In 1965 the United States and the USSR produced almost identical ratios of per capita GNP for each unit of per capita commercial energy consumed (United States—$0.57; USSR—$0.58), but by 1974 the USSR was getting $0.66 while the United States was getting only $0.50.[44]

Defense and Space

In another specific area, that of defense and space, we derive an additional index of comparative economic performance. After experiencing devastation in 1918 and suf-

TABLE 2·18
Expenditures on Defense and Space

	1965	1977
Billion 1976 dollars		
U.S.S.R.	90	133
United States	108	92
U.S.S.R. as percent of United States		
Dollars	83	145
Geometric mean comparison	72	138

fering tremendous losses during the Second World War—with an estimated 20 million deaths, including 8 million civilians, and property losses in the billions of dollars—the Soviet Union has developed its military in an effort to achieve parity with that of the United States and its NATO allies. The success of that policy may be seen by the fact that by 1976 the USSR was devoting 10.4 percent of its GNP (Table 2–9 p. 77) to space and defense which amounted to 138 percent of the U.S. expenditure.[45]

The growth is explained by the CIA Congressional Report in this way:[46]

The growth in the estimated cost of Soviet defense programs was predominantly due to rising outlays for procurement and maintenance of military hardware and research and development. Perhaps the most remarkable aspect of Soviet economic history over the past 25 years has been the USSR's success in supporting both civilian and military investment so lavishly. But the strain of continuously increasing the volume of production and responding to demand for greater sophistication and quality seems to be wearing on the Soviet machine-building sector. Judging by the discussion in Soviet periodicals, the USSR's perception of the opportunity cost of defense investment in terms of foregone civilian investment may be increasing.

Remembering that CIA analysis of its data should always be viewed with the greatest skepticism,[47] it seems to us that

85

the above interpretation contains a valid insight. We would agree that civilian investment which improves overall production capacities for the sake of internal economic development is the preferred policy in the USSR. Former discussions about the long reach of Soviet hegemony seem to have missed this point. Nevertheless, it would be foolish to ignore a primary guiding principle of Soviet foreign policy, which is that the nation must never again suffer the loss it endured in the two world wars—wars which were not of its making and which brought upon the Soviet Union nearly unbearable losses. To that end the Soviet Union has consistently allocated a large portion of its GNP to the enhancement of its military and striven to ensure that countries on its borders would be governed by friendly regimes. Any wavering by countries on its borders has been the cause for immediate intervention; Hungary in 1956, Czechoslovakia in 1968, and, most recently, Afghanistan.

Administration

Finally, examining the specific area of administration we look briefly at administrative outlays as a portion of the GNP. These outlays include expenses incurred for a variety of services, including police, judiciary, fire protection, and various municipal services such as garbage collection and maintenance of streets and roadways.[48]

In 1955 the United States and the USSR spent roughly the same amount, $44 billion compared to $41 billion, respectively. However, in 1977 U.S. expenditures were over three times larger than they had been in 1955, while USSR expenditures had only doubled. In percentage terms, the USSR expenditures changed from 92 to 58 percent of U.S. expenditures. It may be difficult to account for this differential given the standard characterization of Russia as an immense bureaucratic state; on the other hand, we all recognize the tremendous growth in the American bureaucracy, especially at the local level, during the past two decades. Another partial explanation of a more "efficient"

TABLE 2•19
Expenditures on Administration

	1955	1965	1977
Billion 1976 dollars			
USSR	41	49	80
United States	44	64	137
USSR as percent of United States			
Dollars	92	77	58
Geometric mean comparison	88	74	56

USSR performance is the use in the Soviet Union of systematic social pressure which perhaps lowers the cost of street cleaning, police expenditures, and other administrative costs. The Soviets have placed great significance upon *obshchestvennye* organizations, which are volunteer public or social organizations as opposed to state or governmental organizations. Included in *obshchestvennye* are such organizations as the comrades' courts and the people's police, (*tovarishcheski sud* and *druzhina*, respectively).[49] For example, the writer has observed that a person who dropped a cigarette package on the street was very likely to be tapped on the shoulder by a person with a red arm band and told to pick it up and throw it in the trash can. Were the person to refuse, I have been told, he or she would be required to appear before a committee at the workplace or residence in order to explain this antisocial behavior. The comrades' courts (translated by some as "comradely court") are elected social agencies and, by statute, are charged with

actively contributing to the education of citizens in the spirit of a communist attitude toward labor and socialist property and the observance of the rules of socialist life, and with developing among Soviet people a sense of collectivism and comradely mutual assistance and of respect for the dignity and honor of citizens.[50]

EQUALITY: INCOME DISTRIBUTION AND SOCIAL STATUS

In looking at GNP data, even on a per capita basis, one must be cautious in drawing inferences regarding income distribution. The manner in which income is distributed can conceal gross inequality, or fail to reveal comparative differences. For example, if one considers only earned income, the distribution in the Soviet Union and in capitalist nations appears very similar. Specific examples indicate a lack of equity of distribution in the Soviet Union in the following areas: building trade workers receive 21 percent more than the average wage; transportation workers, 18 percent more; industrial workers, 10 percent more. On the other hand agricultural workers and health and security workers receive wages below the average: 34 percent and 40 percent, respectively.[51] The following Table 2–20 reports an approximate wage scale.[52]

Furthermore, there is an elite group of people who earn greater wages than the ordinary citizen. These are, for example, scientists and scholars engaged in research, university professors, middle-level Party officials, and certainly high Party officials and government ministers. The general secretary, prime minister, and president of the Presidium are reported to earn 900 rubles or more per month.[53] Add the various "perks" which social and political elites enjoy, and a disparity of income among various occupational levels is apparent.

On the other hand, it is easy to exaggerate these differences. In the first place, on a comparative basis, they are far less than similar differences seen in the United States. Government officials, for example, in the United States are paid a great deal more than their Soviet counterparts, nor are the favored groups of scientists, scholars, and Party officials in the Soviet Union as numerous or as well paid as doctors, movie stars, and other entertainers and athletes in the United States, to say nothing of their respective contributions to the public good. The best overall comparison of

TABLE 2·20
Wage Scale for Various Workers in the USSR

	Rubles per Month
Washerwoman or watchman (lowest of category of labor)	60
Unskilled worker in industry or construction	80
Auto mechanic	120
Truck driver or loader working on piecework	130
Engineer or M.D. just starting work	100
Skilled production worker or pieceworker	140
Dentist with 25 years experience	200
Research chemist on doctoral level	300
Pension for a retired engineer who worked 30 years	92
Stipend for an undergraduate university student	40
Stipend for same student if he is a foreigner	80
Stipend for a foreign graduate student from "capitalist" country	100–175

income distribution in the USSR takes into account not merely earned income, but unearned income as well. It is the status and power derived from *unearned* income, which generates profound and deep sources of inequality in capitalist countries. The following Table 2–21 permits such a comparison.[54]

The table indicates that a person living in a European communist country earning a high income—that at the 95th percentile, would earn slightly more than twice the income of a person in the median income level in the same country. In contrast, in a European capitalist country, a person earning an income at the 95th percentile would earn nearly two and one-half times the amount of compatriots at the median level (about 138 percent more). The second part of the table shows that a comparison between communist and noncommunist countries of Europe, which have a relatively high GNP per capita, substantiates the claim that a higher GNP brings greater equality no matter what the system. However, the communist countries continue to have a relatively *greater*

89

TABLE 2·21
Inequality of Income Standardized for Population and Per Capita Income

	95th percentile	90th percentile	25th percentile
European communist systems	202	169	77
Western Europe	238	189	71
Standardized for a higher level of gross national product per capita			
European communist systems	184	155	82
Western Europe	216	173	76

equality of distribution, even when allowing for development.

Another author, attempting to provide estimates of comparisons of income of all kinds after taxes excluding capital gains and farm income in the USSR, puts it another way:

...the United States is considerably less egalitarian than the USSR. For each country a ratio is indicated between the income of a person at the 95th percentile and one at the 5th. Thus for Sweden, the former has three times the income of the latter. The results are as follows: Sweden, 3.0; Hungary 4.0; Czechoslovakia, 4.3; United Kingdom, 5.0; USSR, 5.7; Denmark, 6.0; Canada, 12.0; United States, 12.7.[55]

Regarding equity of distribution of income, it appears reasonable to conclude that although the distribution of income in the USSR is not equal, it is considerably more equal than in the United States or in nearly every capitalist country in Western Europe. Furthermore, income equity is increasing in the Soviet Union, remarkably so since the death of Stalin. In addition, a strong argument can be made that, aside from equity considerations, distribution of income in the Soviet

90

Union is more rational in terms of the provision of socially important services, such as the promotion of scientific research and inducement of talent for government jobs.

It would be desirable to compare other economic categories in attempting to measure comparative success in equity and distribution. The quality of economic life certainly contains dimensions beyond income distribution. Establishing equivalence for other dimensions and finding comparative data is, unfortunately, very difficult. We will attempt to look at two further categories.

A comparison of the cost of living in the United States and in the USSR is somewhat difficult because patterns of expenditure are very different. For example, the Soviet citizen spends as much as one-third to one-half of the family budget on food, but about only 2.6 percent of the budget on housing (the comparable U.S. figures are 21 to 30 percent and 20 to 24 percent, respectively), according to 1973 calculations.[56] Another factor making comparisons difficult is what might be thought of as the "repressed inflation" of the Soviet economy. Because of the state administration of prices, the price of many items are well below what they would be in a market economy, where demand would raise the price. The goods so priced disappear from the shelves and the person does not spend the money. A measure, then, of this "repressed inflation" is the large amount of money held in saving accounts in the Soviet Union. In 1974 savings amounted to over $78 billion, nearly a fivefold increase over the previous ten years.[57] During the same period in the United States we have witnessed a decline in savings and a large increase in consumer credit.

Regarding unemployment, too, the records of the USSR and capitalist economies are difficult to compare. In the Soviet Union, there is no unemployment, as such, but there is underemployment in that much of the production in the Soviet Union is labor intensive rather than capital intensive. The use of unskilled labor and, in some areas, obsolete tools, in a sense, "underemploys" labor in terms of potential productive yield. Nevertheless, at the same time, a labor shortage has existed in the Soviet Union since the Second World

War and has resulted in the rapid increase in numbers of women in the workforce along with an extensive development of child-care facilities.

Before leaving this brief discussion of equality, we would do well to direct our attention to the treatment of women as well as minorities in the Soviet Union. Progress in these areas appears to be similar to the progress toward establishing material equity. The USSR has not solved the problem of equal treatment for women and minorities, but it has made considerable progress. For example, regarding women in particular, according to the 1970 census women in the USSR represented 50 percent of the workforce compared to 37 percent in the United States. (While we are well aware that the United States has increased its proportion of women in the workforce since that census, comparative census data from the 1980 census was not available in time for publication.) In contrast to occupational trends in the United States, women in the Soviet Union dominate such fields as health and banking where they constitute, for example, 77 percent of all dentists and 74 percent of all doctors. In addition, the 1970 census reveals that women made up 32 percent of directors of state and public institutions, 32 percent of educational institutions, and 16 percent of enterprise directors.[58] While these statistics are impressive by Western standards they also indicate that in proportion to their numbers, women are still living in a male-dominated society, particularly when one considers that representation of women in political elite and managerial or directoral positions does not reflect the good proportion of women in lower and middle-level positions. For example, while woman constitute approximately 23 percent of Party membership, they represented only 14 members of the 241-member Central Committee as of 1976.[59]

Article 34 of the 1977 Draft Constitution of the Soviet Socialist Republics states:

Citizens of the USSR shall be equal before the law, irrespective of origin, social and property status, nationality or race, sex, education, language, attitude to religion, type or character of occupation, domicile or other particulars.

> Equality of rights of citizens of the USSR shall be ensured in all fields of economic, political, social and cultural life.

Moreover, there are statutes specifically prohibiting the utterance of antisemitic remarks and discrimination against Jews. But in the case of dissent, for example, the government crackdown on such people as Alexander Ginzberg, there is evidence that officials made use of the traditional ethnic antipathy toward Jews in efforts to isolate and discipline dissenters.[60] Add to this the fact that approximately 125,000 Jews have emigrated since 1970 and the plight of Jews in the USSR becomes apparent. For very practical reasons Soviet officials have taken steps to ameliorate these conditions and to curb Russian chauvinism but with only limited success.

Regarding the long-term record of the USSR in the area of economic growth and equity, one would have to conclude that in terms of their own goal of achieving a modern, industrialized economy they have been remarkably successful. While one might expect slower growth in the future, there is certainly no reason to perpetuate the myth that the Soviet economy is basically unsound or incapable of showing relatively strong performance. In fact, in the crucial area of energy, which has become a source of increasing difficulty for the West in the past decade, the USSR is an exporter of oil, selling a great deal of their surplus to Eastern European communist countries below the world market price. While this surplus may not continue—some estimates suggest that by the mid-eighties the USSR may itself become an importer—Soviet developments in the area of nuclear energy, including the extensive development of breeder reactors, promise an energy-independent status within a world of shrinking energy resources. Furthermore, the Soviet ratio of energy usage to productive energy-efficient sectors, as noted earlier (p. 84), has been steadily improving.

Regarding income distribution, the data suggest that the twin goals of ensuring that all income is earned and that through wage inducement differentials in income are equalized or based upon contributions to the well-being of society as a whole are being met. Even though the achievement of total equity has never been a primary goal in the Soviet Union, the present system of wage allocation has resulted in a distribution which is considerably more equal than that of capitalist countries.

Finally, regarding social equality, the Soviet Union has not overcome various discriminatory practices such as those toward minorities and women. However, here, too, the period of communist rule has been one of *de jure* equality and steady *de facto* improvement over past conditions. The greatest progress seems to be in the treatment of women and the worst in the intractable and traditional antisemitism and the Greater Russian chauvinism.

THE FUTURE OF SOVIET COMMUNISM*

W. Arthur Lewis writes that the key to understanding the development of a self-generating industrial society is:

to understand the process by which a community is converted from being a 5 percent saver to a 12 percent saver—with all the changes in attitudes, in institutions and in techniques which accompany this conversion.[61]

That the Soviet Union has achieved this conversion or transformation is undeniable. As Andrew Martin has recently pointed out, the mechanism by which this industrialization took place was established by "a process compressed within about a half decade from the inception of the First Five Year Plan in 1929 to the Seventeenth Party Congress in 1934."[62] The costs of such a transformation were, of course, enormous. As has been well documented, these costs were incurred in both human and material resources, but the command economy developed by Stalin relying on Lenin's

*We acknowledge our indebtedness to an article by Andrew Martin, "Political Constraints on Economic Strategies in Advanced Industrial Societies," *Comparative Political Studies* 10,3 (October 1977): 323.

model of Party rule did result in the phenomenal transformation of a primitive economy into a modern military-industrial state economy. It was not until Stalin's death that the question of political rule became an issue in the Soviet Union—or to be more accurate, previous attempts to question Stalin's authority and tactics were forcibly stifled by Stalin in the 1930s, and most of those who had the courage to raise these issues carried their dissent to their early graves.

Drawing from Martin's analysis, we might offer one scenario for the future of Soviet communism which may be termed the "logic of industrialization." Within this scenario a further transformation will follow the industrialization of the Soviet economy, namely, a transformation to a pluralist society, indistinct from societies under capitalism. The theory underlying this scenario argues that during a country's passage from an agricultural to an industrial economy it is functionally necessary for popular democratic forces to be suppressed. These popular democratic forces must be restrained in their push for freedom which carries with it a demand for a more consumer-based economy than would be compatible with the need for capital accumulation and an increased rate of savings. Self-generating industrialization absolutely requires this initial surge, so the argument goes. Following the transition, according to our scenario, and once a fully industrialized and integrated economy is established, the "politics" of the situation changes. The "mature" phase will now require increased rates of political participation. Participation now becomes a functional necessity rather than a liability. Furthermore, the political structures which facilitate participation are likely to be very similar among nations of similar levels of industrial development. Talcott Parsons, an early proponent of the so-called "convergence thesis" believed, in 1964, that the political structures of all advanced industrial societies were bound to become essentially "democratic."

An alternative scenario, suggested by Martin, challenges the pluralist theory:

An alternative view of what happens to the political structures through which industrialization takes place might run as follows. The successful implementation of the industrialization strategies made possible by the political structures reinforces the political resources of those who have power in those structures. This gives them both a stake in preserving those structures and the means for doing so, even in the face of economic costs or political tensions that might result. Their political dominance and command of the fruits of industrialization permit them to minimize such costs by accommodating to the pressures for increased participation and reduced inequality that may be generated in advanced industrial societies. However, they retain the political resources needed to keep changes in the scope of participation and the pattern of economic development within limits that do not threaten the political universe on which their power is based, and even to reverse such changes should they come to threaten the political structures. Thus, advanced industrial societies are not likely to become effectively democratic or, to the extent that they become democratic, to remain so.[63]

Based on this argument, one can anticipate that the dual character of the Party which Lenin forged will continue. That is to say, the "organizational weapon"—the bureaucracy, the Party apparatus—will continue to control the machinery of government, dominate the planning process, maintain an authoritarian economic allocation, and generally administer the government. On the other hand, the Party is a political instrument of power in the Soviet Union and the mechanism by which political decisions, in contrast to administrative decisions, will continue to be made. There will continue to be tension between these two loci of decision making, *but not necessarily a destructive tension*; and perhaps even a creative tension will emerge between the dual Party elements of bureaucracy and politics. It was precisely the restoration of an equilibrium between the elements or roles of the Party which Khrushchev tried to achieve in the post-Stalin era. This restoration involved structural changes as well—changes to ensure that another Stalin would not arise and changes that recognized a new Party supremacy.

The new-found institutionalization of both the organizational weapon and the political control of the Party may be observed in the manner in which decisions regarding the direction the economy would take in the seventies. As has been noted, the command economy which the USSR has developed has made possible growth rates which have far exceeded the 12 percent Lewis believed necessary for the transformation of society (p. 94). But the mid-1970s, however, the Soviet economy was experiencing difficulty in maintaining efficiency, and there was a need to rethink its mode of operation. Martin summarizes this process as follows:

Inherent in both the process by which the detailed annual plans are drawn up and in the system of targets based on the plans which production units are required to meet, the interaction of these flaws sets up a vicious circle that inhibits technological innovation and combines chronic shortage and bottlenecks with widespread waste. Although these flaws had been present all along, they did not exact so heavy a toll at earlier stages of industrialization, when the ability to take large increments to productive capacity was the major source of gains. However, as the amount of unutilized resources diminished and the sheer size and complexity of the economy grew, continued growth became increasingly dependent on efficient allocation and utilization of resources. The obstacle to this built into the centralized control of production had an increasing impact. At the same time, the regime's goal intensified the need to make the utmost of productive possibilities.[64]

In the debate that followed, two options seemed available to the Soviets: one may be described as "computopia," in Martin's words, and the other "market socialism." The first alternative was a solution which did not endanger the central control actors or mechanisms. It held out the promise of a remedy for the weakness in a command economy without *fundamental* change. The second solution, that of market socialism, appeared to represent a serious threat in the development of new political elites outside the Party. An official of Gosplan, the central planning agency, rejected market socialism out of hand with the statement that "in practice it means a weakening of the role of the socialist state and the party of the working class in the management of the economy"[65] (shades of the early debates surrounding the implementation of NEP). It is, therefore, not surprising that the Party elite opted for the computopia solution, even in the face of strong warning from several Soviet economists who had developed the most sophisticated models but nevertheless cautioned that creating ever-more sophisticated models could not solve the problem, which was the centralized economy itself. While the warning may be correct, the choice of the option of computopia does not spell imminent breakdown. Rather it means that the Party elite has decided to incorporate a measure of economic waste rather than endanger either political control or socialist integrity.

If the foregoing analysis is correct, one can expect to see the future of Soviet communism as an extrapolation from the trend of the last thirty years toward increased stability of Party control. An institutionalized Party, ruling without terror but exercising a monopoly over political decision making and exercising decisive control over the command economy, would be expected to maintain its policy of cautious growth in consumption while continuing to place a large share of the country's expanding wealth in new fixed investment in capital. One might expect not an increase in "popular participation" but greater and more managed democratic centralism along the lines advocated by Lenin, together with an increased effort at political and social integration of the society through an extension of the partisan ranks. The coming succession of leadership, which will be quite massive due to the age and numbers of the present leadership, will not bring about a very great change in the Soviet system, except perhaps to further strengthen the institutionalization of Party rule and induce a closer merger of bureaucratic and political functions. The USSR should continue to be encouraged in the belief that rational central planning by a highly educated and ideologically committed Party elite is the course to follow to achieve Marxian goals.

NOTES

1. Charles E. Lindblom, *Politics and Markets, The World's Political—Economic System* (New York: Basic Books, 1977), p. 247.
2. Ibid., p. 260.
3. For the classic definition of polyarchy, see Robert A. Dahl, *A Preface to Democratic Theory* (Chicago: University of Chicago Press, 1956), and Robert A. Dahl, *Polyarchy* (New Haven, Conn.: Yale University Press, 1971).
4. Lindblom, *Politics and Markets*, p. 248.
5. *UNESCO Statistical Yearbook* (Paris: UNESCO Press, 1975), pp. 642–47, as reported in Richard L. Siegel and Leonard B. Weinberg, *Comparing Public Policies: United States, Soviet Union and Europe* (Homewood, Ill.: Dorsey Press, 1977), p. 115.
6. John A. Armstrong, *Ideology, Politics, and Government in the Soviet Union, An Introduction*, 3rd ed. (New York: Praeger, 1974), pp. 56–59.
7. David F. Roth and Frank L. Wilson, *The Comparative Study of Politics* (Boston: Houghton Mifflin Company, 1976), p. 233.
8. Armstrong, *Ideology, Politics and Government in the Soviet Union*, p. 57.
9. Ibid.
10. *Pravda*, 25 February 1976, p. 7, as reported in Donald D. Barry and Carol Barner-Barry, *Contemporary Soviet Politics* (Englewood Cliffs, N.J.: Prentice-Hall, 1978), p. 105.
11. Roth and Wilson, *The Comparative Study of Politics*, p. 291.
12. Armstrong, *Ideology, Politics and Government in the Soviet Union*, p. 78.
13. Office of Economic Research, Central Intelligence Agency, *Soviet Economy in a Time of Change, A Compendium of Papers Submitted to the Joint Economic Committee, Congress of the United States*, Vol. 1, 10 October 1979 (Washington, D.C.: U.S. Government Printing Office, 1979), p. 370 (hereafter cited as CIA *Compendium*).
14. Zbigniew Brzezinski and Samuel P. Huntington, *Political Power: USA/USSR* (New York: Viking Press, 1968), p. 161.
15. Roth and Wilson, *The Comparative Study of Politics*, p. 233. See also, Armstrong, *Ideology, Politics and Government in the Soviet Union*, p. 92.
16. Robert H. Donaldson, "The 1971 Soviet Central Committee: An Assessment of the New Elite," *World Politics* XXIV (April 1972): 382–409, as reported in Roth and Wilson, *The Comparative Study of Politics*, p. 291.
17. Armstrong, *Ideology, Politics and Government in the Soviet Union*, p. 98.
18. Gary K. Bertsch, Robert P. Clark, and David M. Wood, *Comparing Political Systems: Power and Policy in Three Worlds* (New York: John Wiley and Sons, 1978), p. 276.
19. Central Committee powers are spelled out in *Rules of the Communist Party*, Part IV, "Higher Party Organs," adopted by the Twenty-sec-

ond Party Congress, 31 October 1961, and amended through the Twenty-fifth Party Congress, March 1976.

20. Brzezinski and Huntington, *Political Power: USA/USSR*, pp. 240–52.
21. Leonard Schapiro, *The Communist Party of the Soviet Union* (New York: Random House, 1960), p. 543.
22. Bertsch, Clark, and Wood, *Comparing Political Systems*, p. 266.
23. Lenin in a series of letters considered his "last will and testament," as quoted in John G. Gurley, *Challengers to Capitalism*, 2d ed. (New York: W. W. Norton and Company, 1979), p. 97.
24. Schapiro, *The Communist Party of the Soviet Union,* pp. 213–30.
25. Lindblom, *Politics and Markets*, p. 295, citing Simon Kuznets, *Modern Economic Growth* (New Haven, Conn: Yale University Press, 1966), pp. 64–65.
26. Claire Wilcox et al., *Economics of the World Today*, 3d ed. (New York: Harcourt, Brace, Jovanovich, 1976), p. 19, based on *World Bank Atlas*, as cited in Lindblom, *Politics and Markets,* p. 296.
27. CIA *Compendium*, p. 370.
28. Ibid., p. 383.
29. Ibid., p. 384.
30. Ibid., p. 371.
31. Ibid., p. 385.
32. Ibid.
33. Siegal and Weinberg, *Comparing Public Policies*, pp. 220–21; and Christopher David and Murray Feshback, *Rising Infant Mortality in the USSR in the 70's*, Bureau of The Census, Series P–95, No. 74.
   These reports are from the *World Health Statistics Report 27*, no. 10 (1974), pp. 654–57, 678, 699: *World Health Statistics Annual, 1971*, vol. 3, 1975, p. 49, and pp. 172–76.
34. John Frey, *Medicine in Three Societies* (New York: American Elsevier Publishing, 1970), as discussed in Siegel and Weinberg, *Comparing Public Policies*, n. 44, p. 221.
35. Siegel and Weinberg, *Comparing Public Policies*, pp. 257–58.
36. Ibid., p. 257.
37. Ibid., p. 258.
38. CIA *Compendium*, p. 370.
39. Ibid., p. 386.
40. See, for example, the "Text of President Reagan's Address to the Nation reporting on the State of the Nation's Economy" as he appeared on television networks, 5 February 1981, and the text as reported in the *New York Times*, 6 February 1981, p. A12.
41. Siegel and Weinberg, *Comparing Public Policies*, p. 115, based on *UNESCO Statistical Yearbook, 1974* (Paris: UNESCO Press, 1975), pp. 642–47.
42. Ibid.
43. Charles A. McCoy, letter to the *New York Times*, 12 February 1978.

44. Siegel and Weinberg, *Comparing Public Policies*, computed from Tables 4–8 and 4–11, pp. 114 and 116.
45. CIA *Compendium*, p. 387.
46. Ibid.
47. See Alexander Cox, "The C.I.A.'s Tragic Error," *New York Review of Books*, vol. XXVII, no. 17, 6 November 1980, pp. 21–24.
48. CIA *Compendium*, p. 388.
49. Frederick C. Barghoorn, *The USSR* (Boston: Little, Brown and Company, 1966), pp. 339–46.
50. Harold J. Berman and James W. Spindler, "Soviet Comrades' Courts," *Washington Law Review*, 38,4 (Winter 1963): 895, which also contains a translation of the 1961 RSFR Statute on Comrades' Courts, pp. 587–88, as cited in Barghoorn, *The USSR*, p. 344.
51. Barry and Barner-Barry, *Contemporary Soviet Politics*, p. 186.
52. John Scott, *Detente Through Soviet Eyes* (New York: Radio Liberty Committee, 1974), p. 57, as cited in ibid., p. 187.
53. Barry and Barner-Barry, *Contemporary Soviet Politics*, p. 188.
54. Lindblom, *Politics and Markets*, p. 271, based on estimates standardized for population and per capita income by Frederic L. Pryor, *Property and Industrial Organizations in Communist Nations* (Bloomington: Indiana University Press, 1973).
55. Peter Wiles, *Distribution of Income, East and West* (Amsterdam: North-Holland Publishing Co. and New York: Elsevier Publishing Co., 1974), pp. xiv, 48, as noted in Lindblom, *Politics and Markets*, p. 271.
56. Barry and Barner-Barry, *Contemporary Soviet Politics*, pp. 191–97.
57. Ibid., p. 195.
58. *Moscow Statistics*, 1973, as cited in ibid., p. 181.
59. Ibid., p. 124.
60. Natalia Gorbanevskaya, *Red Square at High Noon* (New York: Holt, Rinehart and Winston Publishing Co., 1972) as quoted in ibid., pp. 228–29.
61. As quoted in Andrew Martin, "Political Constraints on Economic Strategies in Advanced Industrial Societies," *Comparative Political Studies* 10,3 (October 1977): 323.
62. Ibid., p. 327.
63. Ibid., p. 333.
64. Ibid., pp. 338–39.
65. Ibid., p. 340, quoting Ellman (1973).

BIBLIOGRAPHIC NOTE

Recent scholarship on the Soviet Union has followed remarkably closely the developments (fads) in American political science. In the first phase the emphasis was on the totalitarian nature of the Soviet Union and coincided with the cold-war period of American history. Three outstanding examples of this approach are Friedrich and Brzezinski's *Totalitarian Dictatorship and Autocracy* (1956), substantially revised by Friedrich in the second edition in 1966; Brzezinski and Huntington's *Political Power: USA/ USSR* (1968) and Friedrich, Curtis, and Barber's *Totalitarianism in Perspective: Three Views* (1969).

It would be a mistake to assume that American radical scholars have escaped the anti-Soviet bias which has affected so much of American writing on the Soviet Union. In fact, American radicals have been quite outspoken in their objection to Soviet ("Bolshevik") expressions of either theoretical Marxism or socialism. Nicolaus's recent critique as well as the consistent and long-standing criticism of the *Monthly Review* writers are expressions of the left's hostility to Russian communism. It is asserted by the left that Russia has betrayed Marxism through a retrogression into state capitalism or through the creation of a new bureaucratic form of state exploitation. These assertions are not without rebuttal (see Julius Jacobson's *Soviet Communism and the Socialist Vision*, for example).

A second phase in the course of Sovietology might be labeled the "convergence" period. During this time it was fashionable to view the USSR and the USA as developing historically along tracks which would meet at some place and time in the future of post-industrial societies. This convergence perspective began to emerge at the same time as the "end-of-ideology" notion became current in the United States. Daniel Bell played a leading role in both developments. Perhaps the most influential works in the convergence literature are Bell's "Post-Industrial Society: The Evolution of an Idea" (*Survey*, Vol. 17. no. 2, Spring 1971) which was subsequently expanded into a book, *The Coming of Post-Industrial Society: A Venture in Social Forecasting* (1973), and P. A. Sorokin's "Mutual Convergence of the United States and the USSR to a Mixed Sociological Type" (*International Journal of Comparative Sociology*, Vol. 1, no. 1, 1960).

The next development in Soviet studies was an attempt to utilize pluralist interest group theory in analyzing Soviet politics. Hammer's work is representative of this genre. He combines Politburo politics, described as oligarchic, with the maneuverings of the large Soviet bureaucracies, which he labels "bureaucratic pluralism."

Recent work on the Soviet Union seems to focus upon two main themes: the influence of political culture (typified by White's work, *Political Culture and Soviet Politics*), which parallels the interest in socialization and political culture in contemporary U.S. political science; and a more dominant theme of leadership and the orderly transition of leadership during change of regimes. (Once again we would alert the reader to the possible domestic influences shaping these foci of Soviet studies. The Kennedy assassination and subsequent assassination attempts on successive presidents, the Johnson withdrawal from presidential politics, and Nixon's resignation to escape impeachment, and the problem of one-term presidencies indicate a problem of orderly transition of leadership in America.)

It is fitting to conclude this bibliographical note with a comment on Merle Fainsod's seminal work, *How Russia is Ruled* (1953). No other work has done so much to shape the American image of the Soviet Union. It is a pleasure to note that this work has been rewritten by the well-respected Jerry Hough, whose refinements are indicated in the title, *How The Soviet Union Is Governed*. While Mr. Hough had received some critical reviews complaining that the book (in terms of its temperance toward the Soviet Union) was not "faithful" to the Fainsod edition, we are encouraged in thinking that this generation of Soviet scholars will be better served by the closer approximation to reality that Mr. Hough is able to offer. If the cold-war mentality of the 1950s is indeed returning to academia as well as to the nation, its strain will be less virulent, perhaps, due to the temperance of good scholarship.

BIBLIOGRAPHY

Armstrong, John A. *Ideology, Politics, and Government in the Soviet Union, An Introduction.* New York: Praeger, 1974.

Barghoorn, Frederick C. *Politics in the USSR*, 2d ed. Boston: Little, Brown, 1972.

Barry, Donald D. and Barner-Barry, Carol. *Contemporary Soviet Politics.* Englewood Cliffs, N.J.: Prentice-Hall, 1978.

Bell, Daniel. *The Coming of Post-Industrial Society: A Venture in Social Forecasting.* New York: Basic Books, 1973.

Bergson, Abram. *The Economics of Soviet Planning.* New Haven: Yale University Press, 1964.

Berman, Harold J. and Spindler, James W. "Soviet Comrades' Courts." *Washington Law Review*, Vol. 38, no. 4 (Winter 1963).

Bertsch, Gary K., Clark, Robert P., and Wood, David M. *Comparing Political Systems: Power and Policy in Three Worlds.* New York: John Wiley, 1978.

Brown, Emily Clark. *Soviet Trade Unions and Labor Relations.* Cambridge, Mass: Harvard University Press, 1966.

Brzezinski, Zbigniew and Huntington, Samuel. *Political Power: USA/ USSR*. New York: Viking Press, 1968.

Central Intelligence Agency, Office of Economic Research. *Soviet Economy in a Time of Change*, "A Compendium of Papers submitted to the Joint Economic Committee, Congress of the Unites States," Vol. 1 (10 October 1979). Washington, D.C.: U.S. Government Printing Office.

Christensen, L. R., Cummings, D., and Jorgenson, W. D. "An International Comparison of Growth in Productivity, 1947–1973." *SSRI Workshop*, No. 7531. Madison, Wisc: University of Wisconsin (Oct. 1975).

Claudin, Fernando. *The Communist Movement from Comintern to Cominform*. New York: Monthly Review Press, 1975.

Cox, Alexander. "The C.I.A.'s Tragic Error." *New York Review of Books*, Vol. 26, no. 17 (November 6, 1980).

Dahl, Robert. *A Preface to Democratic Theory*. Chicago: University of Chicago Press, 1956.

———*Polyarchy*. New Haven: Yale University Press, 1971.

Davis, Christopher and Feshback, Murray. *Rising Infant Mortality in the USSR in the 70's*. Bureau of the Census, Series P–95, no. 74. Washington, D.C.: U.S. Government Printing Office.

Donaldson, Robert H. "The 1971 Soviet Central Committee: An Assessment of the New Elite." *World Politics*, Vol. 24 (April 1972).

Fainsod, Merle. *How Russia is Ruled*, 2d ed. Cambridge, Mass.: Harvard University Press, 1963 (first edition, 1953).

Frey, John. *Medicine In Three Societies*. New York: American Elsevier, 1970.

Friedrich, Carl J., Curtis, Michael, and Barber, Benjamin. *Totalitarianism in Perspective: Three Views*. New York: Praeger, 1969.

——— and Brzezinski, Zbigniew. *Totalitarian Dictatorship and Democracy*, 2d ed. New York: Praeger, 1969.

Gorbanevskaya, Natalya. *Red Square at High Noon*. New York: Holt, Rinehart and Winston, 1972.

Gregory, Paul and Stuart, Robert. *Soviet Economic Performance*. New York: Harper & Row, 1970.

Gurley, John G. *Challengers to Capitalism*. New York: W. W. Norton, 1979.

Hammer, Darrell P. *USSR: The Politics of Oligarchy*. Hinsdale, Ill.: Dryden Press, 1974.

Hohmann, Hans-Hermann, Kaser, Michael C., and Thalheim, Karl C. eds. *The New Economic Systems of Eastern Europe*. Berkeley: University of California Press, 1975.

Hough, Jerry. *Soviet Leadership in Transition*. Washington, D.C.: The Brookings Institute, 1980.

———*The Soviet Prefects: The Local Party Organs in Industrial Decision-Making*. Cambridge, Mass.: Harvard University Press, 1969.

———— "Political Participation In the Soviet Union." *Soviet Studies*, Vol. 38, no. 1 (January 1976).

———— and Fainsod, Merle. *How the Soviet Union Is Governed*. Cambridge, Mass.: Harvard University Press, 1979.

Hunt, E. K. "Socialism and the Nature of the Soviet Union." *Socialist Revolution*, Vol. 7, no. 2 (March-April 1977).

Jacobson, C. G. *Soviet Strategy—Soviet Foreign Policy: Military Considerations Affecting Soviet Policy-Making*. Glasgow, Scotland: The University Press, 1972.

Jacobson, Julius, ed. *Soviet Communism and the Socialist Vision*. New Brunswick, N.J.: Transaction Press/ Dutton & Co., 1972.

Kuznits, Simon. *Modern Economic Growth*. New Haven, Conn.: Yale University Press, 1966.

Laibman, David. "The 'State-Capitalist' and 'Bureaucratic-Exploitative' Interpretations of the Soviet Socialist Formation: A Critique." *Review of Radical Political Economy*, Vol. 10, no. 4 (Winter 1978).

Lindblom, Charles E. *Politics and Markets, The World's Political-Economic System*. New York: Basic Books, 1977.

Mao Tse-tung. *A Critique of Soviet Economics*. Trans. Moss Roberts. New York: Monthly Review Press, 1977. (This collection of critical comments by Mao regarding Soviet economics is derived from the Chinese collection *Long Live the Thoughts of Mao Tsetung* which first appeared in 1967. They were first articulated by Mao in 1958 and then between 1961 and 1962.)

Marcuse, Herbert. *Soviet Marxism: A Critical Analysis*. New York: Columbia University Press, 1958.

Martin, Andrew. "Political Constraints on Economic Strategies in Advanced Industrial Societies." *Comparative Political Studies*, Vol. 10, no. 3 (October 1977).

Matthews, Mervyn. *Class and Society in Soviet Russia*. London: Allen Lane; New York: Penguin, 1972.

Meyer, Alfred. *Leninism*. Cambridge, Mass.: Harvard University Press, 1957.

Moore, Barrington. *Soviet Politics—The Dilemma of Power*. Cambridge, Mass.: Harvard University Press, 1950.

Nove, Alec. *The Soviet Economy: Its Organization, Growth, and Challenge*. Boston: Houghton-Mifflin, 1966.

Osborn, Robert. *Soviet Social Policies*. Homewood, Illinois: Irwin, 1970.

Pares, Bernard. *A History of Russia*, 5th ed. New York: Knopf, 1949.

Prior, L. Frederick, *Property and Industrial Organizations in Communist Nations*. Bloomington, Ind.: Indiana University Press, 1973.

Reddaway, Peter and Schapiro, Leonard, eds. *Lenin: The Man, the Theorist, the Leader*. New York: Praeger, 1967.

Reed, John. *Ten Days that Shook the World*. Foreward by V. I. Lenin. New York: International Publishers Press, 1967 (first edition, 1919).

Rigby, T. H. "Soviet Party Membership Under Brezhnev." *Soviet Studies* (July 1972).

Roth, David F. and Wilson, Frank L. *The Comparative Study of Politics.* Boston: Houghton-Mifflin, 1976.

Schapiro, Leonard. *The Communist Party of the Soviet Union.* New York: Random House, 1960.

Schwartz, Harry. *An Introduction to the Soviet Economy.* Columbus, Ohio: Charles E. Merrill, 1968.

Sherman, Howard. *The Soviet Economy.* Boston: Little, Brown, 1969.

Skilling, H. Gordon and Griffiths, Franklyn. *Interest Groups in Soviet Politics.* Princeton, N.J.: Princeton University Press, 1971.

Spindler, James W. and Berman, Harold J. "Soviet Comrades' Courts." *Washington Law Review,* Vol. 38, no. 4 (Winter 1963).

Szymanski, Albert. "The Class Basis of Political Processes in the Soviet Union." *Science and Society,* Vol. 42, no. 4 (Winter 1978–79).

Tucker, Robert C., ed. *The Lenin Anthology.* New York: W. W. Norton, 1975.

Ulam, Adam B. *Stalin, The Man and His Era.* New York: Viking Press, 1973.

Wesson, Robert, ed. *The Soviet Union Looking to the 1980's.* Millwood, N.J.: KTO Press, 1979.

White, Stephen. *Political Culture and Soviet Politics.* London: Macmillan, 1979.

Wilcox, Claire, et al. *Economies of the World Today,* 3rd ed. New York: Harcourt Brace Jovanovich, 1976.

Wilczynski, J. *The Economics of Socialism,* 3rd ed. Studies in Economics Series. London: Allen & Unwin, 1977.

Wiles, Peter. *Distribution of Income, East and West.* New York: Elsevier; Amsterdam: North-Holland Publishing Co., 1974.

Wolfe, Bertram, *Three Who Made a Revolution,* rev. ed. New York: Dell, 1964.

Yanowitch, Murray. *Social and Economic Inequality in the Soviet Union.* White Plains, N.Y.: M. E. Sharpe, 1977.

3

LIBERALISM

As the old feudal order crumbled and the power of the landed aristocracy declined, a new philosophy emerged which served to justify the ascending and dominant class— the bourgeoisie.

One necessary ingredient that served the needs of the new class was freedom—freedom to travel, freedom of inquiry, and, above all, the freedom of commerce, a condition free from the hindrances and shackles of old customs and old hierarchies. The new freedom was, in a sense, a condition of equality—freedom from special favors and licenses granted by a monarch on grounds of blood or simple and often capricious largess. The new conditions of freedom and equality were needed by the new merchant class and the emerging bourgeoisie and manufacturing class to overtake and secure the domain of "rule" left by the declining aristocracy. The cornerstone of the new ideology was liberty. This was liberty of a special kind, however. It was a liberty defined by the absence of restraint, or a "negative freedom"; that is, the belief that freedom meant being left alone, and, in particular, being free of state-imposed restrictions. This new freedom has had a tremendous and lasting impact. It is a view very much alive in contemporary society, some three hundred years later.*

*The original statement of the division between negative and positive liberalism was made by Isaiah Berlin in his essay "Two Concepts of Liberty," an inaugural lecture delivered before the University of Oxford 31 October 1958.

There is another view of freedom, however, namely, "positive freedom." In this view, one which has never successfully challenged the former and more conservative definition, freedom is conceived as the realization of one's potential as a human being rather than as a condition of the absence of restraint. In this view a person is considered to be most free who has come closest to realizing his or her full human potential.

In recent years those who adhere to the second, or "positive," definition of freedom, and support a more active role for the state which is derived from that view of freedom, are called "liberals." Those who adhere to the dominant negative definition are called "conservatives." These two terms have caused much confusion in Americans' understanding of politics. Mistakenly, "liberal" and "conservative" have been seen as two polar opposites. A more correct view would be that what we call liberal and conservative are two different attitudes toward freedom and that they are *both* merely different aspects of liberalism. This chapter will focus upon these two different definitions of freedom and the ideologies which emanate from them.

NEGATIVE FREEDOM AND THE CONSERVATIVE VIEW

In the seventeenth century, the old feudal order was in a state of decay and the emerging needs of commerce and trade could no longer be confined by the traditional political and social relationships of the feudal order. Professor Heilbroner documents the case of a German merchant in the sixteenth century as follows:

Andreas Ryff, a merchant, bearded and fur-coated, is coming back to his home in Baden; he writes a letter to his wife that he has visited thirty markets and is troubled with saddle burn. He is even more troubled by the nuisances of the times; as he travels he is stopped approximately once every six miles to pay a custom toll; between Basle and Cologne he pays thirty-one levies.

And that is not all. Each community he visits has its own money, its own rules and regulations, its own law and order. In the area around Baden there are 112 different measures of length, 92 different square measures, 65 different dry measures, 163 different measures for cereals and 123 for liquids, 63 special for liquor, and 80 different pound weights.[1]

The insular condition and autonomy of each of the communities described in Herr Ryff's journey make it clear that a new economic and political order is needed. The specific need is for an environment congenial to the development, indeed maturation, of capitalism: an environment which provides mobility and easy exchange, an environment conducive to the development of markets and capital accumulation. Old traditions such as the divine right of kings, and the accompanying systems of hierarchy and rule would be required to give way to a freer, more liberating way of acting and thinking.

Thomas Hobbes (1588–1679)

No one in the seventeenth century was more perceptive about the need for change than Thomas Hobbes, and the clarity of his definition of freedom stands today as perhaps the most masterful treatise on the subject.[2] The appeal of Hobbes's definition of freedom is its natural and reasonable "fit"—it seems even today, to contain an obvious rightness; it is intuitively acceptable. Hobbes defines freedom as follows:

> ...*A FREEMAN is he that in those things which by his strength and wit he is able to do is not hindered to do what he has a will to do.*[3]

It should be noted at this point that Hobbes, by his own confession was motivated by a consideration of fear rather than by a primary concern with liberty. In his own time he understood that there existed a great danger to the civil order of Britain, a civil order which permitted Britain to become one of the most advanced and prosperous nations on the earth. After the defeat of the Spanish Armada, coincidentally, on Hobbes's birthdate in 1588, England had succeeded in becoming the world leader in commerce and industry. A remarkable market society was developed which contained the freedom of trade and commerce and the enforcement of contracts in the king's courts. However, as the seventeenth century began, those happy times seemed greatly endangered. The war which had begun on the continent in 1618 continued until 1648 and became known as the Thirty Years War. Moreover, the English had no need to look overseas to see the approaching danger to their civil order, for the religious strife between the Puritans and the Church of England was imminent. Thomas Hobbes thought, and rightly so, that of all wars, civil war was the worst; and civil wars fought on religious grounds were the worst of all. He was astute enough to realize that the days in which a divine right of kings could command the necessary authority to legitimize a government were over. He, therefore, set for himself the task of trying to justify authority without reference to the traditional moral code of monarchial divinity.

Hobbes's justification of authority is best understood by following the geometric logic of his argument. Let us begin by imagining what life would be like if all authority were suddenly removed. Imagine a condition where there would be no law, no police, no courts, no prisons, no military, no civil authority whatsoever. Hobbes believed, as well might we, that such a condition, which he described as the "state of nature," would be a "state of war" of "every man against every man." It would be such an intolerable condition that life itself would be endangered, and for Hobbes the first law of nature was to preserve one's life.

Whatever, therefore, is consequent to a time of war where every man is enemy to every man, the same is consequent to the time wherein men live with the other security than what their own strength and their own invention shall furnish them withal. In such condition there is no place for industry, because the fruit thereupon is uncertain, and consequently no culture of the earth;

no navigation nor use of the commodities that may be imported by sea; no commodious building; no instruments of moving and removing such things as require much force; no knowledge of the face of the earth; no account of time; no arts; no letters; no society; and, which is worst of all, continual fear and danger of violent death; and the life of man solitary, poor, nasty, brutish, and short.[4]

The fear of violent death and the desire to preserve not only life but "commodious living," leads people to form a civil state ruled by a sovereign, composed of one or many, with sufficient authority to maintain law and order. Although not even the state can remove entirely the "general inclination of all mankind; a perpetual and restless desire of power after power that ceases only in death."[5] The state does bring a check on such desires so that they do not endanger all. The liberal state provides a framework in which those seeking power will not endanger the domestic tranquility needed for commerce and industry. Hobbes, with his usual clarity, states the proper role of liberty which the sovereign would grant to his subjects:

The liberty of a subject lies, therefore, only in those things which, in regulating their actions, the sovereign has pretermitted; such as is the liberty to buy and sell and otherwise contract with one another; to choose their own abode; their own diet, their own trade of life; and institute their children as they themselves think fit; and the like.[6]

It becomes clear that the freedom so dear to Hobbes is freedom of contract: a condition of "armistice," in a sense, where contenders for power could agree to conditions for further agreement. He realized that freedom could not be preserved without a state of sufficient *legitimacy* and *power* to *command obedience*. He comprehended what a contemporary theorist has so well summarized: "He understood that men are not born but are made sociable, that there is no justice without law, and no law without discipline, and no discipline without sanctions."[7]

Although Thomas Hobbes's ideas of freedom and contract provide a liberating influence, his idea of sovereignty appeared less attractive in a world of new power seekers. The new elite was growing in strength and was able to challenge and unseat the landed aristocrats in some cases, or at the very least to force the aristocracy to share power. They were fearful, these contentious elites, of a sovereignty such as Hobbes advocated which would be not only unlimited but self-perpetuating. Sovereigns so powerful and self-perpetuating could, after all, fall under the control of forces which were opposed to the new elites, namely, the masses of liberated serfs who now lived in poverty in cities. Organized groups such as the Diggers and the Levellers,* who challenged the ascendancy of the new ruling class, aroused in the new bourgeoisie a fear which surpassed the feelings of confidence following their defeat of aristocratic rule.

John Locke (1632–1704)

In the writings of John Locke[8] the merchants and manufacturers found the apology for their rule they desired. Locke's manuscripts, especially his *Second Essay on Civil Government* asserted that: (1) private property is a natural right; (2) the reason governments are established is for the protection of private property; (3) only men of property should control the state; and (4) the state should not interfere in the lives of people more than was necessary for the enforcement of contractual obligations under law.

Locke, using the form of reasoning begun by Hobbes, affirms that there is a "natural right" to property:

...I shall endeavour to show how men might come to have a property in several parts of that which God gave to mankind in common, and that without any express compact of all the commoners.

*Leveller activity reached its peak and was relatively short-lived, from 1646 to 1649. The Diggers, followers of Gerrard Winstanley, published their *Law of Freedom* in 1652 and thereafter were responsible for providing only a residue of agrarian utopia.

26. God, who hath given the world to men in common, hath also given them reason to make use of it to the best advantage of life and convenience. The earth and all that is therein is given to men for the support and comfort of their being. And though all the fruits it naturally produces, and beasts it feeds, belong to mankind in common, as they are produced by the spontaneous hand of nature, and no body has originally a private dominion exclusive of the rest of mankind in any of them, as they are thus in their natural state, yet being given for the use of men, there must of necessity be a means to appropriate them some way or other before they can be of any use, or at all beneficial, to any particular man. The fruit or venison which nourishes the wild Indian, who knows no enclosure, and is still a tenant in common, must be his, and so his—i.e., a part of him, that another can no longer have any right to it before it can do him any good for the support of his life.

27. Though the earth and all inferior creatures be common to all men, yet every man has a property in his own person. This nobody has any right to but himself. The labour of his body and the work of his hands, we may say, are properly his. Whatsoever, then, he removes out of the state that nature hath provided and left it in, he hath mixed his labour with it, and joined to it something that is his own, and thereby makes it his property.[9]

It should be noted that this right to property is individualistic and derives from one's right to the use of one's own body and labor. It acknowledges no debt to anyone or to society. This claim of absolute sovereignty over one's body is what C. B. Macpherson[10] has labeled *possessive individualism*. If one held that a person had the sole domain over his or her own body, owing nothing to others, then it would follow that individuals had an equal right to alienate themselves from the product of their labor. That is, they could be separated from what they produced, and in such a manner would no longer be able to even identify that which they had made. Even more than this, one could sell one's labor to others; then the product of this labor would be theirs and not one's own. At that time the alienation of the individual from his or her labor would be complete. What a convenience—no, more than that, what a necessary fiction for the development of capitalism!

One can easily recognize that there exist two serious limitations to this natural right of property. These two limitations were recognized by Locke as: (1) that an individual may appropriate only that amount of nature's bounty which leaves "enough and as good"[11] for others, and (2) that one should only appropriate that which can be used before it spoils.

As a contemporary student of Locke has explained, one of Locke's main purposes in the *Second Treatise* is to overcome these two limitations.[12] Macpherson demonstrates how, by the introduction of money as natural to the state of nature, Locke is able to overcome the limitation of spoilage.

> ...by compact transfers that profit, that was the reward of one man's labour, into another man's pocket. That which occasions this, is the unequal distribution of money; which inequality has the same effect too upon land, that it has upon money.... For as the unequal distribution of land, (you having more than you can, or will manure, and another less) brings you a tenant for your land;...the same unequal distribution of money, (I having more than I can, or will employ, and another less) brings me a tenant for my money....[13]

> The chief end of trade is Riches & Power which beget each other. Riches consists in plenty of moveables, that will yield a price to foraigner, & are not like to be consumed at home, but espetially in plenty of gold & silver. Power consists in numbers of men, & ability to maintaine them. Trade conduces to both these by increasing y^r stock & y^r people. & they each other.[14]

Furthermore, it is clear that Lock views money not merely as a medium of exchange but as capital necessary for the development of trade and commerce.

The second limitation—that there be ample store in nature for all—required a more intricate argument by Locke than the mere introduction of money. The root of his argument is that if property was privately held, rather than held in common, the cultivation of this privately held property would be so much more intensive that the wealth created would be abundant. The fruits of the land would be so multiplied by private cultivation that all could be richer, and therefore the taking of property for oneself did not lessen but instead increased the total bounty of nature. As a clinching argument, he blames the poor state of the American Indians on their lack of private property, which he contrasts with the high stage of development in England where private property is the norm.

41. There cannot be a clearer demonstration of anything than several nations of the Americans are of this, who are rich in land and poor in all the comforts of life; whom nature, having furnished as liberally as any other people with the materials of plenty, i.e., a fruitful soil, apt to produce in abundance what might serve for food, raiment, and delight; yet, for want of improving it by labour, have not one hundredth part of the conveniences we enjoy. And a king of a large and fruitful territory there feeds, lodges, and is clad worse than a day labourer in England.[15]

This ingenious defense of private property and its unlimited accumulation as a matter of natural right remains today a bulwark of liberal political theory. What was also needed was the justification of the formation of the state for the protection of this property right. Locke states the reasons for a necessary state formation in the following passages:

124. The great and chief end therefore of men's uniting into commonwealths, and putting themselves under government, *is the preservation of their property*; to which in the state of nature there are many things wanting.

First, There wants an established, settled, known law, received and allowed by common consent to be the standard of right and wrong, and the common measure to decide all controversies between them. For though the law of nature be plain and intelligible to all rational creatures, yet men, being biased by their interest, as well as ignorant for want of study of it, are not apt to allow of it as a law binding to them in the application of it to their particular cases.

125. Secondly, In the state of nature there wants a known and indifferent judge, with authority to determine all differences according to the established law. For everyone in that state being both judge and executioner of the law of nature, men being partial to themselves, passion and revenge is very apt to carry them too far, and with too much heat in their own cases, as well as negligence and unconcernedness, make them too remiss in other men's.

126. Thirdly, In the state of nature there often wants power to back and support the sentence when right, and to give it due execution. They who by any injustice offended, will seldom fail where they are able by force to make good their injustice. Such resistance many times makes the punishment dangerous, and frequently destructive to those who attempt it.

127. Thus mankind, notwithstanding all the privileges of the state of nature, being but in an ill condition while they remain in it, are quickly driven into society. Hence it comes to pass, that we seldom find any number of men live any time together in this state. The inconveniences that they are therein exposed to by the irregular and uncertain exercise of the power every man has of punishing the transgressions of others, make them take sanctuary under the established laws of government, and therein seek the preservation of their property.[16]

Locke's concern to protect the natural right of property is clear in the list of limitations on state power, which appears in Book XI of the *Extent of the Legislative Power*. Nothing could be more explicit of his interest than the first sentence of section 138: "The Supreme Power cannot take from any man any part of his property without his consent."[17] Constitutionalism, about which there has been so much comment with regard to John Locke, is primarily a limitation on the role of the state for the protection of property rights.

A final element of Locke's political theory is needed to affirm the class bias of his liberal theory. A question arises: Who shall control the state? Upon whom does the ultimate sovereign authority rest—including the right to revolt should that drastic step prove necessary for the protection of property? Locke's answer, as interpreted by C. B. Macpherson, is:

Everyone, whether or not he has property in the ordinary sense, is included, as having an interest in preserving his life and liberty. At the same time only those with "estate" can be full members, for two reasons: only they have a full interest in the preservation of property, and only they are fully capable of that rational life— that voluntary obligation to the law of reason—which is the necessary basis of full participation in civil society. The labouring class, being without estate, are subject to, but not full members of, civil society. If it be objected that this is not one answer but two inconsistent answers, the reply must be that both answers follow from Locke's assumptions, and that neither one alone, but only the two together, accurately represent Locke's thinking.[18]

The right to rule (more accurately, the right to control any government) is given to the men of estate only; it is they who are given the decisive voice about taxation without which no government can exist.[19] On the other hand, the obligation to be bound by law and subject to the lawful government is fixed on all, whether or not they have property, as is made abundantly clear when Locke speaks of tacit consent.

...every Man, that hath any Possession, or Enjoyment, of any part of the dominions of any Government, doth thereby give his *tacit Consent*, and is as far forth obliged to Obedience to the Laws of that Government, during such Enjoyment, as any one under it; whether this his Possession be of Land, to him and his Heirs for ever, or a Lodging only for a Week; or whether it be barely travelling freely on the Highway; and in Effect, it reaches as far as the very being of any one within the Territories of that Government.[20]

It remains necessary to document Locke's view that the laboring class, in addition to *lacking a property interest* sufficient to entitle them to a role in governing the commonwealth, also *lacked the rational capacity* to be permitted to govern society. We have been taught to think of Locke as the liberal guardian of individual rights, which we have mistakenly taken to be a benign defense of human dignity. We forget that he is the same person who believed that "the children of the unemployed 'above the age of three' were unnecessarily a burden on the nation; they should be set to work, and could be made to earn more than their keep."[21] The following two quotations of the liberal Locke should be sufficient to disabuse even the most ardent Lockian of a view which mistakes Locke for an egalitarian democrat:

...the labourer's share [of the national income], being seldom more than a bare subsistance, never allows that body of men time, or opportunity to raise their thoughts above that, or struggle with the richer for theirs, (as one common interest) unless when some common and great distress, uniting them in one universal ferment, makes them forget respect, and emboldens them to carve to their wants with armed force: and then sometimes they break in upon the rich, and sweep all like a deluge. But this rarely happens but in the male-administration of neglected, or mismanaged governments.[22]

Locke continues in Book IV:

...a religion suited to vulgar capacities; and the state of mankind in this world, destined to labour and travel.... The greatest part of mankind have not leisure and logick, and superfine distinctions of the schools. Where the hand is used to the plough and the spade, the head is seldom elevated to sublime notions, or exercised in mysterious reasoning. 'Tis well if men of that rank (to say nothing of the other sex) can comprehend plain propositions, and a short reasoning about things familiar to their minds, and nearly allied to their daily experience. Go beyond this, and you amaze the greatest part of mankind.[23]

Adam Smith (1723–1790)

Adam Smith developed a liberal economic and political theory which harmonized very nicely with Locke's negative liberalism. Adam Smith's unbounded faith was that the division of labor coupled with unbridled competition would achieve greater wealth than could be imagined. This would occur because the division of labor would increase productivity by an almost infinite factor.

The greatest improvement in the productive powers of labour, and the greater part of the skill, dexterity, and judgement with which it is any where directed, or applied, seem to have been the effects of the division of labour....

This division of labour, from which so many advantages are derived, is not originally the effect of any human wisdom, which foresees and intends that general opulence to which it gives occasion. It is the necessary, though very slow and gradual, consequence of a certain propensity in human nature which has in view no such extensive utility; the propensity to truck, barter, and exchange one thing for another....[24]

The division of labor would be so beneficial because it was in harmony with the natural liberty which Smith saw as guiding the proper destiny of humankind.

All systems either of preference or of restraint, therefore, being thus completely taken away, the obvious and simple system of natural liberty establishes itself of its own accord. Every man, as long as he does not violate the laws of justice, is left perfectly free to pursue his own interest his own way, and to bring both his industry and capital into competition with those of any other man, or order of men....[25]

The uniform, constant, and uninterrupted effort of every man to better his condition, the principle from which publick and national, as well as private opulence is originally derived, is frequently powerful enough to maintain the natural progress of things toward improvement, in spite both of the extravagance of government, and of the greatest errors of administration....[26]

Every individual is continually exerting himself to find out the most advantageous employment for whatever capital he can command. It is his own advantage, indeed, and not that of the society, which he has in view. But the study of his own advantage naturally, or rather necessarily leads him to prefer that employment which is most advantageous to the society.... I have never known much good done by those who affected to trade for the publick good....[27]

It may come as a surprise that Smith could write so

optimistically at a time when the lot of the average working person was so bad. Once again Professor Heilbroner's description of the working conditions in Smith's time is most vivid:

A sixteen-hour working day was not uncommon, with the working force tramping to the mills at six in the morning and trudging home at ten at night. And as a crowning indignity, many factory operators did not permit their work-people to carry their own watches, and the single monitory factory clock showed a strange tendency to accelerate during the scant few minutes allowed for meals. The richest and most far-sighted of the industrialists may have deplored such excesses, but their factory managers or hard-pressed competitors seem to have regarded them with an indifferent eye.[28]

Nor can Adam Smith plead ignorance of the circumstance of the working class, for he observed:

Of mankind the half die under 7, and of these the children of the vulgar most commonly. It is not unusual in Wales, Ireland, and the Highlands to see women without a child who have borne above a dozen, which is owing to their poverty which renders them unfit to bring up the most tender of all animals, viz infants.[29]

While Smith was moved by the conditions of the poor, he regarded their condition as unchangeable and necessary. A modern student of Smith, explains Smith's thinking:

...without there being profits from the value which workmen add to the materials, the capitalist would have no interest to employ them, nor...is the compensation...no more than a very moderate compensation for the risk and the trouble of employing the stock.[30]

However, the profits of these early capitalists, as well as later ones, were often quite large indeed. The success of one Richard Arkwright, for example, who rose from a barber's apprentice to die a wealthy man leaving an estate worth 500,000 pounds in 1792, is a story worth retelling:

Richard Arkwright, who had gotten together a little capital ped-
dling women's hair to make wigs, invented (or stole) the spinning
throstle. But, having constructed his machine, he found it was not
so easy to staff it. Local labor could not keep up with the "regular
clerity" of the process—wagework was still generally despised and
some capitalists found their new-built factories burned to the
ground out of sheer blind malice. Arkwright was forced to turn
to children—"their small fingers being active." Furthermore,
since they were unused to the independent life of farming or
crafts, children adapted themselves more readily to the discipline
of factory life. The move was hailed as a philanthropic gesture—
would not the employment of children help to alleviate the condition of the "unprofitable poor"?[31]

The freedom enjoyed by the early capitalists is impressive.
    The condition of children or of the poor, while a source
of constant worry because of the threat to peace and domestic tranquility it posed, was not the proper concern of
the state within Smith's view of natural liberty:

According to the system of natural liberty, the sovereign has only
three duties to attend to; three duties of great importance, indeed,
but plain and intelligible to common understandings: first, the
duty of protecting the society from the violence and invasion of
other independent societies; secondly, the duty of protecting, as
far as possible, every member of the society from the injustice or
oppression of every other member of it, or the duty of establishing
an exact administration of justice; and, thirdly, the duty of erect-
ing and maintaining certain public works and certain public institutions, which it can never be for the interest of any individual,
or small number of individuals, to erect and maintain; because
the profit could never repay the expense to any individual or
small number of individuals, though it may frequently do much
more than repay it to a great society.[32]

It should be noted, however, that even Smith recognized
that the state was essential for providing a degree of infrastructure beneficial to the accumulators of capital, those
necessary services which they could not provide for themselves or for others at a profit.

It should be recalled that during Smith's day he was renowned not as the founder of capitalism but as a moral philosopher. Upon the publication in 1759, sixteen years before the *Wealth of Nations*, of *The Theory of Moral Sentiments* Adam Smith gained almost instant fame. Nowhere is the contradiction or paradox in liberalism more apparent than when Smith the distinguished moral philosopher can see that the only reason freedom is preferable to slavery is because "free" miners "voluntarily" agreed to work "below ground and live there for years."

When men are constrained to work for another they will not work as if at liberty....In the Mines of Silesia...(where free labor is used in contrast to English salters and colliers whose wages are fixed by law and who are confined to one trade and one master)...the miners go *voluntarily* below ground and live there for years.[33]

These sentiments of Smith were a part of his Glasgow lectures on jurisprudence. It would appear that the *freedom so valued by liberals like Smith was no more than the increase in utility gained by free labor over slave labor, and it has changed little since that time.*

Another even harsher proponent of negative freedom was the nineteenth-century Englishman, Herbert Spencer. He, too, like Smith, saw great virtue in negative freedom and viewed it as part of the grand design of nature.

Herbert Spencer (1820–1903)

It remained for Herbert Spencer to take negative freedom to its logical conclusion. Drawing upon Charles Darwin's discoveries of natural selection as the process for the evolution of the species, Spencer developed what has become known as social Darwinism, and the phrase "survival of the fittest" was given a social application. Spencer states his view on the beneficence of letting laissez-faire work its "will" regardless of the harshness of the results:

The well-being of existing humanity, and the unfolding of it into this ultimate perfection, are both secured by that same beneficient, though severe discipline, to which the animate creation at large is subject: a discipline which is pitiless in the working out of good: a felicity-pursuing law which never swerves for the avoidance of partial and temporary suffering. The poverty of the incapable, the distresses that come upon the imprudent, the starvation of the idle, and those shoulderings aside of the weak by the strong, which leave so many 'in shallows and in miseries' are the decrees of a large, far-seeking benevolence....[34]

Spencer, always on his guard against state intervention, writes similarly to contemporary "libertarian" indictments of state intervention:

If an Institution undertakes not two functions, but a score—if a government, whose office is to defend citizens against aggressors, foreign and domestic, engages also to disseminate Christianity, to administer charity, to teach children their lessons, to adjust prices of food, to inspect coalmines, to regulate railways, to superintend house-building, to arrange cab-fares, to look into people's stink-traps, to vaccinate their children, to send out emigrants, to prescribe hours of labour, to examine lodging houses, to test the knowledge of mercantile captains, to provide public libraries, to read and authorize dramas, to inspect passenger-ships, to see that small dwellings are supplied with water, to regulate endless things from a banker's issue down to the boat fares on the Serpentine [was] it not manifest that its primary duty must be ill discharged in proportion to the multiplicity of affairs it busies itself with?[35]

While the negative freedom school of liberalism has not, heretofore, won control of modern government and gone as far as Spencer's doctrinaire approach, it was and is the dominant strain of liberalism, especially as practiced in the United States. Both the necessary development of the modern welfare state and the counterposition of a positive liberal school of thought have "sheltered" state developments.

UTILITARIANS

Two other giants of liberal theory, Jeremy Bentham[36] and John Stuart Mill,[37] stand at the watershed between negative freedom and positive liberty.

Jeremy Bentham (1748–1832)

Jeremy Bentham adhered most closely to a negative view of freedom. While he was anxious to abandon the metaphysical elements of the earlier liberals such as Locke (and spoke of natural law as "nonsense upon stilts"), he nevertheless shared their atomistic concept of society. He denied that there existed a moral order to be discovered in nature; rather he argued, in his introduction to the *Principles of Morals and Legislation*:

Nature has placed mankind under the governance of two sovereign masters, pain and pleasure. It is for them alone to point out what we ought to do, as well as to determine what we shall do. On the one hand the standard of right and wrong, on the other the chain of causes and effects, are fastened to their throne. They govern us in all we do, in all we say, in all we think: every effort we can make to throw off our subjection will serve but to demonstrate and confirm it.[38]

In terms of public policy, it would seem to follow that if what we call right, just, moral, or good is merely that which gives us pleasure, then government ought to follow those policies which give the "greatest happiness to the greatest number." While logically this frame of mind might, indeed *has*, led to the "welfare state" which functions to meet the demands of the people, such a result was not so clearly favored by Jeremy Bentham. He shared the individualist and negative view of freedom of his predecessors. Developing what has become known as the "Benthamite Calculus," he viewed the individual as a machine which processed for each decision, a series of calculations that determined an ultimate course of action (what in today's model of "rational-actor" choice is called "maximization"). Bentham tells us there are fourteen simple pleasures, such as sense, wealth, and skill, and twelve simple pains such as privation and awkwardness. Each, in turn, is divided into components; for example sensations are broken down into touch, sight, hearing, and sex. These simple pains and pleasures may be combined to produce complex pains or pleasures. An individual processes these pains and pleasures according to further criteria: intensity, duration, certainty or uncertainty, propinquity or remoteness, fecundity, and purity. While this rational calculus may seem to us absurd, today's reliance on quantification and the belief that what are fundamentally moral choices can be reduced to an amoral calculus have become a major "skill" and tenet of liberalism. There still exists in liberalism a very strong tendancy to deny qualitative differences and to insist along with Bentham that "Pushpin is as good as Pushkin if it gives as much pleasure."[39]

John Stuart Mill (1806–1873)

Mill's break with the individualistic, self-centered, and narrow utilitarism of Bentham is nowhere more apparent than in his essay on utilitarianism:

It is better to be a human being dissatisfied than a pig satisfied; better to be Socrates dissatisfied than a fool satisfied. And if the fool, or the pig, are of a different opinion, it is because they only know their own side of the question. The other party to the comparison knows both sides....

...The happiness which forms the utilitarian standard of what is right in conduct, is not the agent's own happiness, but that of all concerned. As between his own happiness and that of others, utilitarianism requires him to be as strictly impartial as a disinterested and benevolent spectator. In the golden rule of Jesus of Nazareth, we read the complete spirit of the ethics of utility. To do as you would be done by, and to love your neighbour as yourself, constitute the ideal perfection of utilitarian morality.[40]

In spite of the more expansive, or positive, idea of utilitarianism found in Mill's writings, he never completely overcame utilitarianism's legacy of negative, self-interested freedom. The strength of Mill's individualism shows this. Nevertheless, there is evidence that Mill believed that the intellectual and moral development of the individual was the highest goal of society. And it is clear that an important concern of Mill's influential book, *Representative Government*, is that only through political participation can individuals achieve the highest development of which they are capable. Furthermore, Mill argued that one of the chief functions of democratic participation is education. On the other hand, Mill strongly believed that for the present and probably for a long period of time in the future the progress of humankind depended not on the masses but on the elite few who possessed the intellect and discernment required for rule:

The initiation of all wise and noble things comes and must come from individuals; generally at first from some one individual. The honor and glory of the average man is that he is capable of following that initiative; that he can respond internally to wise and noble things, and be led to them with his eyes open.[41]

The uncultivated cannot be competent judges of cultivation. Those who most need to be made wiser and better, usually desire it least, and if they desired it, would be incapable of finding the way to it by their own lights.

In the matter of education, the intervention is justifiable, because the case is not one in which the interest and judgment of the consumer are a sufficient security for the goodness of the commodity.[42]

Mill's famous defense of free speech in his essay *On Liberty* may well be read as a plea to the masses to not curb the freedom of the intelligensia upon whom the whole civilized world is dependent. Mill stresses where the danger to freedom of expression is most likely to come in the introduction to his famous essay:

Like other tyrannies, the tyranny of the majority was at first, and

still is vulgarly, held in dread, chiefly as operating through the acts of the public authorities...
[a]gainst the tyranny of the magistrate is not enough; there needs protection also against the tyranny of the prevailing opinion and feeling; against the tendency of society to impose, by other means than civil penalties, its own ideas and practices as rules of conduct on those who dissent from them; to fetter the development, and, if possible, prevent the formation, of any individuality not in harmony with its ways, and compel all characters to fashion themselves upon the model of its own.[43]

One should not read the above as implying that Mill was an opponent of democracy. On the contrary, he was a strong supporter of universal suffrage, although not without qualifications. As he stated, "Though everyone ought to have a voice—that everyone should have an equal voice was a totally different proposition."[44] As he stated in "Thought on Parliamentary Reform," an electoral system is "perfect only when each person has a vote and the well-educated have more than a vote."[45] He did, however, advocate the Hare system of proportional representation to ensure that all interests were represented. For example, on the question of the representation of the working class, Mill had this comment:

In this country, for example, what are called the working classes may be considered as excluded from all direct participation in the government. I do not believe that the classes who do participate in it have in general any intention of sacrificing the working classes to themselves. They once had that intention; witness the persevering attempts so long made to keep down wages by law. But in the present day their ordinary disposition is the very opposite: they willingly make considerable sacrifices, especially of their pecuniary interest, for the benefit of the working classes, and err rather by too lavish and indiscriminating beneficence; nor do I believe that any rulers in history have been actuated by a more sincere desire to do their duty towards the poorer portion of their countrymen. Yet does Parliament, or almost any of the members composing it, ever for an instant look at any question with the eyes of a working man? When a subject arises in which the labourers as such have an interest, is it regarded from any point of view but that of the employers of labour? I do not say that the working men's view of these questions is in general nearer to the truth than the other; but it is sometimes quite as near; and in any case it ought to be respectfully listened to, instead of being, as it is, not merely turned away from, but ignored.[46]

In addition, we must note Mill's relative enlightenment regarding the equality of women. We tend to forget that in the middle of the nineteenth century at the height of the Victorian era, support of women's liberation, as forceful as that advocated by ERA supporters today, was indeed both a farsighted and courageous stand.

In John Stuart Mill one can observe so many of the ambiguities of liberalism. What is observable is that the "democratization of liberalism"[47] (the drive toward freedom, even if primarily the negative kind of Hobbes, Locke, and Smith), made inevitable the demand on the part of the masses for a greater say in the manner of their governance. Thus the emergence of liberal democracy and its grudging acceptance by such as J. S. Mill. The acceptance of liberal democracy by the elites was only secure, however, *after it was tamed.* In the present era, when everyone claims to favor democracy, it is hard to recall that in earlier times democracy was a thing to be dreaded. It was widely believed in the seventeenth and eighteenth century that one must either take the vote away from the masses or the masses would take the wealth away from the few.[48] John Stuart Mill, with skill and liberal eloquence, did more than most in taming that "beast, the people" and making democracy acceptable to the few as well as the many. The chief manner in which liberal democracy's acceptability was ensured was the insistence that the state refrain from playing an active role in the provision of either welfare or political opportunity. Mill stated this in tones which still stand as the heart of liberal ideology:

Everyone who receives the protection of society owes a return for the benefit, and the fact of living in society renders it indispensable that each should be bound to observe a certain line of conduct towards the rest. This conduct consists, first, in not injuring the interests of one another...and secondly, in each person's bearing his share (to be fixed on some equitable principle) of the labours and sacrifices incurred for defending the society or its members from injury or molestation. These conditions society is justified in enforcing, at all costs to those who endeavour to withhold fulfillment.[49]

On the other hand, individuals should, according to Mill, be free to choose their own life-style and not be compelled to improve themselves or to obtain a higher purpose, which may be attainable by the well-born and gifted:

An individual ought not to be compelled even because it will be better for him to do so, because it will make him happier, because, in the opinions of others, to do so would be wise, or even right. These are good reasons for remonstrating with him, or reasoning with him, or persuading him, or entreating him, but not for compelling him, or visiting him with any evil in case he do otherwise.[50]

It is conveniently not remembered that Mill, in the later editions of *Political Economy*, advocated a large measure of state intervention and entertained ideas of socialism. As will be seen in the section on socialism, one of socialism's primary objectives is to maintain Mill's liberal defense of freedom of thought, conscience, and speech, including his defense of the liberty of tastes and life-style. Today's socialism, however, accepts in varying degrees a more active role of the state in aiding self-realization of the individual in society.

POSITIVE LIBERTY

Liberalism, as described in the preceding sections of this chapter and characterized by negative freedom, has been the dominant liberal ideology. There does exist, however, a strand of liberalism which may be called positive liberty. This strand of thought has contended with the traditional or negative school and for a time, in the more recent past, appeared to have gained parity with the older variety of liberalism. In the United States, the older variety of liberalism has come to be called conservatism, while positive liberty, which has become the ideology of the welfare state, has taken as its own the generic term, *liberalism*. (In Europe, however, what is currently called conservatism in America is still known as liberalism.) While these peculiar reversals of the terms liberal and conservative cause the confusion which exists in attempts to identify liberal and conservative tendencies in politics, it is understandable that those who wish to adhere to the philosophy of negative freedom should refer to their position as "conservative" in that they do indeed wish to conserve the status quo from inroads made by the welfare state. It is, in part, because of this confusion that we have chosen to refer to these two versions of capitalist ideology as negative *freedom* and positive *liberty*. As we noted earlier, both negative freedom (conservative in American usage) and positive liberty (liberal in American usage) are but different aspects of *liberalism*.

The ideas of four writers (the first of whom, Rousseau, is really a precursor to the more recent and relevant advocates of positive liberty) will be used to explicate this strand of liberalism. The three main writers are T. H. Green, L. T. Hobhouse, and J. M. Keynes.

Rousseau, the Precursor (1712–1778)

While Rousseau wrote more than a hundred years before the other writers, he, as was his wont, stated most boldly and clearly the concept and moral worth of positive liberty. According to Rousseau the individual is confronted with two conflicting wills within his or her own personality. There is the "particular will" which is egocentric, narrow, and destructive of both civility and freedom in its true sense. There is also in the individual a recognition of the "general will" which is shared by all members of a true community.

It is this general will which can unite people to their fellows and which transcends their particular wills. Replacing the negative view of freedom as the absence from external restraint, the general will provides an alternative positive liberty.

Only a person who lives by common rules can be positively free. Someone who obeys rules from force of habit, fear, or narrow prudential self-interest is not truly free. But by "willing" the rules the individual thinks ought to be obeyed by everyone, including himself or herself, a person becomes doubly free: one obeys oneself and thereby possesses full freedom of choice, and one is also free of all the petty ties of self-interest, narrow clannish loyalties, and mean calculations. To achieve this positive liberty a person must identify with the general will.

In Rousseau's strongest, and perhaps most controversial statement, an individual who refuses to obey the general will can be forced to do so, and this only makes the person freer. In Rousseau's own words: "[W]hosoever refused to obey the general will shall be compelled to it by the whole body; this in fact only forces him to be free."[51]

Although subsequent writers have refrained from going as far as Rousseau in proclaiming that one can be justly forced to be free, in fact, a multitude of rules of the modern welfare state, ranging from compulsory school attendance legislation to the regulations of the Occupational Safety and Health Administration (OSHA), do just that. One need use only a very prosaic example: observe a traffic light which fails to function to see how one's freedom is in fact prevented rather than enhanced by the failure of regulation.

T. H. Green (1836–1882)

The person most frequently associated with the notion of positive liberty is T. H. Green.[52] In 1881 Green expressed his view as follows:

We shall probably all agree that freedom, rightly understood, is the greatest of blessings; that its attainment is the true end of all our effort as citizens. But when we thus speak of freedom, we should consider carefully what we mean by it. We do not mean merely freedom from restraint or compulsion. We do not mean merely freedom to do as we like irrespectively of what it is we like. We do not mean a freedom that can be enjoyed by one man or one set of men at the cost of a loss of freedom to others. *When we speak of freedom ... we mean a positive power or capacity of doing or enjoying something worth doing or enjoying,* and that, too, something that we do or enjoy in common with others.[53]

Green and his associates at Oxford, F. H. Bradley[54] and Bernard Bosanquet[55] drew upon and were part of a revived interest in the German idealists Georg Hegel[56] and Immanuel Kant.[57] Relying more on Kant than Hegel as a source of their idealism these British idealists recognized that freedom consisted mainly of the pursuit of a moral or good will. This pursuit lay beyond the simple absence of external restraints.

Human freedom, it was thought, is achieved *not* by alienating our natural impulses by subjecting them to external restraints or domination but by uniting them with a higher goal. Self-realization becomes, for the British idealists, the *summum bonnum.*

Self-perfection, in this view, can never be achieved in isolation. How far an individual can progress toward fully realizing his or her potential is closely related to the level of civilization in which one lives and the degree to which one interacts with the political and social environment. To be the inhabitant of a corrupt society or to be insulated (through class or geographic sectionalism, for example) from the greater society, is to lack positive liberty—to be unfree.

The state, therefore, becomes a necessary and a positive force for liberty. Unlike Rousseau, Green and his friends believed that the state is not created by the general will; rather it is the state which creates the general will. The state teaches us to prefer that which we ought to prefer, not merely to fight for what we want. It is less an arena than a classroom. The state is not based, therefore, on a mere contract, nor is it based on force. Rather the state embodies the highest reason and serves the common good, according to Green. Only the state can ensure collective well-being as a precondition of individual freedom and responsibility.

For the positive libertarian there are no rights, including property rights, except those which can be justified in terms of their service to the common good. It seemed to these liberals, however, that property rights were nevertheless essential for the common good; essential, so they thought, as the best means of ensuring personal security and individual personality development.

In practice, T. H. Green was very timid about the role of the state and certainly failed to realize or advocate the logical extention of the role of the state warranted by his philosophical position. His position on slavery illuminates his views on property and authority:

Under certain conditions the right of helping the slave may be cancelled by the duty of obeying the prohibitory law. It would do so if the violation of law in the interest of the slave were liable to result in general anarchy....[S]uch a destruction of the state would mean a general loss of freedom, a general substitution of force for mutual good-will in men's dealings with each other, that would outweigh the evil of any slavery under such limitations and regulations as an organized state imposes on it.[58]

Leonard Hobhouse (1864–1929)

Leonard Hobhouse[59] developed and expanded on Green's ideas and, along with that of John Maynard Keynes,[60] his writing represents the current status of positive liberty and the best defense of the welfare state on both theoretical and practical grounds. The following extensive quotations from Hobhouse, written in 1911, could easily have been part of a contemporary American president's campaign rhetoric:

Let us first observe that, as Mill pointed out long ago, there are many forms of collective action which do not involve coercion. The State may provide for certain objects which it deems good without compelling anyone to make use of them. Thus it may maintain hospitals, though anyone who can pay for them remains free to employ his own doctors and nurses. It may and does maintain a great educational system, while leaving everyone free to maintain or to attend a private school....[61]

The ground problem in economics is not to destroy property, but to restore the social conception of property to its right place under conditions suitable to modern needs. This is not to be done by crude measures of redistribution, such as those of which we hear in ancient history. It is to be done by distinguishing the social from the individual factors in wealth, by bringing the elements of social wealth into the public coffers, and by holding it at the disposal of society to administer to the prime needs of its members.[62]

...an individualism which ignores the social factor in wealth will deplete the national resources, deprive the community of its just share in the fruits of industry and so result in a one-sided and inequitable distribution of wealth. Economic justice is to render what is due not only to each individual but to each function, social or personal, that is engaged in the performance of useful service, and this due is measured by the amount necessary to stimulate and maintain the efficient exercise of that useful function. This equation between function and sustenance is the true meaning of economic equality....[63]

...the function of society was to secure to all normal adult members the means of earning by useful work the material necessaries of a healthy and efficient life. We can see now that this is one case and, properly understood, the largest and most far-reaching case falling under the general principle of economic justice. This principle lays down that every social function must receive the reward that is sufficient to stimulate and maintain it through the life of the individual....[64]

The sum and substance of the changes that I have mentioned may be expressed in the principle that the individual cannot stand alone, but that between him and the State there is a reciprocal obligation. He owes the State the duty of industriously working for himself and his family. He is not to exploit the labour of his young children, but to submit to the public requirements for their education, health, cleanliness and general well-

being. On the other side society owes to him the means of maintaining a civilized standard of life, and this debt is not adequately discharged by leaving him to secure such wages as he can in the higgling of the market.[65]

John Maynard Keynes (1883–1946)

The writer who perhaps speaks most clearly to the present generation regarding liberalism is J. M. Keynes. His writings as much as any other exemplify the contemporary positive liberal school. Keynes is forthright in his rejection of laissez-faire economics: the first paragraph of "The End of Laissez-Faire", published in 1926, is an indictment of the basic premises of negative freedom:

Let us clear from the ground the metaphysical or general principles upon which, from time to time, laissez-faire has been founded. It is not true that individuals possess a prescriptive "natural liberty" in their economic activities. There is no "compact" conferring perpetual rights on those who Have or on those who Acquire. The world is not so governed from above that private and social interest always coincide. It is not so managed here below that in practice they coincide. It is not a correct deduction from the Principles of Economics that enlightened self-interest always operates in the public interest. Nor is it true that self-interest generally is enlightened; more often individuals acting separately to promote their own ends are too ignorant or too weak to attain even these. Experience does not show that individuals, when they make up a social unit, are always less clearsighted than when they act separately.[66]

Keynes regards traditional liberalism, with its emphasis on money-making (what Marx called the "money-nexus"), as both morally bankrupt and doomed to failure unless it can be rejuvenated with a higher purpose:

...it seems clearer every day that the moral problem of our age is concerned with the love of money, with the habitual appeal to the money motive in nine-tenths of the activities of life, with the universal striving after individual economic security as the prime object of endeavour, with the social approbation of money as the measure of constructive success, and with the social appeal to the hoarding instinct as the foundation of the necessary provision for the family and for the future.[67]

In his essay, "Why I am a Liberal" (1925), Keynes further points out the limitations of support of the old liberalism, the negative or laissez-faire version. He finds that it

... satisfies no ideal; it conforms to no intellectual standard; it is not even safe, or calculated to preserve from the spoilers that degree of civilization which we have already attained.[68]

In a comment as relevant today as in 1925, Keynes indicts the defenders of economic conservatism:

The difficulty is that the capitalist leaders in the City and in Parliament are incapable of distinguishing novel measures for safeguarding Capitalism from what they call Bolshevism. If old-fashioned Capitalism was intellectually capable of defending itself, it would not be dislodged for many generations.... But fortunately for Socialists, there is little chance of this.[69]

Lest Keynes be misunderstood as a defender of either the USSR or socialism, his stance as a liberal needs to be made clear. First, he was certainly a liberal as a matter of temperament. This becomes apparent when Keynes discusses why he cannot be a Labour supporter:

To begin with, it is a class party, and the class is not my class. If I am going to pursue sectional interests at all, I shall pursue my own. When it comes to the class struggle as such, my local and personal patriotisms, like those of everyone else, except certain unpleasant zealous ones, are attached to my own surroundings. I can be influenced by what seems to me to be Justice and good sense; but the Class war will find me on the side of the educated bourgeoisie.[70]

He further castigates the left with the charge of malevolence:

The passions of malignity, jealousy, hatred of those who have wealth and power... ill consort with ideals to build up a true Social Republic.... It is not enough that he should love his fellow-men; he must hate them too.[71]

Keynes charges liberals with the task of developing new issues for the future, and states that to do so liberalism must abandon its ties with the moribund ideas of extreme individualism and laissez faire economics. No one has done more than he to fashion for liberalism a new role—especially a new role for the state. This is not the place to attempt a summary of the significance of his great work, *The General Theory of Employment, Interest,* and *Money* (1935). We are all aware how his views on fiscal policy have influenced the role of the state. What needs amplification is the philosophical values which underlie his "new" theories of increased state intervention into the economy.

Keynes, from as early as the 1920s to the end of his life, searched for some means of organization and control which would lie somewhere between the leviathan of the state and the haphazardness of the individual. He was optimistic about the opportunity for this reconciliation and discerned models for it in his own contemporary England:

I propose a return, it may be said, towards mediaeval conceptions of separate autonomies. But, in England at any rate, corporations are a mode of government which has never ceased to be important and is sympathetic to our institutions. (It is easy to give examples, from what already exists, of separate autonomies which have attained or are approaching the mode I designate—the Universities, the Bank of England, the Port of London Authority, even perhaps the Railway Companies.)

But more interesting than these is the trend of Joint Stock Institutions, when they have reached a certain age and size, to approximate to the status of public corporations rather than that of individualistic private enterprise. One of the most interesting and unnoticed developments of recent decades has been the tendency of big enterprise to socialise itself.[72]

In pursuit of a way to actualize his ideas concerning positive liberalism, Keynes became the first director of the British Arts Council, whose task it was to allocate certain funds in support of the arts—a function of positive state intervention.

One of Keynes's most challenging suggestions for positive state intervention, *as a functional part of* (state) *capitalism*, is his partially formulated concept of state control over private investment, and direct state control over the "public" decisions of private business. This suggestion, perhaps more than any other, strikes a blow at centralized private decision making—the control of capital in virtually every crucial decision regarding the future of capitalist society, unfettered by public disclosure.

These measures would involve Society in exercising directive intelligence through some appropriate organ of action over many of the inner intricacies of private business, yet it would leave private initiative and enterprise unhindered. Even if these measures prove insufficient, nevertheless they will furnish us with better knowledge than we have now for taking the next step....

I believe that some co-ordinated act of intelligent judgement is required as to the scale on which it is desirable that the community as a whole should save, the scale on which these savings should go abroad in the form of foreign investments, and whether the present organisation of the investment market distributes savings along the most nationally productive channels.

I do not think that these matters should be left entirely to the chances of private judgement and private profits, as they are at present.[73]

While these ideas of Keynes have had great practical impact on European economies, and the Japanese economy as well, they have had only a peripheral and grudging influence in the United States.

In Keynes's *General Theory* he explained the possibility that the return in the future on capital would become zero. However, to Keynes, this falling rate of profit was not the doomsday nightmare suggested by both Marx and many leaders of capitalism. Rather it opened up the possibility for state-economic decisions to turn to the real issues—to those human concerns related to human-realization and dignity:

Now, though this state of affairs would be quite compatible with some measure of individualism, yet it would mean the euthanasia of the rentier, and consequently, the euthanasia of the cumulative oppressive power of the capitalist to exploit the scarcity-value of capital. Interest today rewards no genuine sacrifice, any more than does the rent of land. The owner of capital can obtain interest because capital is scarce just as the owner of land can obtain rent because land is scarce. But whilst there may be intrinsic reasons for the scarcity of land, there are no intrinsic reasons for scarcity of capital. . . .

If I am right in supposing it to be comparatively easy to make capital-goods so abundant that the marginal efficiency of capital is zero, this may be the most sensible way of gradually getting rid of many of the objectionable features of capitalism. For a little reflection will show what enormous social changes would result from a gradual disappearance of a rate of return on accumulated wealth. A man would still be free to accumulate his earned income with a view to spending it at a later date. But his accumulation would not grow.[74]

That these changes in capitalism would produce drastic changes in the future Keynes had no doubt, but he viewed these developments with optimism:

There are changes in other spheres too which we must expect to come. When the accumulation of wealth is no longer of high social importance, there will be great changes in the code of morals. We shall be able to rid ourselves of many of the pseudomoral principles which have hag-ridden us for two hundred years, by which we have exalted some of the most distasteful of human qualities into the position of the highest virtues. We shall be able to afford to dare to assess the money-motive at its true value. The love of money as a possession—as distinguished from the love of money as a means to the enjoyments and realities of life—will be recognised for what it is, a somewhat disgusting morbidity, one of those semi-criminal, semi-pathological propensities which one hands over with a shudder to the specialists in mental disease. All kinds of social customs and economic practices, affecting the distribution of wealth and of economic rewards and penalties, which we now maintain at all costs, however distasteful and unjust they may be in themselves...we shall then be free, at last to discard.[75]

and:

I see us free, therefore, to return to some of the most sure and certain principles of religion and traditional virtue—that avarice is a vice, that the exaction of usury is a misdemeanour, and the love of money is detestable, that those walk most truly in the paths of virtue and sane wisdom who take least thought for the morrow. We shall once more value ends above means and prefer the good to the useful. We shall honour those who can teach us how to pluck the hour and the day virtuously and well, the delightful people who are capable of taking direct enjoyment in things, the lilies of the field who toil not, neither do they spin.[76]

It is fashionable now to speak of the death of Keynesianism, yet such a system has never been fully developed. Keynes still provides what may possibly be the last defense of both liberalism and capitalism, but only if we do not overestimate the importance of economics and sacrifice to the profit motive the really human requirements of life. If social direction of investment can replace profits as the motive for future growth, only then will it be possible to regard economists as "humble, competent people, on a level with dentists."[77]

One final consideration regarding Keynesian liberal economics must be dealt with. Perhaps, after all, American politicians in their die-hard opposition to the implementation of Keynes's policies see better than they are given credit for. Perhaps they instinctively realize that Keynesian thought, if carried through to its logical conclusion, would not refurbish capitalism but replace it with socialism. Perhaps Keynesianism is indeed a transitional ideology. More speculation on this point properly belongs in the next chapter on the United States as the practical model of liberalism. It is important to point out, however, that in over three hundred years in the history of liberalism, the classical or negative-freedom school of liberalism has been dominant for all but the period from the Great Depression of the

1930s to the late 1960s—a mere thirty years. Even during that period there was an unwillingness to pursue the philosophy of positive liberalism to its natural conclusions. Even the "tough-minded line" that Schumpeter[78] derived from Marx, that: "the system is cruel, unjust, turbulent, but it does deliver the goods, and damn it all, it's the goods that you want,"[79] is no longer an available defense of the liberal capitalist system which we have inherited.

NOTES

1. Robert L. Heilbroner, *The Worldly Philosophers*, rev. ed. (New York: Simon and Schuster, 1972), p. 20.
2. Hobbes's most influential works include *Elements of Law* (1650), *De Cive* (1642), *Leviathan* (1651), *De Corpore* (1655), and *De Homine* (1659). It is *Leviathan* that has exerted the greatest impact on liberal thought.
3. Thomas Hobbes, *Leviathan*, Parts I and II (New York: Liberal Arts Press, 1958), Part II p. 171.
4. Ibid., Part I, p. 107.
5. Ibid., Part I, p. 86.
6. Ibid., Part I, p. 173.
7. John Plamenatz, *Man and Society*, Vol 1 (New York: McGraw-Hill Book Company, 1963), p. 154.
8. Locke's most influential works are *Essay Concering Human Understanding* (1690), *The Reasonableness of Christianity* (1695), *Two Treatises of Civil Government* (1690), and *Letters on Toleration* (1689).
9. John Locke, *Treatise of Civil Government, An Essay Concerning the True Original, Extent and End of Civil Government*, (New York: Appleton-Century-Crofts, 1937), Chapter V, secs., 25, 26, and 27, pp. 19–20.
10. C. B. Macpherson, *The Political Theory of Possessive Individualism* (London: Oxford University Press, 1962).
11. Locke, *Treatise of Civil Government*, Chapter V, sec. 27, p. 19, reads:

    For this labour being the unquestionable property of the labourere, no man but he can have a right to what that is once joined to, at least where there is enough, and as good left in common for others.

12. Macpherson, *Possessive Individualism*, pp. 206–211.
13. Locke, *Works* (1759), pp. ii, 19, as quoted in ibid., p. 206.

14. Locke, Bodleian Library ms. Locke c. 30, f. 18, as quoted in ibid., p. 207.
15. Locke, *Treatise of Civil Government*, Chapter V, sec. 41, p. 27.
16. Ibid, Chapter IX, secs. 124–27, pp. 82–64.
17. Ibid., Chapter XI, sec. 138, p. 93.
18. Macpherson, *Possessive Individualism*, p. 248.
19. Locke, *Treatise of Civil Government*, Chapters XI, XII, and XIII, secs. 140–58, pp. 94–107.
20. Ibid., Chapter VIII, sec. 119, p. 79.
21. Macpherson, *Possessive Individualism*, p. 222.
22. Locke, *Works*, pp. ii, 36, as quoted in Macpherson, ibid., p. 223.
23. Ibid., pp. ii, 585–86. Cf. *Human Understanding*, Book IV, Chapter 20, secs. 2–3, in ibid., p. 225.
24. Adam Smith, *The Wealth of Nations*, ed. Edwin Canaan (Chicago: University of Chicago Press, 1977), Book I, Part I, Chapters 1 and 2, pp. 5 and 15 respectively. Originally published in London in 1776 as *An Inquiry Into the Nature and Causes of the Wealth of Nations*.
25. Adam Smith, *The Wealth of Nations*, ed. R. H. Campbell and A. S. Skinner (London: Oxford University Press, 1976), Vol. II, p. 687.
26. Ibid., p. 343.
27. Ibid., pp. 454–56.
28. Heilbroner, *The Worldly Philosophers*, p. 103.
29. Adam Smith, *Glasgow Lectures in Jurisprudence*, Notes from Glasgow University Lectures, 1763–64, eds. D. D. Raphael, P. G. Stein and Ronald Meek, for publication by Glasgow University, Bicentennial, as quoted in Ronald Meek, *Smith, Marx and After* (London: Chapman and Hall, 1977), p. 90.
30. Meek, *Smith, Marx and After*, p. 11.
31. Heilbroner, *Worldly Philosophers*, p. 61.
32. Smith, *Wealth of Nations*, Book IV, Chapter 9, pp. 649–51.
33. Smith, *Glasgow Lectures*, no. 34, in Meek, *Smith, Marx and After*, p. 90.
34. Herbert Spencer, "The Sins of the Legislators," in *The Man versus the State* (1884) (London: Watts, 1909), p. 67.
35. Spencer, "Over-Legislation," in *Essays: Scientific, Political and Speculative*, (London: William & Norgate, 1868), pp. 93–94.
36. Bentham's most influential works are *A Fragment on Goverment* (1776) and *Introduction to the Principles of Morals and Legislation* (1789).
37. Mill is the most influential of all "utilitarians" and was a prolific writer. His most influential works include *Logic* (1843), *Political Economy* (1848), *The Subjection of Women* (1869), and the essays, *Utilitarianism* (1861), *On Liberty* (1859), *Considerations on Representative Goverment* (1861), as well as a prodigious amount of writing appearing in the *Westminster Review*.
38. Jeremy Bentham, *The Collected Works of Jeremy Bentham, Section Two: Principles of Legislation* (New York: Oxford University Press, 1970),

as quoted in Charles A. McCoy and Alan Wolfe, *Political Analysis* (New York: Thomas Y. Crowell Company, 1972), p. 170.

39. John Stuart Mill, *Utilitarianism, Liberty and Representative Government* (New York: Dutton, 1950), p. 1.

40. Ibid.

41. John Stuart Mill, "On Liberty," in *Utilitarianism*, Liberty, *and Representative Government*, p. 166.

42. John Stuart Mill, *Principles of Political Economy* (London: Longmans, People's Edition, 1866), Ib., secs. 8 and 9, pp. 575–77.

43. Mill, "On Liberty," p. 6, the Introduction.

44. John Stuart Mill, "Considerations on Representative Goverment," in *Utilitarianism, Liberty, and Representative Government*, p. 282.

45. John Stuart Mill, "Thoughts on Parliamentary Reform," as quoted in J. N. Robson, *The Improvement of Mankind* (Toronto: University of Toronto Press, 1968), p. 255.

46. Mill, *Utilitarianism, Liberty, and Representative Government*, p. 209.

47. C. B. Macpherson, *The Life and Times of Liberal Democracy* (New York: Oxford University Press, 1979).

48. See, for example, James Harrington, *The Commonwealth of Oceana* (1656), in "The Preliminaries, Showing the Principles of Government," *The Political Writings of James Harrington*, ed. Charles Blitzer (New York: Bobbs-Merrill, 1955), pp. 40–81.

49. Mill, "On Liberty," p. 177.

50. Ibid, p. 96.

51. Jean Jacques Rousseau, *The Social Contract*, ed. Charles Frankel (New York: Hafner, 1947), p. 18.

52. Green's most influential works include *Prolegomena to Ethics* (1883) and *Lectures on the Principles of Political Obligation* (1800).

53. T. H. Green, "Liberal Legislation and the Freedom of Contract," in *Political Theory of T. H. Green*, ed. John R. Rodman (New York: Appleton-Century-Crofts, 1964), pp. 51–52, as quoted in Dante Germino, *Modern Western Political Thought* (Chicago: Rand, McNally, 1972), pp. 264–65.

54. Bradley's contribution to a Hegelian conception of the state was "My Station and Its Duties," which appeared in 1876 in *Ethical Studies*.

55. Bosanquet's chief contribution is *The Philosophical Theory of the State* (1889).

56. Hegel's influence has been enormous and his writings extremely dense and prodigious. They include *Phenomenology of Mind* (1807), *Science of Logic* (1816), *Encyclopedia of the Philosophical Sciences* (1817), *Philosophy of Right* (1821), and *Philosophy of History* (1837).

57. Kant's works include *Critique of Pure Reason* (1781), *Critique of Practical Reason* (1788), *Fundamental Principles of the Metaphysics of Morals* (1785), *Metaphysical Foundations of the Philosophy of Law* (1797), and *Eternal Peace* (1795).

58. Green, "Lectures on the Principles of Political Obligation," in *Political Theory of T. H. Green*, p. 138, as quoted in Germino, *Modern Western Political Thought*, p. 271.

59. For Hobhouse's critique of the British idealist school, see *The Metaphysical Theory of the State: A Criticism* (1918).

60. John Maynard Keynes's *General Theory of Employment, Interest and Money* (New York: Harcourt, Brace & World, 1936) is, of course, the foundation of all subsequent "Keynesian economics" and contains a programmatic application of his positive liberal views. For a more popular and accessible version, see a volume containing what Keynes himself describes as the "croakings of twelve years," *Essays in Persuasion* (New York, W. W. Norton and Company, 1963).

61. Leonard T. Hobhouse, "The State and the Individual," in *Liberalism* (New York: Oxford University Press (originally published in London in 1911), 1964), p. 75.

62. Ibid., p. 98.

63. Ibid., p. 99.

64. Ibid., p. 105.

65. Ibid., p. 86.

66. Keynes, "The End of Laissez-Faire" (1926), in *Essays in Persuasion*, p. 312.

67. Keynes, "A Short View of Russia" (1925), in *Essays in Persuasion*, p. 308.

68. Keynes, "Am I a Liberal?" (1925), in *Essays in Persuasion*, p. 324.

69. Ibid., p. 327.

70. Ibid., p. 324.

71. Ibid., p. 328.

72. Keynes, "The End of Laissez-Faire," p. 314.

73. Ibid., pp. 318–19.

74. Keynes, *General Theory of Employment, Interest and Money*, p. 376, as quoted in Joan Robinson, *Economic Philosophy* (New York: Doubleday, 1964), p. 104.

75. Keynes, "Economic Possibilities for Our Grandchildren" (1930), in *Essays in Persuasion*, pp. 369–70.

76. Ibid., 371–72.

77. Ibid., p. 373.

78. See, generally, Joseph Schumpeter, *History of Economic Analysis* (New York: Oxford University Press, 1954).

79. Robinson, *Economic Philosophy*, p. 140.

BIBLIOGRAPHIC NOTE

During the last decade, the literature on liberalism has continued to mirror the divisions between negative freedom and positive liberty, discussed in this chapter. Works which reflect a commitment to negative freedom, extreme individualism, and, concomitantly, a reduced role for the state in the provision of social welfare, have gained an acceptance and increasingly large audience—unequaled prior to the twentieth century. Peter Steinfels provides an introduction to these proponents of negative freedom in his *Neo-Conservatism: The Men Who Are Changing American Politics* (1979). For those who wish to go directly to the writings of the new conservatives, the following authors provide a representative sample: Alexander Bickel, *The Morality of Consent* (1975); Nathan Glazer and Irving Kristol, eds., *The American Commonwealth* (1976); and Robert Nisbit, *The Twilight of Authority* (1975). Journals such as *Public Interest* and research institutes such as the American Enterprise Institute also provide a source of conservative writings and statements.

In contrast to the radical individualism of the "new conservatives" are those who continue to press the desirability and, according to some, necessity, of a sense of community. The sense of community which these authors feel is lost or endangered is an "organic" attachment through law or custom (either psychological or functional) to the larger society. Three volumes among the contemporary works dealing with communitarian themes are Benjamin Barber, *The Death of Communal Liberty* (1974); Wilson Carey McWilliams, *The Idea of Fraternity in America* (1973); and Christopher Lasch, *The Culture of Narcissism* (1979). Analyses exploring impediments to the communitarian impulse are also available. Two of the least polemical and most innovative in combining the psychology of individual economic decision making in a modern society are Mancur Olsen's *The Logic of Collective Action* (1965) and Fred Hirsch's *The Social Limits to Growth* (1976).

Liberal literature has produced a corpus of work regarding the theoretical discussion of rights and justice in the past decade. Ronald Dworkin's *Taking Rights Seriously* (1977) and Richard Flathman's *The Practice of Rights* (1976) are representative of these enduring liberal concerns. It is Rawls' *A Theory of Justice* (1971), however, that has provoked the most vigorous debate and elaboration. This work is reminiscent of John Stuart Mill's *Utilitarianism* in that it too attempts to provide a viable base for liberal/utilitarian philosophy in contemporary society, and like Mill's earlier work it is only partially successful, perhaps less so because of the rear-guard defense of liberalism that Rawls must attempt in the face of conservative criticism of the real-world failure of liberal social reforms. Robert Nozick's *Anarchy, State, and Utopia* is representative of the attack upon and theoretical vulnerability of contemporary liberalism.

The liberal perspective in terms of economics has been provided by the post-Keynesians. Joan Robinson's leadership and intellectual vitality have given an impetus to this Cambridge-based movement, whose impact has shaped democratic socialist reforms in Europe but made little progress in the United States, where Samuelsonian revisions of Keynes' original formulations remain the most liberal articulation of American economics.

BIBLIOGRAPHY

Arneson, Richard J. "Prospects for Communists in a Market Economy." *Political Theory*, Vol. 9, no. 2 (May 1981).

Ashcraft, Richard. "Revolutions, Politics and Locke's Two Treatises of Civil Government: Radicalism and Lockean Political Theory." *Political Theory*, Vol. 8, no. 4 (Nov. 1980).

Barber, Benjamin. *The Death of Communal Liberty: A History of Freedom in a Swiss Mountain Canton*. Princeton, N.J.: Princeton University Press, 1974.

Barry, Brian. *The Liberal Theory of Justice*. Oxford: Clarendon Press, 1973.

Barry, Norman D. *Hayek's Social and Economic Philosophy*. Atlantic Highlands, N.J.: Humanities Press, 1979.

Becker, Carl. *The Declaration of Independence: A Study in the History of Political Ideas*. New York: Random House, 1957.

—— *The Heavenly City of the Eighteenth Century Philosophers*. New Haven, Conn.: Yale University Press, 1932.

Bell, Daniel. *The Coming of Post-Industrial Society: A Venture in Social Forecasting*. New York: Basic Books, 1937.

—— *The Cultural Contradictions of Capitalism*. New York: Basic Books, 1975.

—— *The End of Ideology, on the Exhaustion of Political Ideas in the 50's*. New York: Free Press, 1960.

Bentham, Jeremy. *A Fragment on Government*. Oxford: Clarendon, 1948. (Written in 1776.)

—— *An Introduction to the Principles of Morals and Legislation*. Oxford: Clarendon, 1948. (Written in 1789.)

—— *Handbook of Political Fallacies*. Harold A. Larrabee, ed. New York: Harper & Row, 1962.

—— *The Collected Works of Jeremy Bentham*. New York: Oxford University Press, 1970.

Berlin, Isaiah. *Against the Current: Essays in the History of Ideas*, Four Volumes, Henry Hardy, ed. New York: Viking Press, 1980.

—— *Concepts and Categories*. New York: Viking Press, 1979.

—— *Four Essays on Liberty*. New York: Oxford University Press, 1969.

———— *Russian Thinkers*. New York: Viking Press, 1978.

———— *The Hedgehog and the Fox; An Essay on Tolstoy's View of History*. New York: Simon & Schuster, 1953.

Bickel, Alexander. *The Morality of Consent*. New Haven, Conn.: Yale University Press, 1975.

Birnbaum, Pierre, Lively, Jack, and Parry, Geraint. *Democracy, Consensus and Social Contract*. Beverly Hills, Ca.: Sage, 1978.

Bosanquet, Bernard. *Philosophical Theory of the State*, 4th ed. London: Macmillan, 1923. (Written in 1899.)

Bradley, F. H. *Ethical Studies: Selected Studies*. Intro. by Ralph Ross. New York: Liberal Arts Press, 1951. (Written in 1876.)

Bramstead, E. K. and Melhuish, K. J., eds. *Western Liberalism: A History in Documents from Locke to Croce*. New York: Longman, 1978.

Bullock, Alan and Shock, Maurice, eds. *The Liberal Tradition from Fox to Keynes*. London: Adam and Charles Black, 1956.

Burke, Edmund. *Appeal from the New to the Old Whigs*. John M. Robson, ed. New York: Liberal Arts Press, 1962. (Written in 1794.)

———— *Reflections on the Revolution in France*. Russell Kirk, ed. Chicago: Regnery, 1955. (Written in 1790.)

———— *Selected Works of Edmund Burke*. Wallace J. Bate, ed. New York: Random House, 1960.

———— *The Philosophy of Edmund Burke: A Selection from His Speeches and Writings*. L. I. Bredvold and R. G. Ross, eds. Ann Arbor, Michigan: University of Michigan Press, 1961.

Cassirer, Ernst. *The Philosophy of the Enlightenment*. F. C. A. Koelln and J. P. Pettegrove, trans. Boston: Beacon Press, 1955.

Chapman, John W. *Rousseau—Totalitarian or Liberal?* New York: Columbia University Press, 1956.

Cobban, Alfred. *In Search of Humanity: The Role of the Enlightenment in Modern History*. New York: Braziller, 1960.

———— *Rousseau and the Modern State*. Hamden, Conn.: Shoe String Press, 1961.

Coleman, Frank M. *Hobbes and America: Exploring the Constitutional Foundations*. Toronto: University of Toronto Press, 1977.

Connolly, William E. *Terms of Political Discourse*. Lexington, Mass.: Heath, 1974.

Cook, Terence E. "Rousseau: Education and Politics." *Journal of Politics*, No. 37 (February 1975).

de Crespigny, Anthony and Cronin, J. P., eds. *Ideologies of Politics*. New York: Oxford University Press, 1976.

Dallmayr, Fred R., ed. *From Contract to Community: Political Theory at the Crossroads*. New York: Marcel Dekker, 1978.

Dewey, John. *The Public and Its Problems*. New York: Holt, Rinehart and World, 1927.

Downs, Anthony. *An Economic Theory of Democracy*. New York: Harper & Row, 1957.

Downs, Michael. *James Harrington*. Boston, G. K. Hall, 1977.

Duncan, Graeme. *Marx and Mill: Two Views of Social Conflict and Social Harmony*. Cambridge, England: Cambridge University Press, 1973.

Dworkin, Ronald. *Taking Rights Seriously*. Cambridge, Mass.: Harvard University Press, 1977.

Eichner, Alfred S., ed. *A Guide to Post-Keynesian Economics*. New York: M. E. Sharpe, 1979.

Flathman, Richard E. *The Practice of Rights*. Cambridge, England: Cambridge University Press, 1976.

Frank, Joseph. *The Levellers; A History of the Writings of Three Seventeenth-Century Social Democrats: John Lilburne, Richard Overton, William Walwyn*. Cambridge, Mass.: Harvard University Press, 1955.

Franklin, Julian H. *John Locke and the Theory of Sovereignty*. Cambridge, England: Cambridge University Press, 1978.

Freeden, Michael. *The New Liberalism: An Ideology of Social Reform*. Oxford: Clarendon Press, 1978.

Friedman, Milton and Friedman, Rose. *Capitalism and Freedom*. Chicago: University of Chicago Press, 1962.

————— *Free To Choose: A Personal Statement*. New York: Harcourt Brace Jovanovich, 1980.

Friedman, Milton and Schwartz, Anna. *A Monetary History of the United States, 1867–1960*. Princeton, N.J.: Princeton University Press, 1963.

Galbraith, John Kenneth. *American Capitalism*, rev. ed. Boston: Houghton-Mifflin, 1956.

————— *The Affluent Society*. Boston: Houghton-Mifflin, 1958.

————— *The New Industrial State*. Boston: Houghton-Mifflin, 1967.

Gay, Peter. *The Enlightenment: An Interpretation*. New York: Knopf, 1966.

Gerimino, Dante and von Beyme, Klaus. *The Open Society In Theory and Practice*. The Hague: Martinus Nijhoff, 1975.

Glazer, Nathan and Kristol, Irving, eds., *The American Commonwealth*. New York: Basic Books, 1976.

Godwin, William. *Enquiry Concerning Political Justice*. Issac Kramnick, ed. New York: Penguin Press, 1976.

Golding, Milton. "Mill's Attack on Moral Conservatism." *Midwest Studies in Philosophy*, No. 1 (1974).

Gourevitch, Victor. "Rawls on Justice." *Review of Metaphysics*, No. 28 (March 1975).

Green, Thomas Hill. *Lectures on the Principles of Political Obligation*. Intro., A. D. Lindsay. London: Longmans, Green, 1941. (Written in 1800.)

————— *The Political Theory of T. H. Green*. John R. Rodman, ed. New York: Appleton-Century-Crofts, 1964.

Halevy, Elie. *The Growth of Philosophic Radicalism*. Mary Morris, trans. Boston: Beacon Press, 1955.

Harcourt, Geoffrey. *Some Cambridge Controversies in the Theory of Capital*. Cambridge, England: Cambridge University Press, 1972.

Harrington, James. *The Political Writings of James Harrington*. Charles Blitzer, ed. New York: Bobbs-Merrill, 1955.

Hartz, Louis. *The Liberal Tradition in America*. New York: Harcourt Brace and World, 1955.

Hayek, F. A. *New Studies in Philosophy, Politics, Economics and the History of Ideas*. Chicago: University of Chicago Press, 1978.

———— *The Road to Serfdom*. Chicago: University of Chicago Press, 1944.

Hegel, G. W. F. *Phenomenology of Mind*. J. B. Baillie, trans., ed., and rev. London: Allen & Unwin, 1961. (Written in 1807.)

———— *Philosophy of History*. J. Silbree, trans. New York: Dover, 1955; reprint of English ed., Bell, 1905. (Written in 1837.)

———— *Philosophy of Right*. T. M. Knox, trans. Oxford: Clarendon Press, 1953. (Written in 1821.)

———— *The Philosophy of Hegel*. Carl Friedrich, ed. New York: Random House, 1954.

———— *Selections*. Lowenberg, J. ed. New York: John Wiley, 1944.

Heilbroner, Robert L. *The Worldly Philosophers*. New York: Simon & Schuster, 1972.

———— "The New Economics." *New York Review of Books* (February 21, 1980).

Held, Virginia. "John Locke and Robert Nozick." *Social Research*, No. 43 (Spring 1976).

Himmelfarb, G. *On Liberty and Liberalism: The Case of John Stuart Mill*. New York: Random House, 1976.

Hirsch, Fred. *The Social Limits to Growth*. Cambridge, Mass.: Harvard University Press, 1976.

Hobbes, Thomas. *Leviathan*, A. D. Lindsay, ed. New York: E. P. Dutton, 1950. (Written in 1651.)

———— *Leviathan*. C. B. Macpherson, ed. New York: Penguin Books, 1975.

———— *Leviathan*. Michael Oakeshott, ed. Oxford: Blackwell & Mott, 1946.

———— *The English Works of Thomas Hobbes*. William Molesworth, ed. 11 Volumes. London: Bohn, 1839–1845.

Hobhouse, Leonard. *Social Evolution and Political Theory*. New York: Columbia University Press, 1911.

———— *The Metaphysical Theory of the State*. London: Allen & Unwin, 1918; New York: Barnes & Noble, 1960.

Hofstadter, Richard. *Social Darwinism in American Thought*. Philadelphia: University of Pennsylvania Press, 1944; Boston: Beacon Press reprint, 1955.

Hume, David. *An Enquiry Concerning Human Understanding*. L. A. Selby-Bigge, ed. Oxford: Clarendon Press, 1894. (Written in 1751.)

———— *David Hume's Political Essays*. Charles W. Hendel, ed. New York: Liberal Arts Press, 1953.

James, Michael. "Public Interest and Majority Rule in Bentham's Democratic Theory." *Political Theory*, Vol. 9, no. 1 (February 1981).

Kariel, H. S. *Beyond Liberalism*. New York: Harper & Row, 1978.

Kaufmann, Walter. *Hegel: A Reinterpretation*. Garden City, New York: Doubleday/Anchor Books, 1966.

Keane, John. "The Legacy of Political Economy: Thinking With and Against Claus Offe." *Canadian Journal of Social and Political Theory*, No. 2 (Fall 1978).

Kendall, Wilmoore. *The Conservative Affirmation*. Chicago: Regnery Press, 1963.

Keynes, John Maynard. *Essays in Persuasion*. New York: W. W. Norton, 1963.

—— *General Theory of Employment, Interest and Money*. New York: Harcourt, Brace & World, 1935.

Kirk, Russell. *The Conservative Mind; From Burke to Santayana*. Chicago: Regnery Press, 1953.

Kramnick, Isaac. *The Rage of Edmund Burke: Portrait of an Ambivalent Conservative*. New York: Basic Books, 1977.

Lasch, Christopher. *The Culture of Narcissism: American Life in an Age of Diminishing Expectations*. New York: W. W. Norton, 1978.

Laski, Harold. *A Grammar of Politics*. London: Allen & Unwin, 1925.

—— *Authority in the Modern State*. New Haven, Conn.: Yale University Press, 1919.

—— *Liberty in the Modern State*. New York: Harper & Row, 1930.

—— *Political Thought in England; Locke to Bentham*. London: Oxford University Press, 1920.

—— *The Rise of European Liberalism*. London: Allen & Unwin, 1936.

—— *The State in Theory and Practice*. New York: Viking Press, 1935.

Lieberson, Jonathan and Marganbesser, Sidney. "The Choices of Isaiah Berlin." *New York Review of Books* (20 March 1980).

Lindblom, Charles E. *Politics and Markets*. New York: Basic Books, 1977.

Lippmann, Walter. *Essays in the Public Philosophy*. New York: New American Library/Mentor, 1957.

—— *Public Opinion*. New York: Harcourt, Brace, 1922.

Locke, John. *A Letter Concerning Toleration*. J. W. Gough, ed. Oxford: Blackwell & Mott, 1947. (Written in 1685.)

—— *A Treatise of Civil Government: An Essay Concering the True, Original, Extent and End of Civil Government*. Charles L. Sherman, ed. New York: Appleton-Century-Crofts, 1937. (Written in 1690.)

—— *An Essay Concerning Human Understanding*. Alexander Campbell Fraser, ed. Oxford: Clarendon Press, 1894, 2 vols. (Written in 1690.)

—— *Two Treatises of Government*. Peter Laslett, ed. London: Cambridge University Press, 1960. (See this edition for Laslett's discovery dating the *Two Treatises* in 1679–1681, and not a decade later, as had been thought.)

Lukes, Steven. *Power: A Radical View*. New York: Humanities Press, 1974.

Macpherson, C. B. "Class, Classlessness and the Critique of Rawls." *Canadian Journal of Political Science*, No. 6 (September 1976).

―― "The Economic Penetration of Political Theory." *Journal of the History of Ideas*, No. 39 (January/March 1978).

―― "Humanist Democracy and Elusive Marxism." *Canadian Journal of Political Science*, No. 9 (May 1978).

―― *The Life and Times of Liberal Democracy.* New York: Oxford University Press, 1979.

―― *The Political Theory of Possessive Individualism: Hobbes to Locke.* New York: Oxford University Press, 1962.

Mansfield, Harvey C. *The Spirit of Liberalism.* Cambridge, Mass.: Harvard University Press, 1978.

McWilliams, Wilson Carey. *The Idea of Fraternity in America.* Berkeley, Ca.: University of California Press, 1974.

Mill, John Stuart. *Essays on Politics and Society*, 2 Vols. J. M. Robson, ed., Toronto: University of Toronto Press, 1976. (Written in the mid-nineteenth century.)

―― *Disquisitions and Discussions*, 4 vols. London: Longmans, Green, 1859–75.

―― *Principles of Political Economy.* London: Longmans, Green/People's edition, 1866.

―― *The Collected Works of John Stuart Mill*, 2 vols. J. M. Robson, ed. Toronto: University of Toronto Press, 1978.

―― *Three Essays: On Liberty; Representative Government; The Subjection of Women*, intro., Richard Wolheim. New York: Oxford University Press, 1975.

―― *Utilitarianism, Liberty, and Representative Government.* New York: Dutton, 1950.

Minogue, Kenneth. *The Liberal Mind.* London: Methuen, 1963.

Montesquieu. *Oeuvres complètes.* 7 vols. Edouard Laboulaye, ed. Paris: Garnier, 1875–79.

Nisbet, Robert. *The Twilight of Authority.* New York: Oxford University Press, 1975.

Nozick, Robert. *Anarchy, State and Utopia.* New York: Basic Books, 1974.

Oakshott, Michael. *Rationalism in Politics.* New York: Basic Books, 1962.

Olson, Mancur, Jr. *The Logic of Collective Action.* Cambridge, Mass.: Harvard University Press, 1965.

Ortega y Gasset, José. *The Revolt of the Masses.* New York: W. W. Norton, 1932.

Parry, Geraint. *John Locke.* London: Allen and Unwin, 1978.

Pateman, Carole. "Sublimation and Reification: Locke, Wolin and the Liberal Democratic Conception of the Political." *Politics and Society*, No. 5 (Winter 1975).

―― *The Problem of Political Obligation: A Critical Analysis of Liberal Theory.* New York: John Wiley, 1979.

―― "Women and Consent." *Political Theory*, Vol. 8, no. 2 (May 1980).

Pennock, J. Roland. *Democratic Political Theory.* Princeton, N.J.: Princeton University Press, 1980.

Plamenatz, John. *Democracy and Illusion: An Examination of Certain Aspects of Modern Democratic Theory.* New York: Longman, 1977.

—— *Man and Society*, 2 Vols. New York: McGraw-Hill, 1963.

—— *The English Utilitarians.* London: Oxford University Press, 1949.

Pocock, J. G. A. *The Political Works of James Harrington.* New York: Cambridge University Press, 1977.

Polanyi, Karl. *The Great Transformation.* Boston: Beacon Press, 1957.

Rawls, John. *A Theory of Justice.* Cambridge, Mass.: Harvard University Press, 1971.

Reed, Gary Frank. "Berlin and the Division of Liberty." *Political Theory*, Vol. 8, no. 3 (August 1980).

Richter, Melvin. *The Politics of Conscience: T. H. Green and His Age.* Cambridge, Mass.: Harvard University Press, 1964.

Robinson, Joan. *Collected Economic Papers*, 5 Vols. Oxford: Basil, Blackwell, 1979.

—— "Understanding The Economic Crisis." *New York Review of Books* (21 December 1978).

Robson, J. M. *The Improvement of Mankind.* Toronto: University of Toronto Press, 1968.

Rousseau, Jean-Jacques. *Émile.* Barbara Foxley, trans. New York: Dutton Everyman's Library, 1948.

—— *On the Social Contract, with the Geneva Manuscript and Political Economy*, R. D. Masters, ed. and J. R. Masters, trans. New York: St. Martin's Press, 1978.

—— *The First and Second Discourses.* Roger D. Masters and Judith Masters, eds. New York: St. Martin's Press, 1964.

—— *The Social Contract and Discourses.* G. D. H. Cole, trans. New York: Dutton, 1950.

—— *The Social Contract.* R. W. Crosby, trans. Brunswick, Ohio: Kings Court, 1979.

—— *The Social Contract.* Charles Frankel, ed. New York: Hafner, 1947.

Ryan, Alan, ed. *The Idea of Freedom: Essays in Honour of Isaiah Berlin.* New York: Oxford University Press, 1980.

Schaar, John H. *Legitimacy in the Modern State.* New Brunswick, N.J.: Transaction Press, 1979.

Schumpeter, Joseph. *History of Economic Analysis.* New York: Oxford University Press, 1954.

—— *Capitalism, Socialism and Democracy.* New York: Harper, 1962.

Skinner, Quentin. *The Foundation of Modern Political Thought*, Vol. I: *The Renaissance*; Vol. II: *The Age of Reformation.* Cambridge, England: Cambridge University Press, 1979.

Smith, Adam. *An Enquiry Into the Nature and Causes of the Wealth of Nations.* R. H. Campbell, A. S. Skinner and W. B. Todd, eds. New York: Oxford University Press, 1976.

—— *Glasgow Lectures in Jurisprudence.* D. D. Raphael, P. G. Stein and

Ronald Meek, eds. Published by Glasgow University for the Bicentennial of the original publication, 1776.

—— *The Theory of Moral Sentiments.* D. D. Raphael and A. L. MacFie, eds. New York: Oxford University Press, 1976.

Sombart, Werner. *Why Is There No Socialism in the United States.* Patricia M. Hocking and C. T. Husbands, trans. White Plains, N.Y.: M. E. Sharpe, 1978. (First published in 1905 as a series of articles in the *Archevfür Sozialwessenschaft und Sozialpolitik,* in Germany.)

Spencer, Herbert. *Essays: Scientific, Political and Speculative,* 3 Vols. London: William & Norgate, 1868–1874.

—— *Social Statics.* New York: Appleton Century Crofts, 1864.

—— *The Man versus the State.* Caldwell, Idaho: Caxton, 1940; London: Watts, 1909. (Written in 1884.)

Steinfels, Peter. *Neo-Conservatives: The Men Who Are Changing American Politics.* New York: Simon & Schuster, 1979.

Stephen, Leslie. *History of English Thought in the Eighteenth Century,* 3rd ed. New York: Harcourt, Brace & World/Harbinger, 1962.

—— *Hobbes.* New York: Macmillan, 1904.

—— *The English Utilitarians,* 3 vols. London: Duckworth, 1900.

Sumner, William Graham. *Essays,* 2 vols. A. G. Keller and M. R. Davie, eds. New Haven, Conn.: Yale University Press, 1934.

de Tocqueville, Alexis. *Democracy in America.* H. S. Commager, ed. London: Oxford University Press, 1946. (Written and published in France, 1835; English translation, 1863.)

Vernon, Richard. "The 'Great Society' and the 'Open Society': Liberalism in Hayek and Popper." *Canadian Journal of Political Science,* No. 9 (June 1976).

Von Hayek, Friedrich A. *The Constitution of Liberty.* Chicago: University of Chicago Press, 1960.

Walzer, Michael. "The New Masters." *New York Review of Books* (March 1980).

Warrender, Howard J. *The Political Philosophy of Hobbes; His Theory of Obligation.* Oxford: Clarendon Press, 1957.

Wiltshire, David. *The Social and Political Thought of Herbert Spencer.* Oxford: Oxford University Press, 1978.

Winch, Donald. *Adam Smith's Politics: An Essay in Historiographic Revision:* Cambridge, England: Cambridge University Press, 1978.

Wolff, Robert Paul. *Understanding Rawls: A Reconstruction and Critique of 'A Theory of Justice.'* Princeton, N.J.: Princeton University Press, 1977.

.4.
LIBERALISM: THE CASE OF THE UNITED STATES

The United States has become the foremost bastion of liberalism, exercising hegemony over the entire capitalist world. More than other capitalist nations, it has adhered to the early formulation of liberalism, described in the previous chapter as negative freedom. The four sections of this chapter will describe the process and results of the United States adherence to liberal ideology.

The first section will describe how James Madison's "Grand Design" has prevented majority rule and ensured that the state would serve the interest of the propertied classes while being only of limited service to the great mass of citizens.

The next section presents the transformation of America from the pluralism of the nineteenth and first half of the twentieth century to the corporate domination of the present era. In addition, this section will look at the means that the corporations use to control the state, the political process, the market, and the ideology of the people.

The third section will consider the results of this domination of United States society by the corporate elite. It will document the inequitable distribution of income and wealth and how the state has failed to provide adequately for the needs of its citizens while consistently coming to the relief of the corporations.

The final section of the chapter will point out that in spite of the support provided by the state, capitalism is

155

nevertheless in serious trouble. The liberal system established two hundred years ago in accordance with the liberal principles described in the previous chapter is having difficulty maintaining its legitimacy. The time may be coming when a choice, long avoided, will be forced upon us. Shall we respond to democratic pressure for a more positive interpretation of liberalism, positive liberty, which many believe will inexorably lead to some form of socialism? Or shall we abandon democracy, even the limited liberal form developed in the United States, in order to ensure the continued rule of the established elite?

THE GRAND DESIGN

The American Constitution is often read and taught as an instrument for guarding against the tyranny of kings; however, one need only briefly look at *The Federalist Papers* to learn otherwise. *The Federalist Papers* by James Madison, John Jay, and Alexander Hamilton were written to defend the newly proposed Constitution and to urge that the thirteen states ratify the new system of government. To this day these papers stand as the best theoretical writing on politics produced in the United States. While many of the papers could be used to defend the thesis of this section, *Federalist* No. 10, written by James Madison—rightly known as the "Father of the Constitution"—will be chosen, because it is the boldest of the documents and does not attempt to conceal its intent.

It is our contention that the system of government designed at the Constitutional Convention had as its core the twin goals of preventing majority rule and ensuring that the state would be in the hands of the propertied classes.

James Madison describes his aim as follows:

Among the numerous advantages promised by a well constructed Union, none deserves to be more accurately developed than its tendency to break and control the violence of faction.[1]

Madison makes clear which faction must be controlled only a few paragraphs further on:

The diversity in the faculties of men from which the rights of property originate, is not less an insuperable obstacle to a uniformity of interests. The protection of these faculties is the first object of Government. From the protection of different and unequal faculties of acquiring property, the possession of different degrees and kinds of property immediately results; and from the influence of these on the sentiments and views of the respective proprietors, ensues a division of the society into different interests and parties.

But the most common and durable source of factions, has been the various and unequal distribution of property. Those who hold, and those who are without property, have ever formed distinct interests in society. Those who are creditors and those who are debtors, fall under a like discrimination.[2]

This division of society into two factions—a majority of "have-nots" and a minority of men of property—constituted the danger which Madison sought to guard against by preventing those without property from combining to gain control over the state. It is the acquisition of power by the disenfranchised which would constitute a threat of "faction." Faction, as Madison understood, is a constant potential in a class society. Controlling the effect of faction is the aim of the American Constitution.

On the other hand, there are "legitimate" interests in society. The chief requisite, "domestic tranquility," and services from the state such as the enforcement of contracts support and promote this legitimacy. Madison describes these legitimate interests in the tenth *Federalist* paper.

A landed interest, a manufacturing interest, a monied interest, with many lesser interests grow up of necessity in civilized nations, and divide them into different classes, actuated by different sentiments and views....

The regulation of these various interests forms the principal task of modern legislation and involves the spirit of party and faction in the necessary and ordinary operations of government....[3]

The task, therefore, is clearly to provide for the active role of the state in mediating the disputes which will unavoidably develop among "legitimate" interests and to provide access to the state, even control over the state, to these "legitimate" interests while at the same time preventing from uniting into an effective political force that most dangerous faction—the majority of the citizens who lack both property and, in the judgment of the framers, good sense. Again, in Madison's words it was necessary to...

refine and enlarge the public views, by passing them through the medium of a chosen body of citizens, whose wisdom may be to discern the true interests of the country...[I]t may well happen that the public voice pronounced by the representatives of the people, will be more consonant to the public good, than if pronounced by the people themselves....[4]

The techniques of achieving control over the people are numerous, but essentially they resolve into a set of institutional relationships for dividing the polity both geographically and functionally.

We are so accustomed to these divisions and to hearing celebrations of praise that we seldom reflect on their purpose or on the radical nature of their design. Since the time of the Greek city-states, political philosophy has held that only a small homogeneous community could provide the social basis necessary for good government. Here, James Madison affirms the opposite. The larger the nation, perhaps—he evisions one spanning a continent—the more numerous and varied the interests are and the less likely a factious majority could unite. It was almost impossible then, and nearly as difficult now, to imagine the debtor in Massachusetts joining forces with the sharecropper, to say nothing of the slave or free black in Georgia, to form an effective political force. To this day the skill with which the people have been divided is remarkable: the skilled against the unskilled, the old against the young, the men against the women, the Catholic against the Protestants and both against the Jew. The list could go on indefinitely.

It would be a mistake to think that this process of division has been merely an historical development and not part of a conscious design. Again the tenth *Federalist* paper demonstrates Madison's intention:

The influence of factious leaders may kindle a flame within their particular States, but will be unable to spread a general conflagration throughout the other States.... The rage for paper money, for the abolition of debts, for an equal division of property, or for any other improper or wicked project, will be less apt to pervade the whole body of the Union.[5]

Of course, federalism was not the sole or even the chief means of keeping the republic from the control of the majority. Nor were the various states left unaided and at the mercy of those factious indigent masses. The Constitution restricted the powers of the states so that they could not respond to popular demands. Most important, the states were prohibited from passing any laws which impaired the obligations of contracts. Furthermore, they were prevented from issuing paper money and the Full Faith and Credit Clause (Article IV, Section 1) of the Constitution enabled creditors to pursue debtors across state borders and prevented states from providing a sanctuary for debtors.

On the other hand, the national government was given more than enough power to protect property and promote commerce (see, for example, the eighteen paragraphs of Article I Section 8 of the Constitution). However, to ensure that no factious majority would gain control of the central government with its extensive power, the government was also divided functionally. Our familiarity blinds us to the degree that these familiar devices prevent *majority* rule rather than tyrannical impulse. It should also be remembered that senators were not popularly elected until 1914, that women did not receive the vote until 1920; that slavery was condoned by the Constitution and blacks were not effectively enfranchised until the civil rights movement forced the enactment of the civil rights laws by the Johnson administration.

The most extreme example of the screening of the majority will is provided by the elaborate scheme which the Constitution originally provided for the election of the president, the only office representing a national constituency, and, potentially, the least autonomous branch. First, the Constitution requires that the state legislature shall appoint electors in a manner to be determined by the states themselves. Second, the electors shall meet in their respective states, not together as a collective body; third, each elector shall vote for two persons, one of whom is not required to be a citizen of that state. The list of persons and the number of votes received shall be sent to the president of the Senate, who shall count the votes. The process then becomes so complicated that a direct quotation from the Constitution is required to illustrate the extent of the protection against a popular election of the president:

The person having the greatest Number of Votes shall be the President, if such Number be a Majority of the whole number of Electors appointed; and if there be more than one who have such Majority, and have an equal Number of Votes, then the House of Representatives shall immediately choose by Ballot one of them for President, and if no person have a Majority then from the five highest on the List the said House shall in like manner choose the President. But in choosing the President, the votes shall be taken by States, the Representatives from each State having one Vote...and a Majority of all the States shall be necessary to a Choice.[6]

It would be difficult to design a system of election more removed from democratic control, while still maintaining a representative form. With the unique exception of George Washington, there is little doubt that the framers thought that future choices for the presidency would be made by the House of Representatives, from candidates taken from a list of most prominent citizens. The assumptions of the framers regarding the electoral mode have, of course, proven unfounded. Almost at once their system of elite choice broke down. Nevertheless, the spirit and, to a considerable extent, the form obstructing a democratic choice of the executive have survived.

The structure designed by Madison did not, of course, go on unchanged, nor were democratic movements entirely without success. The method of electing the president has changed, although attempts to eliminate entirely the electoral college have failed. Blacks and women have won the right to vote. Workers have won the right to form unions. However, as C. B. Macpherson observes in *The Real World of Democracy*,[7] the extension of the franchise was won at a price. While liberalism was becoming democratized during the nineteenth century, democracy was also in the process of being liberalized. That is, democracy was tamed. The price paid for the acceptance of a measure of popular input into the political system was the acceptance of the Madisonian view of "legitimate" factions. This broader democratized liberalism came to be called pluralism. Politics became the politics of organized groups. The state was seen as merely one group among many with its own interest to protect against those of other groups. Public policy, then, was the result of the pressure of the numerous groups concerned. The only really public role for the state was to see that the groups played according to the rules of the game, that is, acted through accepted channels and by peaceful means. Much of the "progressive" legislation of liberalization was designed to initiate new groups into the rules of the game. The Wagner Act, which brought labor unions legitimacy at the expense of militancy, is perhaps the best example of pluralism at work.

THE INORDINATE POWER OF THE AMERICAN CORPORATION

Size and Economic Output

The American corporation exercises a vast amount of power. Its power has become so concentrated that it now represents in its critics' view a serious threat to democracy

TABLE 4·1
Largest Manufacturing Corporations—Percent Share of Assets Held 1950 to 1978

Year	100 Largest (%)	200 Largest (%)
1950	39.7	47.2
1955	44.3	47.7
1960	46.4	56.3
1965	46.5	56.7
1970	48.5	60.4
1975	45.0	57.5
1979	46.1	59.0

Source: *Statistical Abstract of the United States 1980* (Washington, D.C.: U.S. Government Printing Office, 1980), p. 568, Table 953.

in America. This section will first examine the basis for this undue influence of the American corporation and will then discuss the four ways in which the corporation exercises its influence in American society.

The basis for the corporations' power is its size and contribution to the total economic output of the United States. While we may feel that we have some appreciation of the size of the giant corporation, in fact, we are likely to be surprised when the data are closely examined. The following table (Table 4–1) indicates the total corporate manufacturing assets held by the 100 and 200 largest corporations in the United States and how the share of corporate assets held by those corporations have expanded.

In spite of the slight drop in concentration between 1970 and 1975, it appears that the trend toward greater concentration has started up once more. Since 1977 the ten largest takeovers in American history have occurred. The list is topped by Shell Oil's purchase of Belridge Oil for $3.65 billion in 1979.[8]

Of equal significance are the figures in Table 4–2, which compares the top 500 corporations to the second 500 corporations.

162

TABLE 4·2
Sales, Profits, and Assets of the Top 500 Manufacturing Corporations and the Second 500 (1979)

	Top 500	Second 500	Ratio of Top 500 to Second 500 in 1975	Ratio of Top 500 to Second 500 in 1976	Ratio of Top 500 to Second 500 in 1979
Sales	$1,445.3 billion	$109.9 billion	10.5:1	11.8:1	13.1:1
Profits	18.4 billion	6.1 billion	11.4:1	11.6:1	12.8:1
Assets	1,034.7 billion	78.8 billion	10.4:1	12.0:1	13.1:1

Source: Statistical Abstracts of the United States, 1980, (Washington, D.C.: U.S. Government Printing Office, 1980), pp. 569, 570, Tables 956, 957.

TABLE 4·3
Comparison of the Top 500 Manufacturing Corporations and the Top 100 (1979)

	Top 500	Top 100	Percent Accounted for by Top 100
Employees	16,195 thousand	9,141 thousand	56.4
Sales	$1,445.3 billion	$963.7 billion	66.7
Profits	$78.4 billion	$50.8 billion	64.8
Assets	$1,034.7 billion	$676.3 billion	65.4

Source: Statistical Abstract of the United States, 1980, (Washington, D.C.: U.S. Government Printing Office, 1980), p. 569, 570, Tables 956, 957.

Again, one sees the increase in concentration at the top where the top 500 corporations are more than ten times larger in terms of assets, sales, and profits than those of the second 500 corporations. When one speaks of concentration, therefore, one increasingly refers to a very, very small number of firms—an infinitesimal percentage of the some 170,000 corporations in the United States. The next table 4–3 may seem redundant but it is not, for a further concentration *within* the top 100 manufacturing corporations in relation to the top 500 makes the power concentration of the few even more significant. Furthermore, the concentration of sales, profits, and assets in a smaller number of firms has been increasing over time. "The 100 largest firms in 1972 held as large a share of manufacturing assets as the 200 largest in 1950."[9]

Mere numbers designating a place along the "concentration-scale" fail to tell the whole story of concentration in the United States. The wielding of economic power requires another dimension—that of linkage among corporations which is most clearly seen in the pattern of interlocking directorates. A week after Senator Lee Metcalf's untimely death, his Subcommittee on Reports, Accounting and Management released a news report which stated in part:

Power to vote stock in 122 of the largest corporations in America is concentrated in 21 institutional investors led by Morgan Guarantee Trust Company.... The study also shows that Morgan and other major banks are the principal stockvoters in each other's bank holding companies.

The press release continues:

The 122 corporations studied by the subcommittee are so large that the total market value of their common stock amounts to 41% of the market value of all outstanding common stock in the U.S. The 122 companies and their 2,259 subsidiaries and affiliates include the largest industrial, financial, transportation, insurance, utility and retailing firms in the country.

Morgan Guarantee Trust was the major identified stockholder in twenty-seven of the 122 corporations studied.[10]

In arriving at an accurate conception of the magnitude of those giant corporations, the following description of a familiar corporation will supplement the tabular data presented above:

General Motor's yearly operating revenues exceed those of all but a dozen or so countries. Its sales receipts are greater than the combined general revenues of New York, New Jersey, Pennsylvania, Ohio, Delaware, and the six New England states. Its 1,-300,000 stockholders are equal to the population of Washington, Baltimore, or Houston. G.M. employees number well over 700,-000 and work in 127 plants in the United States and forty-five countries spanning Europe, South Africa, North America, and Australia. The total cash wages are more than twice the personal income of Ireland. G.M.'s federal corporate tax payments approach $2 billion, or enough to pay for all federal grants in fiscal year 1970 for health research. The enormity of General Motors...should not be thought of as unique. Some 175 other manufacturing, merchandising and transportation companies now have annual sales of at least a billion dollars.[11]

This concentration of potential power is alarming in itself, but more threatening are the ways in which and extent to which this power can be and has been used to give the corporate community domination over American political, social, economic, and ideological life. Additional evidence of power concentration is also presented in the next section.

Corporate Influence*

Four ways in which corporations exercise their pervasive influence over American life are as follows: (1) the utilization of their *strategic position as dispensers of public goods* to gain inducement from government; (2) a direct application of old-fashioned "political muscle"; (3) the creation of a *circularity in markets* so that the usual market restraints on the corporation cease to function properly; and (4) the *manipulation of the ideology* of Americans. This last category of influence introduces a *circularity in the polyarchy* which is subversive to democracy.

The strategic position   It must first be recognized that corporations provide public goods and make public, that is, political, decisions. The state has left in private hands (the hands of corporate executives, to be more exact) the determination of level of investment, the nature of the technology to be developed, the location of industry (where and in what sectors growth will occur), the pattern of work organization, income distribution, and to a large degree the levels of employment and the pricing of products. Each and every one of these decisions has great public impact in that these decisions determine the nature of the economic, social, political, and natural environments vital to the standard of living and style of life of citizens. The wrong decision of the corporate leadership means, at the very least, inflation or depression or both, and either or both of these can undermine any government or administration. It is therefore not surprising that it is of major concern to political leaders that the private corporate sector performs its task of providing

*This section is greatly indebted to Charles Lindblom, *Politics and Markets*, 1977.

that "dynamo" which will at least ensure an acceptable level of employment.

Government, itself, is necessarily concerned about corporate performance. However, it should be noted that the provisions of the Constitution and of the laws regarding private property are negative; that is, while regulatory schemes may prevent the corporation from doing something, they cannot *compel* the corporation to do anything. What the state must do is provide the corporate leaders with the proper incentive, or inducement, to persuade them to do what is required to keep the economy afloat. The government officials know full well that if they fail to provide an inducement and the corporations therefore choose not to expand or invest, it is the political leaders and not the business executives who will pay the price in the loss of office.

Charles Lindblom summarizes this in the following paragraphs:

In the eyes of government officials, therefore, businessmen do not appear simply as the representatives of a special interest, as representatives of interest groups do. They appear as functionaries performing functions that government officials regard as indispensable. When a government official asks himself whether business needs a tax reduction, he knows he is asking a question about the welfare of the whole society and not simply about a favor to a segment of the population, which is what is typically at stake when he asks himself whether he should respond to an interest group.

Any government official who understands the requirements of his position and the responsibilities that market-oriented systems throw on businessmen will therefore grant them a privileged position. He does not have to be bribed, duped, or pressured to do so....*Businessmen cannot be left knocking at the doors of the political systems, they must be invited in.*[12]

And what an invitation they have received in recent years! Outstanding federally guaranteed and direct loans to business at the end of 1977 was an astounding $384 billion and new loans of $99 billion were made in 1979.[13] As early as 1963 Lindblom estimated that about 40 percent of business investment was attributable to tax credits.

An even more impressive handout by the government takes the form of tax "loopholes." The U.S. Office of Management and Budget notes that "tax expenditures are estimated revenue losses attributable to provisions of the Federal Tax laws which allow a special exclusion, exemption or deduction from gross income or which provide for a preferential rate of tax or a deferral of tax liability." In 1979 this tax expenditure amounted to a staggering $143,560 million, which represented an increase of $37 thousand million since 1976. In spite of continuous promises of tax reform, the tax loopholes get bigger and bigger. If these exemptions were eliminated, enough taxes would be collected to soak up excessive demand, balance the budget, and leave enough for a substantial tax reduction based on adjusting existing rates downward.[14]

We have seen the great length to which President Carter went to gain the confidence of the corporate world. One merely has to note the connection between Carter's chief aids and the Trilateral Commission. It must be remembered that the Trilateral Commission is a group of influential business leaders from Western Europe, Japan, and the United States organized and financed by Chase Manhattan Bank President David Rockefeller to analyze and recommend public policy. The two most influential members of Carter's administration were both members of the executive committee of the Trilateral Commission. They are Harold Brown, former secretary of defense, and Dr. Brzezinski, who served as the director of the Trilateral Commission. Vice-President Bush was also a member.

The character of the Trilateral Commission can be judged by an essay contained in the report on the *Governability of Democracies*, which has been republished in an abridged form under the revealing title *The Democratic Distemper*. In this report, Samuel Huntington makes the following reservations about democracy:

First, Democracy is only one way of constituting authority and is not necessarily a universally applicable one.... Second, the effective operation of a democratic political system usually requires some measure of apathy and non-involvement on the part of some individuals and groups.... In the past every democratic society has had a marginal population, of greater or lesser size, which has not actively participated in politics.... Marginal Groups, as in the case of the blacks, are now becoming full participants in the political system. The danger of overloading the political system with demands which extend its functions and undermine its authority still remains....

The vulnerability of democratic government in the United States thus comes not primarily from external threats, though such threats are real, nor from internal subversion from the left or the right, although both possibilities could exist, but rather from the internal dynamics of democracy itself in a highly educated, mobilized, and participant society.[15]

Prof. Huntington suggests leaving the governing of society where it has been and where, in the judgment of the corporate world, it belongs—in the hands of the business elite of America.

Direct political role of the corporation The corporation's special strategic position does not impede, but rather enhances its traditional political role in American politics. Indeed its direct involvement in politics dwarfs the role played by any other group in American society. The oft-praised pluralism of America becomes, upon inspection, the *de facto* domination of one element over the entire political realm.

The dollar amounts spent on politics by corporations is difficult to assess because direct corporate expenditure is illegal, although we now know that this did not deter corporations from making under-the-counter contributions to favored politicians and even out-and-out bribes to government officials, both domestic and foreign. On the one hand, the official reported figures show that in the 1972 presidential election unions spent $8.5 million directly and between $4 and $5 million more on "nonpartisan" activities of a political nature, such as registration drives. Business groups, on the other hand, reported spending only approximately $6 million. However, if we look at individual prominent businessmen's contributions we see a different picture. The problem is to account for the difference between the total of almost $500 million campaign expenditures and the estimated $14 million contributed by unions. We do know that members of the president's business council contributed over $1 million and that the directors of five oil companies contributed $1.5 million, and NASA contractors over $2 million. The balance is unaccounted for. However, we should remember that there are at least 40,000 corporations with over 100 employees. In 1964 union committees contributed less than $4 million, while a total of less than 10,000 individuals contributed more than $13.5 million. In 1965, a year with which direct comparisons can be made, contributions of only 742 businessmen equalled the contributions of unions representing 17 million workers.[16]

The House of Representatives made a study of contributions and their conclusion was that 173 corporations spent $32.1 million to influence legislation while farm organizations and unions spent less than $1.5 million.[17]

Of course, it is generally recognized that unions are the only possible organized group which can counterbalance the role of business, but such a notion clearly serves the interest of business for, as has just been shown, political contributions by unions are very small in comparison with those of business. The two organized interests, of course, start from a different financial base; while total union assets in the United States, excluding pension funds which are usually administered by businesses or by banks, are approximately $3 billion, corporate total assets add up to $3 trillion. Anyone who has played even a little poker knows the disadvantage of playing in a game where one's bankroll is so much less than the other players'.

Nearly as important as financial clout is the organizational advantage the corporate community has, which other groups and the general public lack. We tend to forget that businesses have ready-made organizations with a well-defined hierarchical structure, which makes it easy for them to pursue political goals while others must spend most of their energies and resources to create the organization itself before they can pursue any objectives.

Recent Supreme Court decisions acknowledge as a matter of constitutional guarantee the right of corporations to engage in political campaigns on policy matters (see the Belloti case), such as campaigning against antismoking legislation. In addition we are just beginning to witness the promotion by business of PACs (Political Action Committees), on a scale much larger than heretofore. Once again Professor Lindblom summarizes the inordinate power of business and the necessity of such power to keep the "free enterprise" system:

...union demands—far short of those demands that would be pressed successfully if union political influence were stronger—can undercut the entrepreneurial energies on which market-oriented systems depend. To put the point in another way, a market-oriented system may require for its success so great a disproportion of business influence both through the privileged position of business and through business disproportion in electoral and interest-group activity, that even modest challenges to it are disruptive to economic stability and growth. Union power may be "too much" for the survival of private enterprise long before it is great enough to match the privileged position of business. Similarly welfare state demands may be "too much" long before they manifest a political equality in electoral and interest-group activity.[18]

Circularity in markets and values There remain two more ways in which corporations influence the American polity. These influences in their long-term effect are perhaps even more serious to popular democratic control than the deliberate efforts of business we have already examined. The ability of the market to act as a restraint on the corporation is limited by the extent to which the choices made in the market reflect the true volitions of the public. The extent to which consumer choices reflect the desires *not* of consumers themselves, but desires which are artifacts of advertising and sales efforts, mitigates against the equilibrium of supply and demand. The market ceases to perform its function as a restraint on corporate decision making. In the United States it has been calculated that approximately $44 billion a year was spent on advertising and sales promotion—an amount about equal to that spent on higher education ($50.4 billion) or on public health care ($40.6 billion). It is estimated that America spends 2.0 percent of its national income on advertising.[19] Another source reports that the United States spends far more than any other nation on advertising. The United States spends $157 per capita, Sweden $92, West Germany $49, France $47, and the United Kingdom $40.[20] It needs to be said that not all advertising is harmful; certainly some of it does provide needed information and knowledge about the introduction of new products. Whether we need new cereals on the market as frequently as they appear or whether they are as new as the advertising claims is frequently questioned. The central point is that advertising manipulates people's wants for the purpose of implementing what corporations want them to want. In so doing advertising destroys or weakens the essential function of a market, which is to satisfy in the most efficient way the volitions of individuals as distinguished from the wants or choices that the public may be "forced" to make. That this has far-reaching consequences is beyond doubt. Did the public consciously opt for the automobile rather than a mass transit system, or was that decision made not by market forces, but by the oil companies and the automobile manufacturers? The consequences of such unfree decisions are many: supermarkets and shopping malls rather than neighborhoods; energy shortage, foreign dependency, and air pollution are other results which are plaguing us because of that nonmarket decision. (In fact, the secondary and tertiary impact of that decision on the future of America would require book-length treatment to do it justice.)

No less insidious has been the corporate attempt to control the *political* volition of the public. In the circularity created by the corporation in the ideology and values of Americans can be seen the truth of Marx's perceptive comment, "The ideas of the ruling class are in every epoch the ruling ideas: i.e., the class, which is the ruling material force of society, is at the same time its ruling intellectual force."[21]

On many of the issues that businessmen attempt to influence American politics, the divisions that exist among them, while never as effective as Galbraith once believed when he wrote *American Capitalism: A Theory of Countervailing Power*, ensure that there will be some public debate on issues and that the public itself will have some role in determining the outcome. Nevertheless, on the "Grand Issues," as Lindblom refers to them, there is a consensus which makes the view of business omnipresent. These "Grand Issues" are neatly summarized by Professor Lindblom as "private enterprise itself, a high degree of corporate autonomy, protection of the *status quo* on distribution of income and wealth, close consultation between business and government, and restriction of union demands to those consistent with business profitability."[22]

The aim of the corporate world on these issues is to exclude them from the agenda of public debate or discussion. This aim has been largely realized, for it requires nothing of citizens but that they do nothing; that they continue to accept the views that they have heard since they entered kindergarten. The Protestant ethic and the sports-minded competitiveness is made to seem part and parcel of the democratic, American, free enterprise way. American business is seen as being as American as the proverbial baseball and apple pie. To disagree with any of the Grand Issues is to be subversive to the very core of American ideology.

It may seem surprising that many deeply held traditions such as religious beliefs, the sanctity of marriage, the disapproval of premarital sexual relations have all undergone fundamental changes while there has been no serious challenge to the Grand Issues of American business. The drubbing that Senator George McGovern received from the mass media when he dared to question some of these sanctified issues, even in a most tentative and limited manner, was remarkable in its universality.

Of course, much of the attempt to control the ideology of Americans is more subliminal than the attack on Mc-

Govern. Every businessman or woman who heads up a Red Cross or Community Chest drive is doing his or her bit to ensure the permanence of the ideology. Every free grant of materials by a corporation or a public utility to the school system carries with it a subliminal message about the "free enterprise" system.

Every foreign visitor to the United States is struck with the limited scope of public discussion and debate in the United States. This limitation was clearly evident in the choice between Carter and Reagan in the 1980 election.

Nevertheless, as the next section will show, the hegemony so long exercised by the American business community is breaking down. The economic, political, and social disarray in the United States is now all too evident. What the outcome will be is difficult to know, although as the choice between capitalism and democracy becomes inevitable in the United States, the odds are that the hegemony of the business community will be reasserted by suppression of democratic freedom.

THE ECONOMIC DISTRIBUTION OF INCOME AND WEALTH

As has been noted, the fear of majority rule became encased in the Constitution of the United States and memorialized in *The Federalist Papers*. This enshrinement of negative freedom did not, however, prevent state action in behalf of the business community of the United States. A process that began with Hamilton's *Report on Manufacturing* (which concluded on the following note): "...in a community like that of the United States, the public purse must supply the deficiency of private resource. In what can it be so useful, as in prompting and improving the efforts of industry?"[23] This process of state aid to the business community has continued to this day. However, after 1930 the role of the state took a quantum leap. The Great Depression of the thirties marked the beginning of a new era in American politics. In

TABLE 4·4
Government Expenditures from 1950 to 1978
(billions of dollars)

Year	Federal	State	Local	Total
1950	44	11	12	67
1960	100	26	27	153
1965	126	39	38	203
1970	206	69	60	334
1975	302	119	98	519
1978	430	172	131	732

Source: *Statistical Abstract of the United States, 1980,* (Washington, D.C.: U.S. Government Printing Office, 1980), p. 287, Table 480.

comparison with today's role the activity of the federal government in the thirties looks slight for those expenditures ranged from a mere $5 billion in 1932 to a high of only $9 billion in 1937.[24] Table 4–4 shows the growth in government expenditures since 1950.

Paralleling this growth in governmental expenditures has been a growth in government employment.

The data in Table 4–5 do indicate a vast increase in state activities, but nevertheless, as the following material amply demonstrates, the activity has done little to improve the distribution of income or wealth in our society.

TABLE 4·5
Government Employment from 1950 to 1979 (in thousands)

Year	Federal Civilian	State and Local	Total
1950	2,117	4,285	6,402
1960	2,421	6,387	8,808
1970	2,881	10,147	13,028
1979	2,869	13,102	15,971

Source: *Statistical Abstract of the United States, 1980* (Washington, D.C.: U.S. Government Printing Office, 1980), p. 318 Table 519.

Americans have been taught to believe that the United States is a classless or middle-class society, but the reality is rather different. Income in the United States has, for as long as adequate records show, been quite inequitably distributed. The only unusual thing about income distribution in the United States is how constant the share of income received by each segment of society has been, in spite of the introduction of the income tax and the increased role of government. Table 4–6 shows the distribution of income from the end of World War II to 1977.

The major reason for the extreme inequality of income is the inequality of wealth, for it is the unearned income received through the ownership of corporate stock and bonds which provides the basis for the inequality of income.

Table 4–7 provides a clear picture of the distribution of wealth in the United States.[25]

A more recent source provides an even more revealing account. An examination of the wealth held by the extremely wealthy—the top 0.5 and top 1 percent of the people—discloses that the top half of 1 percent owned *49.3 percent of all corporate stock,* and *52.2 percent of all bonds* and *80.8 percent of all trusts.*

Particularly noteworthy is the degree to which the ownership of American corporations is concentrated among the wealthy. That 80 percent of the population owned only 4 percent of the corporate stock undercuts any claims for "stockholder democracy." These data need to be kept in mind when considering the material already presented on the inordinate power of the American corporation.

The income story of Lee Iacocca, past president of the Ford Motor Company and then president of Chrysler, dramatically illustrates the great inequality in American life. In 1976, before he was fired from Ford, Iacocca's salary was $360,000 per year. This was augmented with a bonus of $610,000 for a total compensation in 1976 of $970,000. This averages out to over $19,000 a week, compared with the average production worker's compensation of $174.00 a week.[26] As president of the ailing Chrysler Motor Company, whose continued existence had become dependent on tax-

TABLE 4·6
Money Income of Families. Percent of Aggregate Income and Income at Selected Positions Received by Each Fifth and Highest 5 Percent: 1950 to 1978

Item and Income Bank	1950	1955	1960	1965	1970	1975	1978
Percent of Aggregate Income							
All families	100.0	100.0	100.0	100.0	100.0	100.0	100.0
Lowest fifth	4.5	4.8	4.8	5.2	5.4	5.4	5.2
Second fifth	12.0	12.3	12.2	12.2	12.2	11.8	11.6
Middle fifth	17.4	17.8	17.8	17.8	17.6	17.6	17.5
Fourth fifth	23.4	23.7	24.0	23.9	23.8	24.1	24.1
Highest fifth	42.7	41.3	41.3	40.9	40.9	41.1	41.5
Highest 5 percent	17.3	16.4	15.9	15.5	15.6	15.5	15.6
Income at Selected Positions Current dollars:							
Mean, all families	3,815	4,962	6,227	7,704	11,106	15,546	20,100
Upper limit of each fifth:							
Lowest fifth	1,661	2,221	2,784	3,500	5,100	6,914	8,700
Second fifth	2,856	3,780	4,800	5,863	8,320	11,465	14,700
Middle fifth	3,801	5,082	6,364	7,910	11,299	16,000	20,600
Fourth fifth	5,283	6,883	8,800	10,800	15,531	22,037	28,600
Highest 5 percent	8,615	10,605	13,536	16,695	24,250	34,144	44,900

Source: Statistical Abstract of the United States 1980 (Washington, D.C.: U.S. Government Printing Office, 1980), p. 454, Table 752.

TABLE 4·7
Distribution of Various Types of Personal Wealth, 1962

	Wealthiest 20%	Wealthiest 5%	Wealthiest 1%
Total U.S. wealth	76	50	31
Total corporate stock	96	83	61
Total assets of business and professions	89	62	39

payer largess, Mr. Iacocca's compensation in 1979 was $1,266,000. One million of that compensation was a payment made to compensate him for lost Ford benefits. His salary was $266,000, which represented a cut from $360,000 (his contribution to Chrysler's salary reduction program). However, under a new agreement, he accepted a salary of only one dollar for 1980 and 1981.[27] While it is true that Mr. Iacocca is one of the higher paid executives, it would be a mistake to see him as exceptional. One study of the executives of the top 50 corporations showed that they enjoyed an average salary of $400,000 in 1974 and that the top executives owned on the average $2.6 million worth of stock in their own companies; most of this acquired through bonus and stock options. The stock option exercised by the chairman of the board of General Dynamics, who in 1975 purchased stock from the company for $2 million (which had in 1981 a market value of $4.2 million), is a good illustration of how to make a $2.2 million profit in one transaction.[28]

A more surprising contrast to the wealthy is not the plight of the poor (as shocking as their condition is in a country of such wealth) but the rather meager condition of the average American family.

The U.S. Bureau of Labor Statistics publishes a budget to characterize what it describes as "minimum," "intermediate," and "high" standards of living based on the income necessary for a family of four in an urban environment. In 1977 the average intermediate budget for a family of four

178

TABLE 4·8
Personal Wealth—Value of Assets Held by All Persons, Top 0.5 Percent, and Top 1 Percent: 1972 (In billions of dollars, except as indicated)*

	Value of gross personal assets held by:			Percent held by:	
	All persons	Top 0.5 percent of all	Top 1 percent of all	Top 0.5 percent of all	Top 1 percent of all
Total assets	**4,344.4**	**822.4**	**1,046.9**	**18.9**	**24.1**
Real estate	1,492.6	150.9	225.0	10.1	15.1
Corporate stock	870.9	429.3	491.7	49.3	56.5
Bonds	158.0	82.5	94.8	52.2	60.0
Cash	748.8	63.6	101.2	8.5	13.5
Debt instruments	77.5	30.3	40.8	39.1	52.7
Life insurance	143.0	6.2	10.0	4.3	7.0
Trusts	99.4	80.3	89.4	80.8	89.9
Miscellaneous	853.6	59.5	83.3	6.8	9.8
Liabilities	**808.5**	**100.7**	**131.0**	**12.5**	**16.2**
Net worth	**3,535.9**	**721.7**	**915.9**	**20.4**	**25.9**
Number of persons (million)	**(x)**	**1.04**	**2.09**	**(x)**	**(x)**

*Wealth of all persons derived from national balance sheets. Wealth of top 0.5 percent and 1 percent of all persons estimated by estate multiplier technique.

Source: Statistical Abstracts of the United States 1979 (Washington, D.C.: U.S. Government Printing Office, 1979), Table 775, p. 470.

was put at nearly $17,000, although the median family income as of March 1978 was only $16,009; therefore, somewhat ironically, the intermediate budget was approximately a thousand dollars a year higher than that of half the the families in the United States.

After making an analysis of the intermediate budget, Donald Light summarizes his findings thus:

An examination of the amounts used in the [intermediate] budget shows that they are less than extravagant. Clothes are replaced over a period of two to four years and furniture over a longer period. Transportation is by used-car unless the city has a well-developed public transportation system. There is no hired help for the wife in her housekeeping chores. The recreation allowance permits only a movie every two or three weeks. The education category covers only day-to-day school expenses such as book fees and materials—it does not provide for money to be put away for college or any kind of post-high school training. The entire budget in fact makes no provision for savings of any kind to meet future major expenses. It may be said to be quite un-American in that it does not recognize social mobility as a necessary "good" to be consumed. This budget also makes no provision for legal assistance—people who live under this budget are basically powerless to contest official actions concerning them.[29]

This hardly conforms to the expectations of the average American family. Its failure to include any savings for such purposes as a college education or an illness requiring extensive care should convince us that the average American family is deprived of the things which the more affluent take for granted and mistakenly assume are widely shared.

The picture being described in this section on income and wealth distribution and in the previous section on the power of the American corporation demonstrates that elite status and benefits are highly correlated in American society. The intervention of the state into the economy has failed to make any substantial changes in either the distribution of income or wealth. It can be argued that the plight of the poor and the elderly would be worse than it is if it

TABLE 4·9
Types of Government Expenditures as a Percentage of Gross National Product, 1973

Country	Total Government Expenditures	Education	Health	Social Services	Military
United States	29.9	6.7	2.8	12	6.1
Canada	33.7	8.0	6.0	19	2.0
United Kingdom	34.6	6.3	4.3	17	4.9
West Germany	35.2	4.1	4.6	22	3.4
Sweden	40.6	7.7	6.5	24	3.7
France	35.0	5.3	4.2	19	3.5
Italy	37.0	5.4	1.2	22	3.0

TABLE 4•10
Government Payments to Farms by Value of Farm Sales

Average payment per farm (dollars)	589
Farms with sales of—	
Less than $2,500	54
$2,500–$4,999	165
$5,000–$9,999	252
$10,000–$19,999	383
$20,000–$39,999	841
$40,000–$99,999	1,163
$100,000–$199,999	1,413
$200,000 and over	1,526

Source: Statistical Abstracts of the United States, 1980 (Washington, D.C.: U.S. Government Printing Office, 1980), Table 1225, p. 700.

were not for social security, welfare, and medicaid. It is, however, *more accurate* to argue that the state intervention was the minimum required to ensure the legitimacy of the system.

The United States devotes a smaller proportion of its GNP to government expenditures than any other of the seven industrial nations of Western Europe. Only in the proportion of its income devoted to the military is the United States spending a substantially larger amount than the other nations surveyed. In social services it is spending between a third and a half less in proportion to its GNP than others (see Table 4–9 below).[30]

Moreover, even the social security system is financed out of the earnings of the working class and is regressive in both its tax structure and in the manner in which payments are parceled out.

It is clear that the increased growth of state intervention in the economy since the 1930s has had two functions. First, it has provided subsistence welfare in order to maintain the degree of legitimacy required for the political system to continue to function. Second, state expenditures, as already noted, through direct aid and "tax expenditures" have been used to support the profitability of the capitalist system.

Furthermore, in areas of direct governmental expenditures the payments have served as substantial subsidies not to the poor and the needy but to the more affluent. This is true in terms of housing support, education subsidies, or aid to agriculture. Table 4–10 illustrates how government subsidies have accrued to the wealthy (in this case—wealthy farmers).

As the next and final section on the United States will demonstrate, a truly amazing development of the last two decades is the failure of the system to achieve either of two prime objectives: legitimacy and accumulation. The legitimacy of the system as a whole is under severe strain, probably more severe than anytime since the Depression of the 1930s. In addition, in spite of the state's intervention in behalf of the capitalist system, the economy as measured in profitability, economic growth, and levels of investment has performed very poorly for the past decade. The only indicators of the economy to show steady increases have been unemployment and inflation, results not desired by anyone.

THE PROBLEM OF LEGITIMACY

One of the most striking things about recent American politics has been the decline in support for the major political and social institutions in America. For example, of the following countries the voter turnout was by far the lowest in the United States:[31]

Australia	94.5 percent
Sweden	91.9
West Germany	89.9
France	83.5
Great Britain	72.8
U.S. President	54.4 (1976); 52 (1980)
U.S. midterm	37.0

Furthermore, the voter turnout in the United States has been declining steadily since the 1950s. The presidential

TABLE 4·11
**Percent Turnout in Presidential
and Congressional Elections,
1950 to 1980**

	Office	
Year	President	U.S. House
1950	—	41.1
1952	61.6	57.6
1954	—	41.7
1956	59.3	55.9
1958	—	43.0
1960	62.8	58.5
1962	—	45.4
1964	61.9	57.8
1966	—	45.4
1968	60.9	55.1
1970	—	43.5
1972	55.5	51.1
1974	—	36.3
1976	54.3	49.6
1978	—	37.9
1980	52.5	45.3

election of 1952 brought out 61.6 percent of the eligible voters, and even the U.S. House election that year commanded 57.7 percent of the electorate. Even the Nixon landslide in 1972, with a plurality of 19 million (the largest ever accorded a president) was less impressive if we compare the nonvoting population, which amounted to 62 million, to the turnout of 47 million. The great victory being celebrated by Ronald Reagan begins to pale when it is realized that only 26.7 percent of all eligible voters voted for him in 1980.

Table 4–11 shows the decline in voting since the 1950s.[32]

Voting is only one measure of the increasing lack of legitimacy of the political system. Another index is the decline in party identification.[33]

Louis Harris testified before Congress in December of 1973 as follows:

TABLE 4•12
Changes in Party Attitudes (in percent)

Party Attitude	1960	1964	1972
Strong party identification		38	26
Independent		23	38
Voting split ticket	32		65
Voting straight party ticket	65		33
Negatively evaluating both political parties	29		51
Independent: voters with 20 years' experience			25
New voters			50

On a scale of powerlessness, cynicism, and alienation used by the Harris firm since 1966, an average of 55% of the American people expressed disenchantment, compared with no more than 29% who felt that way only seven years ago. This trend has been steadily and almost unabatingly upward from 29% in 1966 to 36% in 1968 to 42% in 1971 to 49% in 1972 to 55% in 1973, a veritable floodtide of disenchantment, seemingly gaining momentum with each passing year.[34]

Robert Lehman's report on the decline in selected public institutions can be summarized in Table 4–13.[35]

TABLE 4•13
Comparisons of Level of Public Confidence in Selected Institutions, 1966 to 1973
Question: As far as the people in charge of running (institution) are concerned, would you say you have a great deal of confidence, only some confidence, or hardly any confidence at all in them?

	Percent Responding "Great Deal"		
Institution	1966	1972	1973
U.S. House of Representatives	42	21	29
U.S. Senate	42	21	30
U.S. Supreme Court	51	28	33
Executive branch of government	41	27	19

Source: U.S. Senate (1973), Part I, 33.

185

Question: As far as *people in charge of running* (Read list) are concerned, would you say you have a great deal of confidence, only some confidence, or hardly any confidence at all in them?

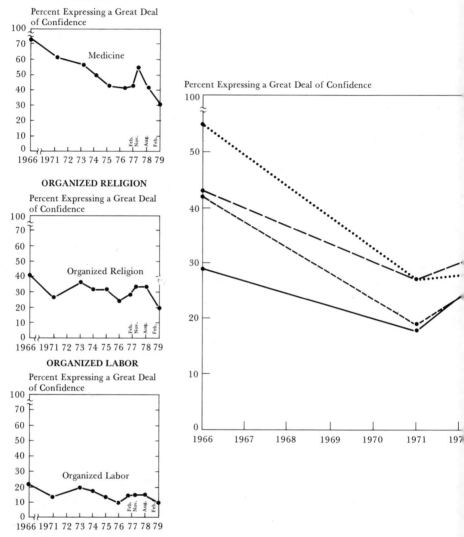

MEDICINE

Percent Expressing a Great Deal of Confidence

ORGANIZED RELIGION

Percent Expressing a Great Deal of Confidence

ORGANIZED LABOR

Percent Expressing a Great Deal of Confidence

Percent Expressing a Great Deal of Confidence

Note: "Average of nine major institutions" is a composite of the following: television news, medicine, the military, the press, organized religion, major companies, Congress, the Executive Branch, and organized labor. In 1979 the following organizations were also listed: higher education 33%, U.S. Supreme Court 28%, law firms 16%, the White House 15%. Question wording varied slightly over time.

Source: Surveys by Louis Harris and Associates, 1966-August 1978; ABC News/Louis Harris and Associates, latest that of February 8-12, 1979.

Figure 4.1   Confidence Rollercoaster

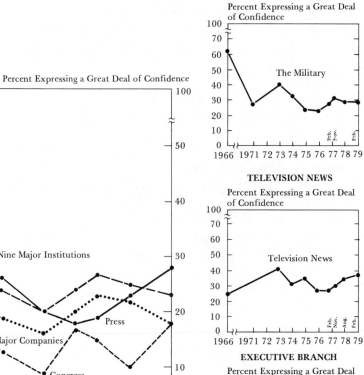

THE MILITARY

Percent Expressing a Great Deal of Confidence

The Military

TELEVISION NEWS

Percent Expressing a Great Deal of Confidence

Television News

EXECUTIVE BRANCH

Percent Expressing a Great Deal of Confidence

Executive Branch

Percent Expressing a Great Deal of Confidence

Average of Nine Major Institutions

Press

Major Companies

Congress

CONFIDENCE IN LEADERS OF INSTITUTIONS

	1966	1971	1973	1974	1975	1976	Feb. 1977	Nov. 1977	1978	1979
Average of nine major institutions	43%	27%	33%	28%	24%	20%	24%	27%	25%	23%
TV news	25	—	41	31	35	28	28	30	35	37
Medicine	73	61	57	50	43	42	43	55	42	30
Military	62	27	40	33	24	23	27	31	29	29
Press	29	18	30	25	26	20	18	19	23	28
Organized Religion	41	27	36	32	32	24	29	34	34	20
Major Companies	55	27	29	21	19	16	20	23	22	18
Congress	42	19	29	18	13	9	17	15	10	18
Executive Branch	41	23	19	28	13	11	23	23	14	17
Organized Labor	22	14	20	18	14	10	14	15	15	10

Of equal importance is the fact that it is not only political institutions which have lost the confidence of the American public; almost all significant social and political institutions have suffered from a loss of confidence and a flight of membership and support.

As Figure 4–1 indicates, there has not been any recovery in confidence since Watergate, Vietnam, and more recent economic disasters. Ideal confidence in American institutions has been even more eroded.

Of particular interest is the extent to which the business community, particularly the large corporations, have lost the confidence of the American public. The following surveys (Figures 4–1 through 4–3) from the American Enterprise Institute publication document the decline in confidence in American corporations.

Furthermore, in response to the following questions, only between 33 and 43 percent were able to agree that business was fulfilling its responsibilities either fully or fairly well:[36]

- Paying their fair share of taxes—43 percent
- Cleaning up their own air and water pollution—43 percent
- Advertising honestly—33 percent
- Charging reasonable prices for goods and services—33 percent
- Keeping profits at a reasonable level—39 percent

Also in 1979 there was a much less favorable attitude toward business than in 1937 when the country was emerging from the Great Depression.

In spite of confidence in business being at or near an all-time low, the public remains as opposed to nationalization of industry now as it was in 1936. One of the more curious characteristics of the present malaise is that there do not seem to be any avenues open—public or private. The citizen has no more confidence in political institutions than in private ones.

EROSION OF CONFIDENCE IN BUSINESS . . .

Question: Would you say your attitude toward business has become more positive, or more negative in recent years?

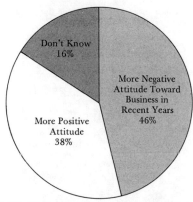

Note: When asked in 1977, 51% of those who were 18-34 years old said they had become more negative toward business and 37% had become more positive. In the 1978 survey, 41% of 18-34 year olds expressed the negative attitude and 46% answered that they had become more positive in their attitudes toward business.

Source: Survey by the Gallup Organization, May 1978.

. . . AND ITS LEADERS OVER TIME

Question: As far as *people in charge of running* (Read list) are concerned, would you say you have a great deal of confidence, only some confidence, or hardly any confidence at all in them? . . . Major companies.

Confidence in Leaders of Institutions

	1966	1971	1973	1974	1975	1976	Feb. 1977	Nov. 1977	1978	1979	1980
Average of nine major institutions	43%	27%	33%	28%	24%	20%	24%	27%	25%	23%	NA
Major companies	55	27	29	21	19	16	20	23	22	18	19

Note: "Average of nine major institutions" is a composite of the following: television news, medicine, the military, the press, organized religion, major companies, Congress, the Executive Branch, and organized labor. In 1980 the other institutions asked were: the military = 33%, television news = 31%, the press = 22%, the White House = 18% and Congress = 11%. Average could not be computed for 1980 since all nine institutions were not included. Question wording varied slightly over time.

Source: Surveys by Louis Harris and Associates, 1966-August 1978; ABC News/Louis Harris and Associates, latest that of January 10-13, 1980.

Figure 4.2   Erosion of Confidence in Business . . .

BLACK EYE FOR BIG BUSINESS

ON SOME ISSUES TIMES HAVE CHANGED

Question: Do you think big business concerns are a good thing or a bad thing for the country?

1937

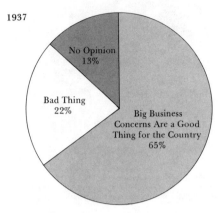

Source: Survey by the Gallup Organization, May 26–31, 1937.

Question: (Hand respondent card*) Here is a set of statements I'd like you to read. After reading each statement, please select the item on the scale on this card (Hand respondent card*) that best describes the extent of your agreement or disagreement with the statement. . . . Big business is a threat because it has become more active politically, and exerts a great deal of influence on government policy.

1979

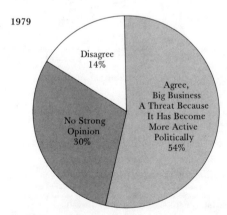

Note: *Respondent given one set with various statements and another card with possible response categories. Agree = strongly agree and agree; Disagree = disagree and strongly disagree; No strong opinion = not sure, but probably agree and not sure, but probably disagree.

Source: Survey by Yankelovich, Skelly and White conducted for the American Council of Life Insurance, May 29-June 22, 1979.

Figure 4.3 Black Eye for Big Business

AMERICANS DELIVER BODY BLOW
TO BIG BUSINESS

Question: (Hand respondent card*) Here is a set of statements I'd like you to read. After reading each statement, please select the item on the scale on this card (hand card*) that best describes the extent of your agreement or disagreement with the statement. . . . If it weren't for big business, our standard of living would be much lower than it is. . . . Despite everything, big business is overly concerned with profits at the expense of good service and good products.

Standard of Living

	Agree	No Strong Opinion	Disagree
1968	64%	26%	10%
1971	56	27	17
1977	45	36	18
1979	44	35	20

Profits

	Agree Big Business Overly Concerned with Profits at Expense of Goods/Services	No Strong Opinion	Disagree
1968	44%	36%	20%
1971	49	32	19
1972	47	34	19
1975	57	29	14
1976	58	25	16
1977	52	32	15
1979	50	31	18

Note: *Respondent given one set with various statements and another card with possible response categories. Agree = strongly agree and agree; Disagree = disagree and strongly disagree; No strong opinion = not sure, but probably agree and not sure, but probably disagree.

Source: Surveys by Yankelovich, Skelly and White conducted for the American Council of Life Insurance, latest that of May 29-June 22, 1979.

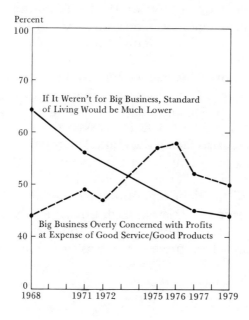

DECLINING ECONOMIC HEGEMONY

It may be argued that although there is an unquestioned loss of legitimacy, this is only an attitude and attitudes are notoriously fickle. Therefore, these attitudes will change as the capitalist economy improves its performance. This relatively optimistic view is based on confidence in the economy. As we shall see, the economy has been in a fairly long and steady decline with no prospects for sudden recovery. This decline has occurred in spite of considerable state intervention on behalf of business and large military and welfare payments designed to maintain aggregate demand.

The success of a capitalist system depends on the ability of the capitalist class to obtain surplus value through the use of labor power. It is also true that for the past fifteen years the rate of exploitation has been on the decline in the United States. Measuring the rate of surplus value as the total of profits, rents, and interest before taxes divided by the total employee compensation (wages and salaries also before taxes), it will be shown that the rate of exploitation has been in a rather steady decline (Table 4–14).[37]

While the rate of exploitation demonstrated some recovery from the recession of 1974–75, all indications are that this improvement was very short, for in 1981 the country was again faced with mounting unemployment and increasing inflation.

Furthermore, this decline has not been merely a phase of the last couple of decades, as a comparison of the periods 1946–66, 1966–76, and 1969–77 will demonstrate.[38]

One final piece of data is necessary to correctly assess the economic crisis facing the United States; this is the extent to which the economy has become dependent upon debt for its maintenance. Figures 4–4 and 4–5 clearly show the expansion of the debt economy since the 1940s.[39]

The Carter administration did make a valiant effort to stem the growth of debt, however, the curtailing effect of a drastic cutback on private debt was such that the pressure

TABLE 4·14
Surplus Value and Corporate Profits: 1955 to 1977

| Year | Rate of Exploitation | Corporate Profits as Percentage of: | | Real Amount of Corporate Profits (in 1972 prices in billions) |
		Surplus Value	Employee Compensation	
1955	27.0%	73.5%	19.8%	$ 68.8
1965	28.4	68.4	19.4	104.5
1966	27.9	67.3	18.8	108.3
1968	25.2	65.4	16.5	104.5
1970	20.4	54.8	11.1	74.5
1972	22.5	57.3	12.9	92.1
1974	19.9	48.0	9.5	71.4
1976	23.1	53.4	12.4	91.6
1977	23.0	52.6	12.1	93.1

Note: The rate of exploitation is surplus value divided by employee compensation. Surplus value includes corporate profits after inventory valuation and capital consumption adjustment, net interst payments of corporations, and rents—all before income taxes. Employee compensation is also taken before taxes. Excluded from both elements of the ratio are incomes of farm proprietors and of unincorporated enterprises. The rate of exploitation is probably understated by the inclusion of executives' salaries and bonuses in employee compensation, for a significant part of these payments may be a form of surplus value. We have not allowed, moreover, for the likelihood that a disproportionate share of taxes serves primarily the interests of the capitalist class. In the last column, corporate profits are shown before taxes and in constant prices. In all calculations, corporate profits are adjusted to eliminate the effects of inflation. While inventory profits are real enough, they do not reflect the ability of corporations over the long run to extract surplus value from their workers. It is for this reason, too, that corporate profits are taken before taxes.
It should be emphasized that the surplus value used here differs from Marx's concept in not being expressed in socially-necessary labor-hours, and in other ways.

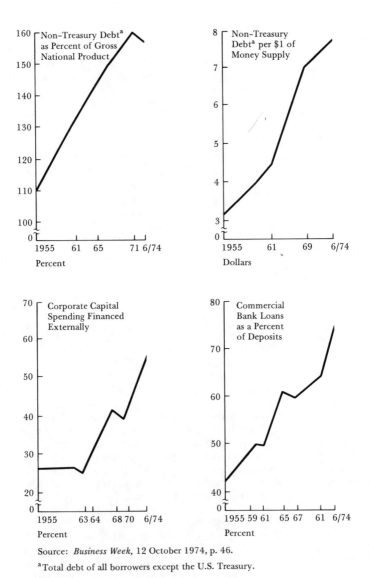

Source: *Business Week*, 12 October 1974, p. 46.

[a] Total debt of all borrowers except the U.S. Treasury.

Figure 4.4   Evolution of U.S. Debt, 1955–1974

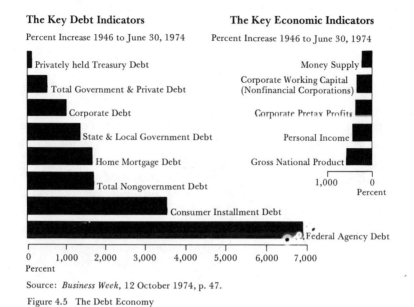

Source: *Business Week*, 12 October 1974, p. 47.

Figure 4.5   The Debt Economy

TABLE 4·15
Data on the Crisis of U.S. Capitalism, Postwar

	Average Annual Rates of Growth		
	1946–1966	*1966–1976*	*1969–1977*
Surplus value (before tax)	5.3%	0.6%	2.1%
Corporate profits (before tax)	5.1	−1.7	−0.1
Gross private domestic investment	4.2	0.7	1.9
Gross national product	3.7	2.7	2.7
Average unemployment rate*	4.7	5.3	6.3
Consumer price index	2.5	5.8	6.5
S & P's 500-stock index	8.4	1.8	0.1

*These are averages of annual data, not rates of growth.

to limit borrowing was soon eased. The growth of governmental debt has shown no sign of lessening. It remains to be seen if Ronald Reagan's economic policies will succeed in the face of tremendous odds.[40]

THE FUTURE OF AMERICAN LIBERALISM

It will be beneficial to review the material just presented on the United States to see to what extent the United States has realized in practice the theoretical aspirations of liberalism, to examine the "fit" of the model to the dimensions of the theory. The observation that the United States is "pragmatic" and therefore nonideological is as commonplace as it is mistaken. The fact is that the United States is highly influenced by its liberal ideology. The United States offers a better climate for the growth of the liberal vision than England, where the liberal nostrums originated some 300 years ago. The absence of an entrenched aristocracy and the scope of a continent both contributed to the acceptance of liberal ideas and ideals. The situation in the United States cried out for a new class based not on privilege and sanguinity but on enterprise and merit. A liberal philosophy which held out the promise to people of being left alone to develop individual entrepreneurial talents to the utmost seemed likely to prevail.

The "Grand Design" encapsulated in the Constitution provided a framework wherein these entrepreneurial abilities could flourish. The United States soon developed a propertied class with both the capabilities and the will to succeed. While the remnants of a feudal order had a foothold in the Southern system with its institution of slavery, it was unable to stand in the way of the developing merchant and industrial class. When the Southern slave owners tried to resist, the issue finally had to be resolved in blood. Under the expansive interpretation of the commerce clause of the Constitution the industrial barons' power grew apace.

Unfortunately, the natural harmony which the liberal

ideology had promised did not occur. There developed a growing tension between the freedom of the industrialist to ravage the environment and exploit the workers and the liberal suggestion of increasing individual control over one's own destiny. The liberalism of Hobbes and Locke with its commitment to the security of contract and sanctity of property (negative freedom) came into conflict with the suggestion of self-realization found in the writings of John Stuart Mill.

In the latter half of the nineteenth century the United States began to choose between the moderate liberalism of Mill with its emphasis on quality instead of mere quantity of pleasure and the "realism" of Herbert Spencer. The United States ultimately took the path of "realism" during the period of the latter half of the nineteenth century and through both repression and expansion put aside the claims of social justice.

In the 1930s the doctrinaire adherence to a negative-freedom style of liberalism, dominated by the harshness of a "survival of the fittest" principle, finally had to give way to the pressures of mass protest. For capitalism to be saved, an American version of positive liberty would have to be reluctantly tried. Unfortunately, the liberalism of T. H. Green, Hobhouse, and Keynes in the hands of American political and business elite, became a form of corporatism. That is, the monopoly corporation became the dominant political as well as economic force in the years following the end of the Second World War. Furthermore, the corporation not only influenced state power, it exercised it.

In the wake of this growth of corporatism in the United States, liberalism became less and less a theory to be practiced and more an "ideology." Liberalism became an ideology in that it was used to rationalize and justify a skewed distribution of income, wealth, and power. The early version of liberalism, negative freedom, was all but abandoned in practice, and positive liberty, with its original aim of using state power for individual self-realization, was adapted to an ironically "illiberal" use of state power to maintain the privilege and influence of the holders of corporate power.

The previous section of this chapter maintained that even with the power of the state behind it, American capitalism is facing a decline in legitimacy which is both moral and material. This present decline, as in the thirties, is posing a dilemma to the custodians of American liberal ideology. In which direction should we turn? Back to the liberalism of John Locke and Adam Smith, or should another attempt be made to develop a welfare state along the lines suggested by Green and Keynes? Or should liberalism be abandoned altogether in favor of some other direction either to the left or the right? Or, again, perhaps there is an absolute unwillingness to change from the corporatism which has developed.

The future seems to offer three diverse scenarios for consideration. The most optimistic one sees the United States evolving along with Western Europe and other liberal-capitalist countries toward a form of controlled economy. The next chapter of this book will describe one form of control: socialism, in theory and practice. The pessimistic scenario sees the United States developing a pathology to which all political and social systems are prone in times of crisis—fascism. This potential alternative will be described in terms of theory and existing pathologies both public and private in the final chapter of this volume.

Perhaps the more likely outcome will be neither as orderly or disorderly as these two scenarios. Instead, there may well be a continuation of the existing system—a somewhat tortuous "muddling through." Keep in mind that the Roman Empire was in a state of decline—even, some say, of crisis—for almost four hundred years, and that the transition from feudalism to capitalism did not come quickly, but was an odyssey of centuries.

We would also do well to keep in mind James Petras's repeated admonition that the United States has great resiliency and capacity for reconstruction.[41] There does exist within the American system great room for further rationalization of the system. An efficient merger of corporate and state power could facilitate national planning and coordination of American production, circulation, and distribution of goods and services, including income and wealth. This would require a coordination of investment and also controls over wages, prices, and profits beyond any imagined by corporate leaders or almost anyone else in the United States. Yet it might be done; certainly the leaders of the Trilateral Commission[42] were headed in that direction.

It is just barely possible that Reagan will assuage the feelings of the public by action on so called moral issues. These are the antiabortion legislation, antiwelfare legislation, anti-Soviet sabre-rattling, or, worse, antifeminism, antidrug, homosexuality, and sexual freedom campaigns of the Reagan administration. While on the other hand the Trilateral Commission's goals of retooling America's industrial plant and coordination of the economy may result in an extraordinarily consolidated and nationalized economy—the staggering bill for the revitalization of the economy is being paid for by the American worker in the form of increased taxes, decreased environmental safeguards, and decreased real income.

NOTES

1. James Madison, *Federalist*, No. 10 (New York: 22 November 1787).
2. Ibid.
3. Ibid.
4. Ibid.
5. Ibid.
6. The Constitution of the United States of America, Article II, Section 1, paragraph 3.
7. C. B. Macpherson, *The Real World of Democracy* (London: Oxford University Press, 1966).
8. Milton Moskowitz, Michael Katz, and Robert Levering, eds. *Everybody's Business: An Almanac* (San Francisco: Harper & Row, 1980), p. 850.
9. *Statistical Abstracts of the United States, 1979,* (Washington, D.C.: U.S. Government Printing Office, 1979), Table 952, p. 573, footnote.
10. Press release from the Subcommittee on Reports, Accounting and

Management, Thursday January 19, 1978, U.S. Senate, Washington, D.C.

11. Richard Barber, *The American Corporation*, (New York: E. P. Dutton, 1970), pp. 19–20, as quoted in Edward S. Greenberg, *Understanding Modern Government* (New York: John Wiley & Sons, 1979), p. 94.

12. Charles E. Lindblom, *Politics and Markets* (New York: Basic Books, 1977), p. 175.

13. *Statistical Abstracts of the United States, 1979,* Table 435, p. 260.

14. Ibid., Table 436, pp. 261–62.

15. Samuel Huntington, "The Democratic Distemper," Nathan Glazer and Irving Kristol, eds., in *The American Commonwealth, Nineteen Seventy-six,* (New York: Basic Books, 1976), pp. 284–85.

16. Lindblom, *Politics and Markets,* p. 195.

17. Ibid.

18. Ibid., p. 199.

19. *Statistical Abstracts of the United States, 1979,* pp. xx, xxi, 595.

20. Moskowitz, Katz, and Levering, *Everybody's Business,* p. 337.

21. Karl Marx And Frederick Engels, *The German Ideology* (1846) (New York: International Publishers, 1970), p. 39.

22. Lindblom, *Politics and Markets,* p. 205.

23. Alexander Hamilton, "Report on Manufacturing," from Henry Cabot Lodge, ed., *The Works of Alexander Hamilton* (New York: G. P. Putnam's Sons, 1904), Vol. I, p. 198.

24. Arthur M. Johnson, *The American Economy* (New York: Free Press, 1974), p. 74.

25. Frank Ackerman et al., "Income Distribution in the United States," *Review of Radical Political Economics,* 3, 3 (Summer 1971), as reported in Edward S. Greenberg, *The American Political System,* (Cambridge, Mass.: Winthrop Publishers, 1980), p. 90.

26. Paul Blumberg, "Another Day, Another $3,000: Executive Salaries in America," *Dissent* (Spring 1978): 157, as reported in Greenberg, *The American Political System,* p. 91.

27. *Business Week,* 12 May 1980, pp. 55–84.

28. Greenberg, *The American Political System,* p. 92.

29. Donald Light, "Income Distribtution," *Review of Radical Political Economy* 3 (Summer 1971): 46, as quoted in ibid., p. 94.

30. Charles F. Andrain, *Politics and Economic Policy in Western Democracies* (North Scituate, Mass.: Duxbury Press, 1980), p. 13, based on OECD, UNESCO, WMSE, and International Studies data, published in 1976.

31. William J. Crotty and Gary C. Jacobson, *American Parties in Decline* (Boston: Little, Brown and Company, 1980), p. 5, based on data compiled by the *Economist,* London, year not supplied by authors.

32. Ibid., p. 7.

33. Norman Nie, Sidney Verba, and John Petrocik, *The Changing Amer-*

ican Voter (Cambridge, Mass.: Harvard University Press, 1976), chapter 4.

34. Robert S. Gilmour and Robert B. Lamb, *Political Alienation in Contemporary America* (New York: St. Martin's Press, 1975), p. 141.

35. Robert G. Lehman, *American Institutions, Political Opinions and Public Policy* (New York: Dryden Press, 1976), p. 165.

36. *Public Opinion* (April/May 1980): 25.

37. John G. Gurley, *Challengers to Capitalism* (New York: W. W. Norton and Company, 1979), p. 200.

38. Ibid., p. 206.

39. Manuel Castells, *The Economic Crisis and American Society* (Princeton, N.J.: Princeton University Press, 1980), p. 117.

40. Ibid., p. 118.

41. James Petras, "Le Mythe du Déclin Américain," *Le Monde diplomatique*, February 1976.

42. The Trilateral Commission is an association of private sector decision makers and corporate leaders from Western Europe, Japan, and the United States who explore the possibilities of "private" public policymaking. They meet regularly, issue reports, establish task forces and advise government officials on such matters as, the "Governability of Democracies." (See their task force report of May 1975, for example.)

BIBLIOGRAPHIC NOTE

The division of the bibliographic entries between the preceding chapter on liberalism and the present chapter is, of necessity, somewhat arbitrary. We have attempted to include in the bibliography for the preceding chapter works that are more general and theoretical in nature. The bibliography for this chapter contains works that focus more specifically upon the historical and contemporary world position of the United States. In some instances we have included references to the same work in both chapters.

In the period from the close of World War II until the 1960s there developed in the United States what was purported to be a unified or general theory of the American system. Like most intellectual enterprise in the United States, this theory was rather more an *approach* to the study of politics, involving the pragmatic application and testing of observations regarding the political behavior of participants in the United States political system and the role of institutions in receiving and shaping behavioral inputs. The elements unifying the approach or "theory" were the foci of observation or units of analysis; an agreement upon certain data collection and measurement techniques; and a collateral insistence upon the development of a value-free science of politics. Decision making and, more generally, the social psychology of political attitudes was the main focus of postwar developments in the new "science of politics." Institutions were also studied and to some extent remained conceptually autonomous from the decision-making modes of analysis, but were more often seen as "receptacles" for decisional inputs (in the form of demands or supports) within a systems-approach to government. The rise in significance of groups as the single most important unit of analysis in the postwar years was due to the contribution of scholars such as David Truman, (*The Governmental Process*, 1951) and Robert Dahl, whose *A Preface To Democratic Theory* (1956) and *Who Governs?* (1961) are regarded as classics of this genre.

The use of survey data and the observation of subject response to political "stimuli" and quasi-experimental questionings and promptings were thought to yield an understanding of the behaviorial "motor" of politics. Both the newly discovered units of analysis (groups and psyche), and the scientific use of observation and measurement techniques were also thought to yield a value-free method of political science. What was discovered in this science was the politics of pluralism. Robert Dahl would use the term polyarchy to describe multiple and dispersed power centers within which pluralism, or the politics of group political interaction, would function. This general theory of pluralism would assert that it was not only descriptively accurate in its account of how liberal democracies (the United States) worked, but also that it was *prescriptively* valuable as both an export (to the rest of the world) and a vision of progress for the future. Stability was regarded as a key virtue in the pluralist notion of politics. Orderly resolution of conflict was, concomitantly, a key function.

In the 1960s, the civil rights movement and later, the Vietnam protest movements penetrated the ivy halls of academe and gave rise to a body of literature which seriously challenged the pluralist general theory. The pluralist approach to politics was challenged in terms of its false universality (both descriptive and prescriptive) and its elitism. Credit, however, should be given to several works which were precursors to the critical theory of the 1960s and 70s. These are Floyd Hunter's study of the politics of Atlanta, Georgia, *Community Power Structure: A Study of Decision-Making* (1953); C. Wright Mills' *The Power Elite* (1956); and E. E. Schattschneider's *Semisovereign People* (1960), which jibed: the "flaw in the pluralist heaven is that the heavenly chorus sings with a strong upper-class accent" (p. 38). Although this jibe has become a classic aphorism of modern political analysis, it remained for the more pointed criticism of the late 1960s and 1970s to provoke a major retreat from the tenets of liberalism—à-la-pluralism. (The 1960s opposition to pluralism is represented in McCoy and Playford's *Apolitical Politics* (1967), which contains articles criticising pluralism from a number of differing perspectives and representing the leading pluralist critics of that decade.) Theodore Lowi's

The End of Liberalism, whose first edition appeared in 1969, has become an extremely influential and comprehensive challenge to pluralism and its ideology of liberalism, bridging the 60s and 70s.

In the 1970s, the pluralism/anti-pluralism debate having exhausted itself, the cutting edge of research and debate in political science in the United States turned to specific areas of public policy. The critical literature in this continuously developing area is very extensive, but several works are representative. One of the finest and earliest policy critiques is Robert Engler's *The Politics of Oil* (1961). More recent, and representative of the seventies are Piven and Cloward's *Regulating the Poor* (1971); Seymour Melman's *The Permanent War Economy* (1974); Robert Alford's *Health Care Politics* (1975); and Laura K. Olson's *Public Policy and Aging; a Critical Approach* (1982).

The late 1970s and these 1980s seem to signal a shift in critical literature. While there is not an abandonment of public policy analysis per se, there appear to be efforts to expand analysis beyond the confines of a specific area concentration in an attempt to develop a theory of the American system reflecting a neo-Marxist critical perspective. Michael Parenti's *Democracy For the Few* (1974) is an early and popular attempt to confront the systemic abuse of politics, as is Murray Edelman's analysis *The Symbolic Uses of Politics* (1964). A more recent and theoretical approach is represented by Alan Wolf's *The Limits of Legitimacy* (1980), which provides a comprehensive, historical analysis of the contemporary dilemma of American capitalism. Recent developments in political economy are very promising, especially in the integration of empirical and theoretical analysis. James O'Connor's *Fiscal Crisis of the State* (1973) and Manuel Castell's *The Economic Crisis and American Society* (1980), along with Harry Braverman's *Labor and Monopoly Capital* (1974) and Charles Anderson's *The Political Economy of Social Class* (1974) are representative of the valuable and creative work being done in this area.

BIBLIOGRAPHY

Ackerman, Frank, et.al. "Income Distribution in the United States." *Review of Radical Political Economics*, Vol. 3, no. 3 (Summer 1971).

Alford, Robert. *Health Care Politics: Ideological and Interest Group Barriers to Reform.* Chicago: University of Chicago Press, 1975.

Andrain, Charles F. *Politics and Economic Policy in Western Democracies.* North Scituate, Mass.: Duxbury Press, 1980.

Aronowitz, Stanley. *False Promises.* New York: McGraw-Hill, 1973.

Bachrach, Peter. *The Theory of Democratic Elitism: A Critique.* New York: Little, Brown, 1967.

Banfield, Edward. *The Unheavenly City Revisited*. Boston: Little, Brown, 1973.

Baran, Paul and Sweezey, Paul. *Monopoly Capital*. New York: Monthly Review Press, 1965.

Barber, Richard. *The American Corporation*. New York: E. P. Dutton, 1970.

Beard, Charles. *An Economic Interpretation of the Constitution*. New York: Macmillan, 1913.

Bell, Daniel. *The End of Ideology*: *On the Exhaustion of Political Ideas in the Fifties*. New York: Free Press, 1960.

Berle, Adolph, Jr. and Means, Gardiner C. *The Modern Corporation and Private Property*. New York: Macmillan, 1932.

Blumberg, Paul. "Another Day, Another $3,000: Executive Salaries in America." *Dissent* (Spring 1978).

Braverman, Harry. *Labor and Monopoly Capital*. New York: Monthly Review Press, 1974.

Carter, Anne. *Structural Change in the American Economy*. Cambridge, Mass.: Harvard University Press, 1970.

Castells, Manuel. *The Economic Crisis and American Society*. Princeton, N.J.: Princeton University Press, 1980.

Cherry, Robert. "Economic Theories of Racism" in David M. Gordon, ed. *Problems in Political Economy*. Lexington, Mass.: Heath, 1977.

——— *MacroEconomics*. Reading, Mass.: Addison-Wesley Publishing Co., 1980.

Cobb, Jonathan and Sennett, Richard. *The Hidden Injuries of Class*. New York: Vintage Books, 1973.

Connolly, William. *The Bias of Pluralism*. New York: Atherton Press, 1969.

Crotty, William J. and Jacobson, Gary C. *American Parties in Decline*. Boston: Little, Brown, 1980.

Dahl, Robert. *Pluralist Democracy in The United States*: *Conflict and Crisis*. Chicago: Rand McNally, 1967.

——— *Who Governs? Democracy and Power in an American City*. New Haven, Conn.: Yale University Press, 1961.

Domhoff, G. William. *The Higher Circles*: *The Governing Class in America*. New York: Random House, 1970.

——— *Who Really Rules?* New Brunswick, N.J.: Transaction Books, 1978.

——— *Who Rules America?* Englewood Cliffs, N.J.: Prentice-Hall, 1967.

Downs, Anthony. *An Economic Theory of Democracy*. New York: Harper & Row, 1957.

Edelman, Murray. *The Symbolic Uses of Politics*. Champaign, Ill.: University of Illinois Press, 1964.

Engler, Robert. *The Politics of Oil*: *Private Power and Democratic Directions*. Chicago: The University of Chicago Press, 1961.

Friedman, Milton. *Capitalism and Freedom*. Chicago: University of Chicago Press, 1962.

——— and Schwartz, A. J. *A Monetary History of the United States*, *1867–1960*. Princeton, N.J.: Princeton University Press, 1963.

Galbraith, John Kenneth. *Economics and the Public Purpose*. Boston: Houghton Mifflin, 1973.

—— *New Industrial State*. Boston: Houghton Mifflin, 1969.

—— *The Affluent Society*. Boston: Houghton Mifflin, 1958.

Gilmour, Robert S. and Lamb, Robert B. *Political Alienation in Contemporary America*. New York: St. Martin's Press, 1975.

Gintis, Herb. "Alienation in Capitalist Society" in Richard C. Edwards, et. al., eds. *The Capitalist System*. Englewood Cliffs, N.J.: Prentice–Hall, 1978.

Glazer, Nathan and Kristol, Irving. *The American Commonwealth*. New York: Basic Books, 1976.

Gold, David. "The Rise and Decline of the Keynesian Coalition. *Kapitalistate*, No. 6 (1977).

Gold, David, et al. "Recent Developments in Marxian Theories of the State." *Monthly Review Press*, Vol. 27, No. 5 (Oct./Nov. 1975).

Gouldner, Alvin. *The Dialectic of Ideology and Technology*. New York: Seabury, 1976.

Greenberg, Edward S. *The American Political System*. Cambridge, Mass.: Winthrop Publishers, 1980.

Hacker, Andrew. *The End of the American Era*. New York: Atheneum, 1970.

Hamilton, Alexander. *Report on Manufacturing* in Henry Cabot Lodge, ed. *The Works of Alexander Hamilton*, Vol. I. New York: Putnam, 1904.

Hartz, Louis. *The Liberal Tradition in America*. New York: Harcourt, Brace and World, 1955.

Heilbroner, Robert. *Limits of American Capitalism*. New York: Harper & Row, 1966.

Hunter, Floyd. *Community Power Structure*. New York: Anchor Books, 1963.

Huntington, Samuel P. "The Democratic Distemper" in Nathan Glazer and Irving Kristol, eds., *The American Commonwealth*. New York: Basic Books, 1976.

Jacobson, Gary C. and Crotty, William J. *American Parties in Decline*. Boston: Little, Brown, 1980.

Keller, Robert. "Monopoly Capital and the Great Depression." *Review of Radical Political Economy*, No. 7 (Winter 1975).

Kolko, Gabriel. *America and the Crisis of World Capitalism*. Boston: Beacon Press, 1974.

—— *Wealth and Power in the United States*. New York: Praeger, 1962.

Kornhauser, William. *The Politics of Mass Society*. Glencoe, Ill.: The Free Press, 1959.

Kotz, Nick. *Let Them Eat Promises, The Politics of Hunger in America*. Englewood Cliffs, N.J.: Prentice-Hall, 1969.

Lamb, Robert B. *Political Alienation in Contemporary America*. New York: St. Martin's Press, 1975.

Lebowitz, Michael A. "Capital and the Production of Needs." *Science and Society*. Vol. 41, no. 4 (Winter 1977–1978).

Lehman, Robert G. *American Institutions, Political Opinion & Public Policy*. New York: The Dryden Press, 1976.

Light, Donald. "Income Distribution." *Review of Radical Political Economy*, No. 3 (Summer 1971).

Lindblom, Charles E. *Politics and Markets, The World's Political-Economic System*. New York: Basic Books, 1977.

Lowi, Theodore. *The End of Liberalism: The Second Republic of the United States*, 2d ed. New York: W. W. Norton, 1979.

———— "The Public Philosophy: Interest-Group Liberalism." *The American Political Science Review* (March 1957).

MacEwan, A. "Changes in World Capitalism and the Current Crisis of the U.S. Economy" in *Radical Perspectives on the Economic Crisis of Monopoly Capitalism*. New York: URPE-PEA (1975).

Macpherson, C. B. *The Real World of Democracy*. London: Oxford University Press, 1966.

Madison, James. "Federalist No. 10." Clinton Rossiter, ed., *The Federalist Papers, Alexander Hamilton, James Madison and John Jay*. New York: Mentor Books, 1961.

Magdoff, Harry and Sweezey, Paul M. "Keynesian Chickens Come Home To Roost." *Monthly Review* (April 1974).

Marcuse, Herbert. "Repressive Tolerance" in Robert Paul Wolff, Barrington Moore, Jr. and Herbert Marcuse, eds. *A Critique of Pure Tolerance*. Boston: Beacon Press, 1965.

McConnell, Grant. *Private Power and American Democracy*. New York: Knopf, 1967.

McCoy, Charles A. and Playford, John, eds. *Apolitical Politics: A Critique of Behavioralism*. New York: Thomas Y. Crowell, 1967.

Melman, Seymour. *The Permanent War Economy: American Capitalism in Decline*. New York: Simon & Schuster, 1974.

Mills, C. Wright. *The Power Elite*. New York: Galaxy Books, 1956.

Moskowitz, Milton, Katz, Michael, and Levering, Robert, eds. *Everybody's Business: An Almanac*. New York: Harper & Row, 1980.

Nie, Norman, Verba, Sidney, and Petrocik, John. *The Changing American Voter*. Cambridge, Mass.: Harvard University Press, 1976.

O'Connor, James. *The Fiscal Crisis of the State*. New York: St. Martin's Press, 1973.

Offe, Claus. "Advanced Capitalism and the Welfare State." *Politics and Society*, No. 2 (Summer 1972).

Olson, Mancur. *The Logic of Collective Action: Public Goods and the Theory of Groups*. Cambridge, Mass.: Harvard University Press, 1965.

Parenti, Michael. *Democracy For the Few*, 3rd ed. New York: St. Martin's Press, 1980.

Petras, James. "Le Myth du Déclin Américain." *Le Monde Diplomatique*, February 1976.

Piore, Michael J., ed. *Unemployment and Inflation: Institutionalist and Structuralist Views.* White Plains, New York: M. E. Sharpe, 1979.

Piven, Francis Fox and Cloward, Richard. *Regulating the Poor: The Functions of Public Welfare.* New York: Pantheon, 1971.

Schattschneider, E. E. *Semisovereign People: A Realist's View of Democracy in America.* New York: Holt, Rinehart and Winston, 1960.

Schorr, D. *Don't Get Sick in America.* Nashville, Tenn.: Aurora Publishing, 1970.

Schumpeter, Joseph. *Capitalism, Socialism and Democracy,* (Originally published in 1942.) 3rd ed. New York: Harper & Row, 1960.

Seltzer, Rick. "The Development of the Crisis in the United States." *U.S. Capitalism in Crisis.* New York: URPE, 1978.

Sennett, Richard and Cobb, Jonathan. *The Hidden Injuries of Class.* New York: Vintage Books, 1973.

Sherman, Howard. "Inflation, Unemployment and the Contemporary Business Cycle." *Socialist Review,* Vol. 9, no. 2 (March–April 1979).

Tabb, William K. "Domestic Economic Policy Under Carter: The Impact of Trilateralism" in *U.S. Capitalism in Crisis.* New York: URPE, 1978.

—— *The Political Economy of the Black Ghetto.* New York: W. W. Norton, 1971.

Thurow, Lester. *The Zero-Sum Society, Distribtuion and the Possibility for Economic Change.* New York: Basic Books, 1980.

Truman, David. *The Governmental Process, Political Interests and Public Opinion.* New York: Knopf, 1951.

URPE. *U.S. Capitalism in Crisis.* New York: Monthly Review Press, 1978.

Wolfe, Alan. *The Seamy Side of Democracy.* New York: David McKay, 1973.

—— *The Limits of Legitimacy: The Contradictions of Contemporary Capitalism.* Riverside, N.J.: Free Press, 1980.

·5

MARKET SOCIALISM

UNDERSTANDING SOCIALISM

A major obstacle confronting socialism, both in theory and in advocacy, is an ambiguous characterization, under which socialism has "fallen between two stools." On the one hand, socialism is characterized by its critics as the harshest of dictatorships of the proletariat. The Stalin era of the Soviet Union is taken as the model and a warning. On the other hand, the proponents of socialism, perhaps due to a reaction in kind to the critics or to the lack of a solid theoretical underpinning, tend to characterize socialism in terms which seem idealistic and unrealizable.

A sentiment often expressed by students, opponents, and "the man on the street" contains a pseudopragmatic reservation: "Socialism is all right in theory, but it can never work in practice." At the same time the proponents of socialism ignore Marx's original warning about the pitfalls of utopian socialism and, for that matter, Mao Tse-tung's more recent and trenchant comment concerning revolution:

209

A revolution is not a dinner party, or a writing essay, or painting a picture, or doing embroidery; it cannot be so refined, so leisurely and gentle, so temperate, kind, courteous, restrained and magnanimous. A revolution is an insurrection, an act of violence by which one class overthrows another.[1]

Two chief obstacles to a successful revolution or simple transition from capitalism to socialism are the unavailability of a socialist blueprint for a transition which preempts dictatorial rule and a blueprint which reduces the "utopian" hope for true and extensive freedom to a set of programmatic reforms.

The aim of this chapter is to introduce a "blueprint" of sorts which attempts to be practical, humane, and radical. In order to do this the various components which form an operative model will be taken from existing elements found in contemporary societies. The nations chosen to represent a collage of socialism are those which are relatively independent of Soviet hegemony.

We here depart from the practice of presenting the theoretical predispositions of a particular ideology in one chapter and examining a real-world application of those principles in another (i.e., communism/Soviet Union; and liberalism/United States). In the case of socialism, no one country represents a complete model.

THE COMPOSITE MODEL

Following are the various components of market socialism to be examined:

1. Public ownership of the means of production coupled with "socialist markets";
2. Worker control at the point of production, that is, in the work place;
3. A fully developed state welfare system which provides care for the ill and indigent, education, and security;
4. A protected natural environment; and

5. A socialist-directed economy stressing full employment, reasonable equity of income distribution, and controls against the structural deficiencies of all market systems, particularly inflation.

This section will draw contrasts between socialist experience with economic controls and that experience of capitalist economies, particularly that of the United States.

This model of socialism claims to be appealing and "utilitarian" in terms of its orderly provision for people's well-being, that is, its primary emphasis on a humane order; however, it is equally important that all evidence in support of the model are drawn from existing systems—every component part is now in existence and, furthermore, these component parts will be shown to be compatible in a general system of socialism.

Public Ownership and Socialist Markets*

A socialist society requires, at the minimum, that the major productive and distributive industries be publicly owned and controlled. Private property must, therefore, be restricted to nonproductive purposes—consumer goods and real personal property. The use and organization of private property for production and profit (surplus accrual) is fundamentally incompatible with socialism and, indeed, with the requirements of democracy. A central element of democracy is that people shall be in control of their own history.

Critics of socialism, especially those in the United States, have developed a very jaundiced view of state ownership and control of the productive economic forces of society. This stems, in part, from the American interpretation of

---

*The greatest part of the data used or adapted in this chapter are from Charles F. Andrain, *Politics and Economic Policy in Western Democracies* (North Scituate, Mass.: Duxbury Press, 1980).

British nationalization of industries. This case of mistaken identity—that is, mistaking British nationalization for socialism—has resulted in a distorted vision of either the intention or operation of socialism. So-called British socialism functions at best as a kind of "trash-can socialism." Trash-can socialism is that form of nationalization wherein the state takes over unprofitable and rundown industries and services which no one in the private sector is willing to invest in or manage, but which are nevertheless essential to both the economy and the political sphere. Nationalization in this sense functions as yet another subsidy to the private corporate sector, both in the provision of needed services and skills and in the assumption of "debt." Railroad nationalization is a prime example of trash-can socialism in both England and the United States. In assuming the responsibilities of subsidy and debt, the state redistributes the burden for maintaining an essentially capitalist order from the corporate sector to the taxpayer, *without providing the taxpayer with the benefits or profits which accrue from increased state subsidy* (hypothetical benefits of a "better life for all" notwithstanding). This practice of socializing the burden of a failing capitalistic order is as antithetical to socialism as competition is to monopoly.

In considering the benefit of public ownership of key industries, the example of West Germany better serves our model than that of Great Britain. Table 5–1 presents an accurate comparison of the United States, with its almost total reliance on private ownership, with Italy, France, Sweden, West Germany and Britain. All of these nations, with the exception of Britain, have demonstrated a growth rate considerably better than that of the United States:[2]

The average annual aggregate output growth rates (by percent) from 1960 to 1973 for these countries is:

United States—4.3
France—5.7
Italy—5.0
West Germany—4.6
United Kingdom—2.9[3]

TABLE 5·1
Ownership of Economic Firms

Economic Firm	Italy	France	Sweden	West Germany	Britain	Canada	United States
Transportation	G						
highways	G	G	G	G	G	G	G
railroads	G	G	M/G	G	G	M/G	M/P
airlines	G	M/G	M/G	M/P	M/C	M/G	P
auto manufacturing	M/P	M/P	P	M/P	M/P	P	P
Communications							
radio/television	G	G	P	G	M/C	M/P	P
telephones	G	G	G	G	G	M/P	P
postal service	G	G	G	G	G	G	M/G
Power industries							
gas	M/G	G	M/G=P	G	G	P	P
electricity	M/G	G	M/G=P	M/G	G	M/G	M/P
coal	M/G	M/G	M/P	P	G	P	P
oil	M/G	M/G=P	M/G=P	M/P	M/P	P	P
steel	M/G	M/P	M/G	M/P	G	P	P
Banks	G	M/G	M/P	M/P	M/P	M/P	P

Note: The table estimates the degree of government ownership during the early 1970s. G refers to ownership by the government, either central or local. P indicates private ownership. Mixed ownership includes three types: M/G means that government ownership predominates; M/P means that private ownership predominates. M/G=P refers to a balance between government and private ownership.

(See following page for Table 5–1 sources.)

Furthermore, with regard to Sweden, one source reports,

...Sweden in the last hundred years has been the world's leader unequalled in any long period by any other country for which data are available....one exception to the above generalization is the USSR for the period 1928–58. Considering the travail suffered in Russia to achieve its growth, the Swedish growth record appears even more outstanding.[4]

It is not simply private ownership which has accounted for even the marginal efficiency demonstrated by capitalist economies. It may be argued that it is the structure of the market which has provided the benefits usually ascribed to capitalist entrepreneurship. Charles Lindblom contrasts the advantages of markets over command systems as follows:

Market systems transform complex decision problems into drastically simplified ones. In the absence of a market system, someone has to face complex problems such as what goods and services are

---

(Continued from preceding page.)

Sources: (1) Anthony King, "Ideas, Institutions and the Policies of Governments: A Comparative Analysis." *British Journal of Political Science* 3 (July 1973):292–96; (2) Martin C. Schnitzer and James W. Nordyke, *Comparative Economic Systems,* 2nd ed. (Cincinnati: South-Western Publishing Co., 1977), pp. 189–93; (3) Stuart Holland, "Europe's New Public Enterprises," in Raymond Vernon, ed., *Big Business and the State: Changing Relations in Western Europe* (Cambridge, Mass.: Harvard University Press, 1974), pp. 25–44; (4) *Encyclopaedia Britannica: Macropaedia* (Chicago: Encyclopedia Britannica, 1975), vol. 3 (Canada), pp. 725–33; vol. 7 (France), pp. 599–601; vol. 8 (Germany), pp. 58–59; vol. 9 (Italy), pp. 1101–02; vol. 15 (Public Enterprises), pp. 198–202; vol. 17 (Sweden), pp. 847–50; vol. 18 (United Kingdom), pp. 880–85; (5) Kevin Allen and Andrew Stevenson, *An Introduction to the Italian Economy* (New York: Barnes and Noble, 1974), pp. 217–63; G. Corti, "Perspectives on Public Corporations and Public Enterprises in Five Nations," *Annals of Public and Co-operative Economy* 47 (January-March 1976): 47–48.

to be produced, and how much of the gross national product should be consumed instead of invested, what sections of the country should specialize in what kinds of economic activity, and whether the society should encourage farming or import agricultural commodities from abroad. In a market system responsive to individual demands, no such questions have to be faced as decision problems by anyone. To "solve" problems like these, each of many persons grapples with a much reduced problem: whether it will be to his advantage to buy or sell.[5]

If capitalism is one type of market system, and one which has demonstrated an imminent cycle of decline at that, market socialism may be considered an alternative type of a market system, one which in terms of longevity and stability appears to be superior. Most significant, market socialism is an alternative whose prototype already exists. Its particular virtues combine the advantages of decentralized decision making in the market with the oversight of public control. Once again, Lindblom's summary of the Yugoslavian practice of socialist markets provides a succinct summary of this method of socialism:

The Yugoslav enterprise produces what it finds profitable to produce. Its new investment funds are routinely obtained, if not from internal enterprise savings or investment by local government, from commercial banks. The banks are instructed to lend not by administrative plan but on considerations of profitability of investment, although there continues to be some governmental and party supervision of the pattern of bank lending. The firm buys its inputs freely on the market, usually, of course, from other firms selling freely on the market. It rents land from government and private owners. It hires labor, but with a difference. Above minimum wages, workers receive income in the form of shares in profits, which vary according to job.

Like a private enterprise in the U.S. economy the Yugoslav enterprise must cover its costs, including minimum level of wages, to stay afloat. It is free to look for new markets, to diversify its production, and to apportion its benefits between wages, including collective benefits to its workers, and reinvestment in the growth of the enterprise.

New firms can be started by any individual or group and are

in fact most often undertaken by units of local government (communes) or existing firms. Except for small private enterprises of less than five employees, enterprises must, once founded, be turned over to social ownership. At least experimentally, some enterprises are constructed as joint ventures combining partial social ownership on the Yugoslavian side and partial private ownership to represent the participation of foreign corporations. The hybrids are required to practice employee self-management.[6]

Obviously, state ownership and socialist markets are not sufficient but only necessary components for a system of market socialism. The components enumerated at the outset of this section are equally important and required. In Yugoslavia the combined components are markets and worker control.

Worker Control: The Case of Yugoslavia

Yugoslavian law requires that all enterprises, except agriculture, which employ five or more persons be of public status. Such businesses are placed under the control of their employees. Within those businesses of less than thirty employees, all workers are members of a workers' council. These councils are the supreme authority within the firm. The usual practice is for the council to elect a management committee from their own members and, in turn, to appoint a manager for the enterprise. These councils have the power to recruit managers from outside the firm and to replace managers as they wish.

There has been criticism of worker control in Yugoslavia. It has been said that too much time is spent in meetings. More significant, it has been charged that councils have tended to grant pay increases of an inflationary nature, exceeding those which might be justified by increased productivity. It has also been charged that managers have frequently not had the necessary managerial experience and skills required for administrative efficiency. Bearing these criticisms in mind and attempting to assess the success of the Yugoslavian experiment, it must be recognized that the

overall record of the Yugoslavian worker-controlled industry is remarkable. Yugoslavia was an almost entirely agricultural country before the Second World War, with all the
hallmarks of underdevelopment, including a very high il-
literacy rate. In spite of the lack of an industrial life experience on the part of the workforce, Yugoslavia has averaged
a growth rate of 6.6 percent a year from 1948 to 1972.
Yugoslavia exports food and has, at the same time, expanded its industrial sector. In 1948 only 18 percent of its
output was industrial; in 1972 the industrial output was 38.1
percent. During the past decade average industrial growth
has been about 10 percent per year. At one point during
this time Yugoslavia was putting an astounding 29 percent
of its GNP into capital investment.[7]

Yugoslavia has made significant gains in the area of
education as well.[8] Greater numbers of people are receiving
an education; a leap from 1 student in 1,000 inhabitants in
1940 to 1 student per 50 inhabitants in 1978 is attributable
to the commitment to increased educational opportunity.
The construction of schools and provision for an expanded
curriculum at higher levels has shown similar growth. Beyond the actual numbers, the commitment to a specifically
socialist education has occurred. As a recent commentator
has observed:

However, there is a trait which the dry statistical data do not
reveal, but one of essential importance. Due to specific historical
circumstances there is an inherent plebian trait in the University.
The young people from poor regions and workers' strata who
rushed to Universities carried with them the vigorous aspirations
for greater social and national equality. The University became
the center of our progressive social and freedom-loving tradition.
Formed in those days of the uprising it was closely linked, in all
the decisive historical upheavals, with the fate and struggle of its
people. From it sprang the generation which, as Ivo Lola Ribar
said, marched toward conscious service to the people, to the social
task of the people's intelligentsia. The fact that a considerable
part of the intelligentsia has its deep roots in the people was the
reason why hardly any of the students movements in the world
had such a share in the revolutionary transformation of its coun-

try. Undogmatic, broad and open attitude toward the freedom of creativity, science and intelligentsia is one of the decisive characteristic traits of Yugoslav socialism. The revolution does not belong to the Party or the State but to the class and the people.[9]

Yugoslavia has, of course, not been free of problems. Its unemployment rate has been high and would be even higher if it weren't for the fact that many Yugoslavians find work as migrant laborers in West Germany, France, and Sweden. It has also been necessary for the Communist party to exercise rather strong control over the worker-control movement, to ensure that investment goals are met and that the poorer southern areas of the country receive economic support. Nevertheless, it is noteworthy that Party meetings are open to the public and that there is considerable cultural pluralism within the Party and the government. There has been a rivalry between the "liberals" who want to move faster down the road to decentralization of worker control and the "conservatives" who are anxious to maintain Communist party domination and producer efficiency. Yet it is important not to exaggerate these differences. Both liberals and conservatives regard themselves as good socialists, and both are protective of their unaligned status—their independence from Soviet hegemony.

Welfare: Sweden, the Model Welfare State

As has been previously noted, Sweden has a lesser commitment to public ownership than many nations of Western Europe, such as West Germany. Nevertheless, when it comes to the provision of social welfare, Sweden is unsurpassed. The following table compares seven nations in terms of their expenditures as a percent of the respective GNPs of each nation. In every category, exdept for military expenditures, Sweden is first by a considerable margin. Somewhat surprisingly, even in the category of military expenditure, Sweden spends a larger proportion of its income than does Canada, West Germany, France, and Italy.[10]

TABLE 5·2
Types of Government Expenditures as a Percentage of Gross National Product, 1973

Country	Total Government Expenditures*	Education†	Health‡	Social Services§	Military**
United States	29.9	6.7	2.8	12	6.1
Canada	33.7	8.0	6.0	19	2.0
United Kingdom	34.6	6.3	4.3	17	4.9
West Germany	35.2	4.1	4.6	22	3.4
Sweden	40.6	7.7	6.5	24	3.7
France	35.0	5.3	4.2	19	3.5
Italy	37.0	5.4	1.2	22	3.0

*Expenditures by all levels of government. See *National Accounts of OECD Countries, 1975* (Paris: OECD, 1977), vol. 2.

†Public education and subsidized private education at all government levels. See *UNESCO Statistical Yearbook* (Paris: UNESCO Press, 1976), pp. 378–88.

‡Medical care and other health services, including national health insurance, public health, and expenditures under workmen's compensation. See Ruth Leger Sivard, *World Military and Social Expenditures 1976* (Leesburg, Va.: WMSE Publications, 1976), pp. 21–22.

§Health care, old-age pensions, unemployment benefits, and family allowances. See *Vision: The European Business Magazine*, no. 66 (May 1976): 33.

**Government spending on defense. See *The Military Balance: 1976–1977* (London: The International Institute for Strategic Studies, 1976), p. 78.

TABLE 5·3
Wealth and Government Spending on Civilian Programs, 1974

Country	GNP per capita (in constant U.S. dollars)	Nonmilitary Government Expenditures* (% of GNP)
Sweden	8,450	41.1
United States	7,099	25.4
Canada	6,935	33.6
West Germany	6,842	34.2
France	6,386	31.8
United Kingdom	4,089	34.0
Italy	3,074	33.9

*Figures obtained by subtracting defense expenditures from total government expenditures at all levels. See *The Military Balance 1976–1977* (London: The International Institute for Strategic Studies, 1976), p. 78; *National Accounts of OECD Countries, 1975* (Paris: OECD, 1977), vol. 2.

Note: The Pearson correlation coefficient between GNP per capita and government expenditures is .13.

Source: Data on GNP per capita from *Statistical Abstract of the United States,* 97th ed. (Washington, D.C.: U.S. Government Printing Office, 1976), p. 877.

Sweden is able to make such large welfare expenditures because it has the highest per capita income of any nation in the world. Table 5–3 compares the per-capita income and the relative percent of GNP spent for non-military purposes by the same seven nations reviewed above. Of course, this level of expenditure cannot be maintained unless the state takes a large part of the national income in the form of taxes. (A later section on income distribution will return to the taxation and spending policies of the same seven countries.) The reader should not forget that a composite picture of socialism is drawn from many nations and in diverse areas of public policy. No one nation can serve by itself as the socialist model.[11]

Sweden and West Germany, respectively, with expenditures of 24 and 22 percent of their GNPs on social services, rank first in the area of income maintenance for the aged and disabled. A commentator recently summarized Swedish leadership as follows:

First with a national pension program for all citizens, Sweden today has exceptional retirement benefits. Its earnings-related supplementary pension, added to a foundational basic grant is designed to provide the majority of retirees with 60 percent of the annual earned income averaged during the last 15 best years before retirement. Unemployment and disability insurance was upgraded in 1974 to provide 90 percent of regular earnings for the average worker. On the basis of somewhat lower benefit levels Wilensky found Sweden's expenditures per recipient in a class of its own—tops by every measure we can devise.

The avant-garde character of the Swedish welfare system is reflected in its recent addition of paternity benefits to its outstanding range of aids to mothers and babies. Further, the active program for combating unemployment through training, relocation, and other means is second to none in expenditure and commitment.[12]

Health Although Swedish governmental expenditure on health is twice that of the United States, its total public and private expenditure, as a percent of GNP, is slightly less than that of the United States: Sweden, 6.7 percent, compared with 6.8 percent for the United States. On the most commonly accepted measures of quality of health care, Sweden surpasses the United States by a considerable margin: infant mortality in Sweden is 13.3 per 1,000 live-born, and in the United States it is 18.5; life expectancy in Sweden is 71.8 years (male) and 76.6 years (female) compared with figures of 66.8 years (male) and 74.1 years (female); hospital beds per 10,000 in Sweden are 149.4 and in the United States, 75.1.[13] In addition, data fail to measure the fact that such factors as the maldistribution of physicians in a strict market allocation system such as that of the United States account for an even harsher deprivation for the rural poor or ghetto residents in such market-controlled countries. Doctors in market systems such as the United States are also "inefficient producers" in relation to their earnings. American doctors, for example, earn considerably more than their European counterparts, who rely upon public sources for their income. For example, the average American physician earns three times as much as the average British physician; yet the comprehensiveness of the British health care system is far greater than that of the American system.[14]

Education The United States in the past has been a world leader in its provision of public education for its citizenry. Education in Sweden has now reached U.S. standards. Government expenditures for education as a percent of GNP, as noted previously, are 6.7 percent in the United States and 7.7 percent in Sweden. In addition, while U.S. levels seem to have remained stable since 1970, Swedish commitment continues to grow. For example, between 1965–66 and 1975–76 the percentage of age-group enrolled in university-level education increased in the U.S. from 26.6 percent to 31.5 percent, while in Sweden the increase went from 11.5 percent to 27.2 percent.[15]

The Environment

It is difficult to summarize the status of quite recent movements in the world surrounding protection of the natural environment. The use and protection of natural environments in terms of their use as factors of production—actual and potential—and in terms of their status as an aspect of human social organization are multivaried. For our immediate purposes we speak of the environment as the natural world, including both productive resources (minerals, fossil fuels, water, and so on) and resources needed to sustain social life (clean air and water, adequate disposal systems, climate, and so on).

In the last decade and a half there has been a reaction to problems of specific degradations of the environment and to problems of ecology in general. Capitalist and socialist countries alike have recognized the need for resource planning and environmental control. Three aspects of the response will be briefly examined in this section. They include the role of political culture as a predisposition for public policy; institutional organization within particular countries with regard to the formulation and implementation of environmental policies; and, finally, the impact of economic growth on conditions in the environment. The argument is basically that ideology shapes these three aspects of the response to the need for remediation of environmental problems. Furthermore, as we are dealing with socialism here, we will argue that socialist ideology (remembering the *composite* nature of our model) is more congenial to environmental reform policies than either capitalist or communist systems as we have defined them in the four previous chapters.

The specific part of a socialist political culture which shapes the political culture of a given nation in a way which makes it sensitive to environmental integrity and capable of implementing environmental reform is the readiness to socialize both the burdens and benefits of economic prosperity, and *to maintain this socialization throughout cyclical economic downswings.* It is recognized that in virtually every industrialized country the burden of increased technology has been threats to the environment. Not only depletion of nonrenewable resources but contamination of the air we breathe and the water we drink, as well as threats to the entire ecological food and life chains have resulted from rapid and extensive industrialization since the turn of the century. While it is true that the extent of environmental pollution depends on the organization of the economy in any given country, it is also true that industrialization itself and the use of high-speed technology create social problems seemingly endemic to *all* industrialized countries, whether they have capitalist, communist, or mixed economies. It is primarily the response to those problems which interests us here. It has been reported that the most comprehensive efforts through legislative enactments in remedying environmental problems have been taken in the United States, Sweden, and East Germany in the last decade.[16] Of these three countries, Sweden appears to remain the most likely to continue to implement its environmental policies:

What is certain, though, is that Swedish reaction to the recent global business recession as it affects the pollution question has been unlike the American reaction. While the tendency in the United States has been to restrict the antipollution commitment in the name of saving jobs and cutting costs, the Swedes have responded to the economic downturn by strengthening their antipollution efforts. Under the Keynesian assumption that more, not less economic public spending is called for during recessionary phases of the business cycle, the government has increased its antipollution expenditures in the hope that this will provide an economic stimulus.[17]

The willingness to "push" this Keynesian assumption *away* from considerations of marginal utility and private profit concerns during recessionary periods may, in turn, be a function of Swedish political culture. The Swedes, like the Germans, are reported to possess collective norms that promote issues such as the environment to the status of a political issue:[18]

A society's political culture determines what a people value highly or treat indifferently. It also shapes the processes by which they convert concerns into issues and then go about resolving them. Here again the Swedish case is instructive. Swedish values downplay mobilized public expression and give professional planners great leverage. Likewise, Swedish egalitarianism has meant Socialist Party regimes in power. This combination of 1) [avoidance] of public demonstration, 2) widespread consensus on welfare programs, and 3) faith in professional planners gave Sweden a head start over other nations in dealing with environmental problems.[19]

In contrast, a country like the United States, with its firm ideological predisposition to negative freedom, minimal government, and private-sector decision making (all of which are the antitheses of socialism), embodies a different political culture:

Among the countries here surveyed the United States is perhaps the most severely underdeveloped in terms of planning and coordinating capacity. While Western European nations such as France, Britain, and Sweden have been pushing ahead with regional development plans and urban planning on a nationwide scale, the American political system cannot digest even a modest land-use planning bill. The cultural preference for laissez-faire relations (and the belief that they still persist when in fact there is increasing, though selective government-business interlocking) and [the avoidance] of ideological modes of debate enshrine pragmatism and ad hoc bargaining; while structural federalism, local home rule, and "subgovernment" specialized policy clusters add further barriers to nationwide planning.

It has been environmental politics, however, which has been the principle factor disclosing the inadequacies of these traditional political modes.[20]

The German Democratic Republic (East Germany) includes an article in its Constitution explicitly protecting the environment. Article 15 reads:

In the interest of the welfare of citizens, the state and society shall protect nature. The competent bodies shall ensure the purity of all water and air, and the protection of flora and fauna and the natural beauties of the homeland; in addition this is the affair of every citizen. (1968)

Going far beyond the model set by the Soviet Union with regard to environmental protection,[21] East Germany directly controls the construction and operation of new plants, as well as inducing compliance with environmental protection standards through fines and subsidies.[22]

The institutional organization of government agencies which both plan and respond to policy alternatives regarding the environment account for a range of variation among countries. Reliance upon central planning regarding key policy alternatives in Sweden has already been mentioned as conducive to comprehensive, well-integrated, and swift policy responses to such social problems as environmental pollution. Combined with the ideological predisposition to provide the socialized benefits of modern life, such as the provision of natural open spaces for the public as well as the protection against environmental contamination, vigorous remedial policies can be enacted. At the same time it must be noted that highly centralized and highly insulated policy rule can work, as well, to inhibit such remedial policies as environmental reform.

The Party-bounded and insular quality of the Soviet Union's decision-making process, while responsible for the tremendous strides in economic development discussed in Chapter 2, has inhibited an environmental policy as vigorous as that of Sweden or East Germany. The solution of environmental problems, of course, requires a fundamental rethinking of the liabilities of rapid and extensive economic growth, the result of rapid heavy industrialization. While the Soviet environmental problems are not nearly as severe as those of advanced capitalist nations like the United States, the Soviets do face increasingly troublesome pollution problems, especially that of water pollution.[23] Its response to the problems have been slower than we might expect from our socialist model. The reason is succinctly stated by a political economist:

The nature of growth in the Soviet economy is two-sided when it comes to its relationship to the environment. On the one hand, Soviet growth is not decided by profit and thus one might expect a clear path to environmental controls despite the costs. If stockholders are not going to be out any money and executives are not going to experience a salary or bonus cut when funds go to pollution controls instead of to profits, what stands in the way of environmental cleanup? In point of fact, nothing, except the demands of growth per se. If factory performance and management reward is measured by quantity of output or filling a quota, directors may go all out to achieve their quota regardless of environmental impacts. This, in fact, has been a tendency in the Soviet Union. Quite aside from directors' personal interests, which as in the capitalist firm plays a prominent role in production decisions, an economy which is characterized by capital scarcity is led to neglect environmental costs. A growth priority system in intermediate stages of development as in the Soviet Union can always be said to have a capital shortage or competition for scarce capital. Even an overdeveloped, stagnating growth economy such as the United States is reluctant to give up funds for the environment.[24]

In a sense we have treated socialist responses to environmental problems as though they were responses to "postindustrial" society, especially when comparing the responses of such developed countries as Sweden and the German Democratic Republic to the Soviet Union. In reality we can recognize as a functional condition no such thing as a "postindustrial" society. The economies of the world are tied to global developmental patterns, which are historically specific and interdependent. To disaggregate the economic models out of the global-historical pattern may be a necessary abstraction in our analysis of competing ideologies but does not serve our attempt to present a composite model of socialism. We conceptualize socialism as a developmental tendency as much as a composite model and must therefore recognize that the impact of economic growth cannot be contained within insulated models.

As a pattern of development our composite model of socialism may be considered as a model which incorporates tendencies that rationalize pure market patterns of economic activity, ameliorate capitalist exigencies, or both. The extent to which socialist organization is capable of rationalization and amelioration is contingent upon both the internal structure of a nation's economy and political system and upon the nature of its dependency within the global economy. We do not wish to explore all of these contingencies here. We note only briefly that the crisis of world capitalism in any given cycle, and indeed the tendencies and contradictions which result from the mechanisms of capital accumulation within capitalism and which are always present as tensions during periods between crises, will tend to have a more severe impact upon mixed "socialist" economies (including the state capitalistic economies such as Sweden and Great Britain) than upon relatively more insulated communist systems (such as the Soviet Union and Cuba).[25] Economic growth and national policies which provide for more or less orderly growth, including such policies as long-range investment planning and various specific inducements for investment, will determine the manner in which the environment enters planning calculations as a factor of production. Socialism, both structurally through its use of central government planning and its "rationalization" policies and in its ideological predispositions, expressed to some as "political culture," is a discreet model, separate and apart from either capitalism with its philosophy of liberalism or Russian "socialism" with its philosophy of communism. Indeed, it appears as a transitional model, which, in part, accounts for the composite nature of the model we present. We would reiterate here that the composite contains *existing* components and has both an explanatory value in its developmental theory and a heuristic value as a middle-range empirical analysis.

A Socialist-Directed Economy

This final section will attempt to demonstrate that in contrast to U.S. economic policy, a socialist policy similar to that followed by Sweden will provide for full employment, a reasonably equitable distribution of income, and an inflation rate that is not excessive. Due to its antipathy to positive state action, let alone socialism, American policy has consistently exercised the option providing for a fiscal and monetary policy allowing for the minimum of state intervention. This nonpragmatic but highly ideological policy has resulted in high unemployment, a poor growth economy of late, and inflation. The socialist composite model which we would use in contrast can be defended on the grounds that in relying upon a high level of state expenditures coupled with a correspondingly high level of taxation, such an economy can provide full employment and an equitable distribution of income and can avoid the pitfall of an unreasonable inflation rate.

American "Keynesianism"   In this section we wish to examine the effects of the very deep-seated resistance of American capital to any expansion in the role of the state beyond facilitating private decision making at the corporate

TABLE 5·4
Levels of Taxes and Expenditures as a Percentage of Gross National Product, 1965–1974

Country	Expenditures		Taxes	
	1965–1969	*1970–1974*	*1965–1969*	*1970–1974*
United States	27.4	30.5	26.4	28.3
Canada	28.0	34.0	30.1	33.9
United Kingdom	32.3	34.9	33.3	34.9
West Germany	32.0	34.3	33.4	35.8
Sweden	33.1	40.3	38.0	42.6
France	34.2	34.7	37.0	37.0
Italy	31.3	35.6	29.8	30.6

Note: Data pertains to all levels of government: central, state-provinical in the three federal systems (United States, Canada, West Germany), and local. Taxes include revenues actually gathered by all governmental levels.

Source: For data, see *National Accounts of OECD Countries, 1975* (Paris: OECD, 1977), vol. 2; *1962–1973* (Paris: OECD, 1975), *1961–1972* (Paris: OECD, 1974); *Revenue Statistics of OECD Member Countries, 1965–1974* (Paris: OECD, 1976), p. 74. Data on the gross national product at market prices appeared in *Revenue Statistics of OECD Member Countries, 1965–1974* (Paris: OECD, 1976), p. 98.

level. We wish to argue that invariably, when the United States has had a choice between an expanded or a retracted role for the state, it has chosen the latter. The resistance to state expansion has operated at the level of restricting state expenditures, thereby constraining both the authority and power of the state to direct economic policy making.[26] For example, when faced with the need to take countercyclical measures during periods of heightened economic tension, the policy has been to favor reduced taxation rather than an increase in government spending. This has occurred even when the evidence suggests that such a policy would result in higher deficits, higher rates of unemployment, and greater inflation than would a policy of increased government expenditure coupled with increased taxation.

Table 5–4 points out that of the nations surveyed the U.S. total expenditures and taxes as a percent of GNP are

229

TABLE 5·5
Unemployment Rates as a Percentage of the Civilian Labor Force

Country	Average Annual Figures		
	1961–1965	1966–1970	1971–1975
United States	5.5	3.9	6.1
Canada	5.4	4.6	6.1
Britain	2.6	3.0	3.8
West Germany	0.4	0.8	1.6
Sweden	1.5	1.9	2.3
France	1.5	2.3	3.3
Italy	3.3	3.8	3.6

Source: Joyanna Moy and Constance Sorrentino, "An Analysis of Unemployment in Nine Industrial Countries," *Monthly Labor Review* 100 (April 1977):15; U.S. Department of Labor, Bureau of Labor Statistics, *Handbook of Labor Statistics, 1975—Reference Edition* (Washington, D.C.: U.S. Government Printing Office, 1975), p. 437; *Handbook of Labor Statistics, 1976* (Washington, D.C.: U.S. Government Printing Office, 1976), p. 332.

the least in the United States and also, that European nations' taxes are higher than their expenditures which result in the United States's experiencing harmful fiscal deficits while the other nations do not.[27]

In large measure, this different fiscal policy accounts for increased levels of unemployment in the United States (see Table 5–5).[28]

A regression analysis of seven nations demonstrates that the fiscal policy pursued by the United States which attempts to combat recession by decreasing taxes and expanding the money supply is less effective than a policy which calls for increased government expenditures matched by increased taxation (see table 5–6).[29]

It appears that the United States has paid a very high price for an inflation rate which is only slightly lower than that of Sweden and France and is even slightly higher than that of West Germany. The United States, as the following table indicates, has a worse economic record than West Germany, Sweden or France in terms of a) growth of GNP, b)

TABLE 5·6
Public Policies and Unemployment Rates

Policy Variables	Pearson $_r$
Government Expenditures as a Proportion of GNP	
1965–1969	−.72
1970–1974	−.63
Taxes as a Proportion of GNP	
1965–1969	−.69
1970–1974	−.65
Annual Percentage Increase in the Money Supply	
1965–1969	.22
1970–1974	−.21

Note: The Pearson $_r$ expresses a correlation between government policies (e.g., the average annual rate of government expenditures as a proportion of the gross national product) and the unemployment rate (the yearly jobless rates during two periods: 1966–1970 and 1971–1975). The values of $_r$ range between −1 and +1. The closer the Pearson $_r$ is to +1 or −1, the higher the association. A minus $_r$ indicates an inverse statistical relationship; for instance, as government expenditures as a proportion of the GNP *increase*, unemployment rates *decrease*. A positive $_r$ shows a positive correlation. Between 1965 and 1970, for example, as annual percentage increases in the money supply rose, unemployment rates also rose slightly. With only seven countries under study, Pearson correlation coefficients should reach at least .75 to be statistically significant at the 5 percent level; that is, in only five instances out of 100 would we expect to obtain an $_r$ of .75 or larger by chance.

wage increase for workers, c) productivity (output per manhour), d) unit labor costs, e) rate of investment in fixed capital, f) real hourly earnings, and g) unemployment:[30]

Only in controlling inflation did the United States demonstrate a better record than the other countries. The attempt by the United States to control inflation was only marginally better than those of Sweden and France and not as successful as that of West Germany. President Reagan said repeatedly that "inflation results, not from *your* living too well, but from *government* living too well." Yet West Ger-

TABLE 5·7
Comparative Measures of Economic Performance, 1971–1975

Nations	Growth rate (%)*	Wages (%)†	Output per worker-hour (%)‡	Unit Labor cost (%)§	Gross Fixed Capital (%)**	Real Hourly Earnings (%)††	Unemployment‡‡	Inflation (%)§§
U.S.	2.4	7.3	1.9	5.5	17.9	0.7	6.1	6.8
West Germany	3.5	14.0	5.4	8.2	25.3	4.3	1.6	6.1
Sweden	3.2	12.7	5.5	7.2	22.0	3.6	2.3	8.0
France	5.3	13.6	5.4	7.8	23.9	5.4	3.3	8.8

*Annual average rates of change in the real gross national product (for Sweden the growth figures indicate changes in the real gross domestic product).

†Annual percentage change in hourly compensation in manufacturing.

‡Annual percentage change in output per hour (total output divided by the number of hours worked by all employees in manufacturing).

§Unit labor costs in national currency indicate the ratio of hourly labor cost to output per hour performed by workers in manufacturing industries.

**Domestic expenditures at current prices on buildings, machinery, and equipment as percentages of the gross national product.

††Figures refer to the percentage changes in the average hourly earnings of wage workers in manufacturing; the earnings have been adjusted for changes in purchasing power since the base period (1967).

‡‡Yearly averages of the number of employed as a percentage of the civilian labor force.

§§Average yearly inflation rate 1971–1975.

Note: Annual percentage change in wages, output per worker-hour and unit labor cost are the key productivity measures.

many has an inflation rate *lower* than the United States' *and* a higher per capita expenditure for social welfare.

In summary, it would appear that inflation is not caused primarily by government policy but is likely to be a product of concentration of industry in the hands of monopolies, whether they be American multinationals or OPEC cartels.

Equality of Income Distribution There are a number of policies which affect income distribution. The best overall index of the degree of income equality is the Gini index.[31] A low Gini coefficient indicates low inequality. A comparison of posttax income inequality standardized for household size shows a Gini index rating of 0.27 for Sweden compared with a rating of 0.37 for the United States.[32] The results of the state spending and taxation policies in Sweden yield a more favorable distribution of posttax income.

A comparison of the United States and Sweden with hourly wages in eight manufacturing industries (see Table 5–8) illustrates the differences between a capitalist and state-interventionist approach with regard to the stabilization and equalization of wage rates.[33]

Sweden's greater equality is a result of a consciously adopted taxation and expenditure policy on the part of the socialist-controlled government from 1932 to 1976. A comparison of the policy outcome of Sweden's taxation/expenditure policy will demonstrate the redistributive results. As Table 5–9 indicates, after taxes and as a result of transfer payments, the ratio of income distribution between the wealthiest 20 percent of the population and the poorest 20 percent in the United States in 1972 changed from 21.3 : 1 to 7.5 : 1. In Sweden the ratio changed from 62.4 : 1 to 3.8 : 1. In simple terms, this means that an average person in the upper 20 percent of Swedish income recipients would have an income which in 1972 was 3.8 times greater than the average (poor) person in the lowest 20 percent of income receivers. A similarly situated person in the United States would have an income which was 7.5 times greater than the average person in the lowest 20 percent level in the United States.[34]

TABLE 5·8
Comparison: United States and Sweden: Hourly Wages in Representative Manufacturing Industries (in U.S. dollars)

	U.S.	Sweden	Difference
"high"	10.75	9.40	+1.35
	(motor vehicles)	(primary metals)	
"low"	4.10	6.95	−2.85
	(footwear)	(apparel)	
mean representative wage across eight industries	6.91	8.06	−1.15
range of pay scales	6.65	2.45	+4.20
standard deviation: "spread" among eight industries	2.58	0.81	+1.77

TABLE 5·9
Share of Money Income in United States and Sweden in 1972

	Poorest 20%	Wealthiest 20%	Ratio: wealthy/poor
United States			
Posttax/pretransfer	2.4	51.2	21.3:1
Posttax/posttransfer	6.3	47.1	7.5:1
Sweden			
Posttax/pretransfer	0.7	43.7	62.4:1
Posttax/posttransfer	9.4	35.6	3.8:1

Note: Government transfers include such payments as social security, pensions, unemployment compensation, family allowances, and public assistance. It is Andrain's conclusion that government expenditures are much more redistributive than governmental taxation policy.

TABLE 5·10
Comparison of Unemployment, Inflation, and Gini Index of Inequality, 1971–1975

	Unemployment (%)	Inflation (%)	Gini Index	GNP per Capita (U.S.$)
U.S.	6.1	6.8	0.37	7,099
Sweden	2.3	8.0	0.27	8,450

Table 5–10 presents a summary of the different outcomes of a mixed "socialist" policy in Sweden compared to a clearly capitalist policy of taxation and expenditure as practiced in the United States.[35]
While Sweden has experienced a somewhat slower growth since 1975, and a higher inflation than reported in data prior to that date, it has nevertheless remained below the United States in the area of inflation and has maintained a slightly higher growth rate.

CONCLUSION

This chapter has attempted to present evidence of a workable socialist composite model by drawing from the experiences of several mixed economies those elements which are congruent with socialist principles of organization and egalitarianism. Our composite has been drawn in an effort to avoid utopian theorizing and confront the charge of idealization with hard evidence.

A glance back through the chapter will show that we have relied primarily on the recent national experiences of two nations. Yugoslavia has provided the example of public ownership and worker control, while Sweden has provided the element of a socialist welfare and income policy. A humane socialism is within the grasp of contemporary societies. Further evidence of the recognition of the potential for country-to-country adaptation and for the programmatic success of market socialism, at least for both the rationalization and amelioration of economic distress, is the march of "Eurocommunism" in Europe.[36] The significant advance of socialist-communist fortunes is marked by the twin electoral victories in May and June 1981. On May tenth France surprised the world by electing François Mitterrand, a socialist, president of France. This startling event was soon to be surpassed by the even more surprising victory of the left in the June 21, 1981 parliamentary election. With the support of the communists who, in those contests where the socialist candidates were ahead on the first ballot, withdrew in favor of the socialists, the Socialist party emerged from the election with an absolute majority in the Parliament. The left coalition had 327 seats out of a total of 471, composed of 283 socialists and 44 communists. President Mitterrand was quick to consolidate the coalition by appointing four communists to the new government.

It is clear already that the new government of France intends to follow policies that will extend public ownership, advance worker control, provide for a more equitable distribution of income, and implement many of the other socialist policies described in this chapter.

NOTES

1. Mao Tse-tung as quoted in John G. Gurley, *Challengers to Capitalism*, 2d ed. (New York: W. W. Norton and Company, 1979), p. 160.
2. Charles F. Andrain, *Politics and Economic Policy in Western Democracies* (North Scituate, Mass.: Duxbury Press, 1980), p. 23.
3. Clair Wilcox et al., *Economies of the World Today*, 3d ed. (New York: Harcourt, Brace, Jovanovich, 1976), based on *World Bank Atlas* data (1975) as reported in Charles Lindblom, *Politics and Markets* (New York: Basic Books, 1977), p. 296.
4. Hugh Helco, *Modern Social Politics in Britain and Sweden* (New Haven, Conn.: Yale University Press, 1974), p. 25.
5. Lindblom, *Politics and Markets*, p. 68.
6. Ibid., pp. 340–41.
7. Yugoslav Federal Office for Statistics, *Materijalni i Drustveni Razvoj, SFR Jugoslavije*, 1947–1942 as reported in Michael Roskin, *Other Governments of Europe* (Englewood Cliffs, N.J.: Prentice-Hall, 1977), p. 123.
8. Miroslav Pecujlic, "The University of the Future," in *Socialist Thought and Practice, a Yugoslavian Monthly*, XX, 9 (September 1980): 29–53, trans., S. Petnifi.
9. Ibid., pp. 44–45.
10. Andrain, *Politics and Economic Policy in Western Democracies*, p. 13.
11. Ibid., p. 45.
12. Richard L. Siegel and Leonard B. Weinberg, *Comparing Public Policies: United States, Soviet Union and Europe* (Homewood, Ill.: Dorsey Press, 1977), p. 210.

13. Ibid., pp. 219–21.
14. Ibid., p. 221. See also, John Fry, *Medicine in Three Societies* (New York: American Elsevier Publishing Company, 1970).
15. Arnold J. Heidenheimer, Hugh Helco, and Carolyn Teich Adams, *Comparative Public Policy, The Politics of Social Choice in Europe and America* (New York: St. Martin's Press, 1975), p. 46, based upon OECD data.
16. Siegel and Weinberg, *Comparing Public Policies*, p. 393.
17. Ibid., p. 397.
18. Cynthia Enloe, *The Politics of Pollution in a Comparative Perspective* (New York: David McKay Company, 1975), p. 13.
19. Ibid., p. 15. See also Siegel and Weinberg, *Comparing Public Policies*, Chapter 11, and their discussion of the stages of development and differential national responses to environmental problems, pp. 382–91.
20. Enloe, *The Politics of Pollution*, p. 326.
21. Peter Sand, "The Socialist Response: Environmental Protection Law in the GDR," *Ecology Law Quarterly* 3 (Summer 1973): 451–505, as cited in Siegel and Weinberg, *Comparing Public Policies*, p. 401.
22. *Governmental Measures in the GDR to Keep Waters Clean and to Rationally Use Ground and Surface Waters* (Stockholm, 1972), as reported in Siegel and Weinberg, ibid., p. 402.
23. Charles H. Anderson, *The Sociology of Survival, Social Problems of Growth* (Homewood, Ill.: Dorsey Press, 1976), p. 240.
24. Ibid., p. 241.
25. See Fred L. Block, *The Origins of International Economic Disorder* (Berkeley: University of California Press, 1977), for a discussion of international monetary policy, for example.
26. For differing analyses regarding this, see Theodore J. Lowi, *The End of Liberalism*, 2d ed. (New York, W. W. Norton and Company, 1979); Manuel Castells, *The Economic Crisis and American Society* (Princeton, N.J.: Princeton University Press, 1980); James O'Connor, *The Fiscal Crisis of the State* (New York: St. Martin's Press, 1973); and Alan Wolfe, *The Limits of Legitimacy* (New York: Free Press, 1977).
27. Andrain, *Politics and Economic Policy*, p. 11.
28. Ibid., p. 66.
29. Ibid., p. 76.
30. This table is compiled from a number of sources and data reported in Andrain, *Politics and Economic Policy*, Chapters 5 and 6, pp. 99–143. The sources include, *International Financial Statistics* 30 (May and October 1977): 334, 362, for growth rate; *National Accounts of OECD Countries*, 1975; for gross fixed capital; *Monthly Labor Review* 100 (July 1977): 15–16, U.S. Department of Labor *Handbook of Labor Statics*, 1976, p. 333, and the *1975 Handbook of Labor Statistics Reference Edition*, p. 438, for wages, output per worker-hour, and labor unit cost; and OECD *Main Economic Indicators, Historical Statistics*:

238

CONTEMPORARY ISMS

1960–1975, and supplements for January 1975, and January 1977 for rises in inflation.

31. The Gini index or coefficient is the most widely accepted method of measuring income equality. Named for the Italian statistician Corrado Gini, the index pegs "0" as perfect equality (or 0 inequality). A coefficient of 1 would indicate absolute inequality. The coefficient is determined by ranking families on a horizontal axis of a graph according to their total income, and the vertical axis indicates the share of income received by them. For example, if 10 percent of all families received 10 percent of all income, 20 percent of all families received 20 percent of all income, and so forth, then there would exist perfect equality of income and the Gini coefficient would be zero. A coefficient of 1 would exist if 1 percent of all families received 100 percent of the total income—the expression within the index of absolute inequality.

32. Andrain, *Politics and Economic Policy*, p. 180.

33. Adapted from ibid., p. 182, based upon *International Economic Report of the President* (Washington, D.C., January 1977), pp. 100–101.

34. Adapted from ibid., pp. 190–91, based upon Malcolm Sawyer, "Income Distribution in OECD Countries," *OECD Economic Outlook: Occasional Studies* (July 1976), and *OECD Studies in Resource Allocation, No. 3: Public Expenditures on Income Maintenance Programs,* 1976.

35. Ibid., p. 45, from *Statistical Abstracts of the United States*, 97th ed., (Washington, D.C.: U.S. Government Printing Office, 1976), p. 877.

36. "Eurocommunism" refers to the changes which have occurred in the posture and policy of the Communist Parties of Western Europe over, roughly, the past fifteen years, and refers particularly to the parties of Italy, France, Spain and Portugal. The essential elements of these developments are: independence from Moscow regarding policy, including the willingness to criticize Moscow—quite vigorously at times; Soviet international activities; adherence to "parliamentarianism" including a willingness to participate in electoral and governing coalitions with socialist and other parties; and a redefinition, by party intellectuals, of the role of the Party particularly with regard to revolutionary transition.

BIBLIOGRAPHIC NOTE

One of the major goals of this chapter is to demonstrate that while socialism cannot be said to exist in any single nation, a componential model can be constructed from the real-world experience and structures of several nations. All of the components, if taken together, would constitute an operative socialism which, if less than ideal, is more than utopian. Therefore, the selections in this bibliography reflect the literature dealing with the existing socialist arrangements in a variety of countries, rather than a theoretical or philosophical approach.

There are roughly three divisions within the literature we cite. Works on the development and growth of the welfare state extend back in time into the last century and cover vast areas of public policy, ranging from the more traditional pension systems to disaggregated policy areas such as health systems, unemployment/incomes policy, child care and education, etc. The extensiveness of Sweden's social welfare system, in this sense, provides the real-world experience in many of these areas.

A second area in which the focus of research has been expanding in recent years has been the subject of worker control and participation in the management of economic production. In this area Yugoslavia has provided a lead although worker control in both Sweden and France and, of course, co-determinism in Germany have existed since the end of World War II. Experience in the United States has centered on the use of various incentive programs (primarily sharing bonuses and investments) to bolster a falling productivity rate.

The third area which might be noted has, to date, produced a relatively smaller contribution in the literature. The development of Eurocommunism, marking the resurgence of the Communist parties of developed countries within a parliamentary system of government is, nevertheless, perhaps the most significant development in the politics of Western Europe.

The programmatic and policy-orientation of much of the literature cited in these three areas suggest that beyond a substantive policy-areas approach, per se (incomes, health, education, etc.), there exists a great potential for an integrated study of the socialist alternative within a market economy. We hope that the model provided may facilitate that approach.

BIBLIOGRAPHY

Adizes, Ichak. *Industrial Democracy: Yugoslav Style.* New York: Free Press, 1971.

Allardt, Erik. "About Dimensions of Welfare. An Explorative Analysis of a Comparative Survey." *Research Report,* No. 1. Helsinki: Research Group for Comparative Sociology, 1973.

Anderson, Charles H. *Sociology of Survival, Social Problems of Growth.* Homewood, Ill.: The Dorsey Press, 1976.

Anderson, Odin W. *Health Care: Can There be Equity?—The United States, Sweden and England.* New York: Wiley, 1972.

Andrain, Charles F. *Politics and Economic Policy in Western Democracies,* North Scituate, Mass.: Duxbury Press, 1980.

Beveridge, William H., *Full Employment in a Free Society.* New York: W. W. Norton, 1945.

Bicanic, Rudolf. *Economic Policy in Socialist Yugoslavia.* New York: Cambridge University Press, 1973.

Block, Fred L. *The Origins of International Economic Disorder.* Berkeley, Ca.: University of California Press, 1977.

Blumberg, Paul. *Industrial Democracy: The Sociology of Participation.* New York: Schocken, 1969.

Boulding, Kenneth E. *The Meaning of the Twentieth Century.* New York: Harper & Row, 1965.

——— "The Shadow of the Stationary State." *Daedalus,* No. 102 (Fall 1973).

Brockmeyer, M. *Yugoslav Workers' Self-Management.* Dordrecht, Holland: D. Reidel, 1970.

Brown, Bernard E., ed. *Eurocommunism and Eurosocialism: The Left Confronts Modernity.* New York: Cyroco Press, 1978.

Bruce, Maurice. *The Coming of the Welfare State,* 4th ed. London: B. T. Batsford, 1968.

Carrillo, Santiago. *Eurocommunism and the State.* Westport, Conn.: Hill & Co., 1978.

Castells, Manuel. *The Economic Crisis and American Society.* Princeton, N.J.: Princeton University Press, 1980.

Castles, Francis. *The Social Image of Society.* London: Routledge & Kegan Paul, 1978.

Childs, Marquis. *Sweden: The Middle Way,* new ed. New Haven, Conn.: Yale University Press, 1961.

——— *Sweden: The Middle Way on Trial.* New Haven, Conn.: Yale University Press, 1980.

Cohen, Stephen. *Modern Capitaliat Planning: The French Model.* Cambridge, Mass.: Harvard University Press, 1969.

Cole, G. D. H. *Chaos and Order in Industry.* London: Methuen, 1920.

——— *Guild Socialism Restated.* London: Parsons, 1920.

——— *Self-Government in Industry.* London: G. Bell & Sons, 1919.

—— *The World of Labor*. London: G. Bell & Sons, 1913.

Commoner, Barry. *The Closing Circle*. New York: Knopf, 1971.

Dahl, Robert A. and Lindblom, Charles E. *Politics, Economics and Welfare*. New York: Harper & Row, 1953.

Daly, Herman E., ed. *Toward a Steady-State Economy*. San Francisco, Ca.: W. H. Freeman & Co., 1973.

Denitch, Bogdan. *The Legitimation of a Revolution: The Yugoslav Case*. New Haven: Yale University Press, 1976.

Djilas, Milovan. *The New Class*. New York: Praeger, 1957.

Durbin, E. F. M. *The Politics of Democratic Socialism*. London: Routledge, 1940.

Duverger, Maurice. *Modern Democracies: Economic Power versus Political Power*. Hinsdale, Ill.: The Dryden Press, 1974.

Edelman, Murray. *Political Language: Words That Succeed and Policies That Fail*. New York: Institute for Research on Poverty, Monograph Series/Academic Press, 1977.

Ehrlich, Paul R. and Holden, Anne H. and John P. *Human Ecology, Problems and Solutions*. San Francisco: W. H. Freeman & Co., 1973.

Einhorn, Eric and Logue, John. *Welfare States in Hard Times*. Kent, Ohio: Popular Press, 1980.

Enloe, Cynthia. *The Politics of Pollution in a Comparative Perspective*. New York: David McKay, 1975.

Frey, John, ed. *Limits of the Welfare State*. Hampshire, England: Gower Publishing, 1980.

Fuchs, Victor R. *Who Shall Live?* New York: Basic Books, 1974.

Furness, Norman and Tilton, Timothy. *The Case For the Welfare State*. Bloomington, Ind.: Indiana University Press, 1977.

Galbraith, John Kenneth. *Economics and the Public Purpose*. Boston: Houghton, Mifflin, 1973.

Gorz, André. *A Strategy for Labor*. Boston: Beacon Press, 1967.

Gouldner, Alvin W. *The Coming Crisis of Western Sociology*. New York: Basic Books, 1970.

Griffiths, Richard T., ed. *Government, Business and Labor in European Capitalism*. London: Europotentials Press, 1977.

Hallett, Graham. *The Social Economy of West Germany*. New York: St. Martin's Press, 1973.

Hamilton, E. E. Ian. *Yugoslavia: Patterns of Economic Activity*. London: G. Bell & Sons, 1968.

Hancock, M. Donald. "Productivity, Welfare and Participation in Sweden and West Germany: A Comparison of Social Democratic Reform Proposals." *Comparative Politics*, Vol. 11, no. 1 (October 1978).

—— *Sweden: The Politics of Post-Industrial Change*. Hinsdale, Ill.: The Dryden Press, 1973.

Hancock, M. Donald and Sjoberg, Gideon. *Politics in the Post-Welfare State: Response to the New Individualism*. New York: Columbia University Press, 1972.

Heclo, Hugh. *Modern Politics in Britain and Sweden.* New Haven, Conn.: Yale University Press, 1974.

Herman, Edward S. *Corporate Control, Company Power.* New York: Cambridge University Press, 1981.

Herman, Edward S. and DuBoff, Richard B. "How Not to Eliminate Poverty." *Monthly Review Press,* No. 25 (February 1974).

Heilbroner, Robert. *An Inquiry Into the Human Prospect.* New York: W. W. Norton, 1974.

Heisler, Martin O., ed. *Politics in Europe: Structure and Processes in Some Post-Industrial Democracies.* New York: David McKay, 1974.

Hunnius, Gerry, Garson, G. David, and Case, John, eds. *Workers' Control.* New York: Random House, 1973.

Janowitz, Morris. "Review Symposium: The Coming of Post-Industrial Society." *American Journal of Sociology.* No. 80 (July 1974).

Kaim-Caudle, P. R. *Comparative Social Policy and Social Security: A Ten-Country Study.* London: Martin, Robertson, 1973.

Kolaja, Jiri. *Workers' Councils: The Yugoslav Experience.* New York: Praeger, 1966.

Korpi, Walter. *The Working Class in Welfare Capitalism.* London: Routledge and Kegan Paul, 1978.

Landes, David. *The Unbound Prometheus: Technology, Change and Industrial Development in Western Europe from 1790 to the Present.* Cambridge, England: Cambridge University Press, 1969.

Lange, Oskar and Taylor, Fred M. *On the Economic Theory of Socialism.* New York: McGraw-Hill, 1964.

Leibfried, Stephan "Public Assistance in the United States and the Federal Republic of Germany." *Comparative Politics,* Vol. 11, no. 1 (October 1978).

Lindbeck, Assar. *Swedish Economic Policy.* Berkeley, Ca.: University of California Press, 1974.

Lindberg, Leon, ed. *Politics and the Future of Industrial Society.* New York: 1977.

———— ed. *Stress and Contradiction in Modern Capitalism.* Cambridge, Mass.: Harvard University Press, 1975.

Lindblom, Charles E. *Politics and Markets.* New York: Basic Books, 1977.

Lowi, Theodore. *The End of Liberalism,* 2d ed. New York: W. W. Norton, 1979.

Martin, Andrew. "Is Democratic Control of Capitalist Economies Possible?" in Lindberg, Leon, ed. *Stress and Contradiction in Modern Politics.* New York: Harper & Row, 1953.

———— *The Politics of Economic Policy in the United States.* Beverly Hills, Ca.: Sage, 1973.

Martin, E. W., ed. *Comparative Development in Social Welfare.* London: Allen & Unwin, 1972.

Meadows, Donnella H., et.al. *The Limits to Growth.* New York: Universe Books, 1960.

Milenkovitch, Deborah. *Planning and Market in Yugoslav Economic Thought.* New Haven, Conn.: Yale University Press, 1971.

Miller, S.M. and Rein, Martin. "Can Income Redistribution Work?" *Social Policy*, Vol. 6, no. 1 (May/June 1975).

O'Connor, James. *The Fiscal Crisis of the State.* New York: St. Martin's Press, 1973.

Pateman, Carole. *Participation and Democratic Theory.* New York: Cambridge University Press, 1970.

Pecujlic, Miroslav. "The University of the Future." *Socialist Thought and Practise: A Yugoslavian Monthly*, Vol. 20, no. 9 (September 1980).

Pryor, Frederic. *Public Expenditures in Communist and Capitalist Nations.* Homewood, Ill.: Irwin, 1968.

Rein, Martin and Miller, S. M. "Can Income Redistribution Work?" *Social Policy.* Vol. 6, no. 1 (May/June 1975).

———— and Hugh Heclo. "What Welfare Crisis? A Comparison of Britain, Sweden and the United States." *Public Interest.* No. 33 (Fall 1973).

Rimlinger, Gaston V. *Welfare Policy and Industrialization in Europe, America, and Russia.* New York: Wiley, 1966.

Ringer, Stein, "Welfare Studies in Scandinavia." *Scandinavian Political Studies*, No. 9 (1974).

Rodgers, Barbara N., Greve, John, and Morgan, John S. *Comparative Social Administration* ed. London: Allen & Unwin, 1971.

Rosenberg, Nathan. "Science, Invention, and Economic Growth." *The Economic Journal*, No. 84 (March 1974).

Roskin, Michael. *Other Governments of Europe.* Englewood Cliffs, N.J.: Prentice-Hall, 1977.

Sand, Peter, "The Socialist Response: Environmental Protection Law in the GDR." *Ecology Law Quarterly*, No. 3 (Summer 1973).

Scase, Richard. *Social Democracy in Capitalist Society.* London: Croom, Helm. 1977.

Schnitzer, Martin. *East and West Germany: A Comparative Economic Analysis.* New York: Praeger, 1972.

———— *The Economy of Sweden.* New York: Praeger, 1970.

Siegel, Richard L. and Weinberg, Leonard B. *Comparing Public Policies: United States, Soviet Union, and Europe.* Homewood, Ill.: The Dorsey Press, 1977.

Sjoberg, Gideon and Hancock, M. Donald. *Politics in the Post-Welfare State: Response to the New Individualism.* New York: Columbia University Press, 1972.

Tanzer, Michael. *The Energy Crisis: World Struggles for Power and Wealth.* New York: Monthly Review Press, 1974.

Taylor, Arthur J. *Laissez-faire and State Intervention in Nineteenth-Century Britain.* London: Macmillan, 1972.

Taylor, Fred M. and Lange, Oskar. *On the Economic Theory of Socialism.* New York: McGraw-Hill, 1964.

Titmuss, Richard M. *Commitment to Welfare.* London: Allen & Unwin, 1968.

—— *Essays on the Welfare State,* 2d ed. London: Allen & Unwin, 1958.

—— *Problems of Social Policy.* London: His Majesty's Stationery Office, 1948.

Tomasson, Richard F. *Sweden: Prototype of Modern Society.* New York: Random House, 1970.

Vacca, Roberto. *The Coming of the Dark Age.* New York: Anchor Books, 1974.

Vanek, Juroslav. *The Participatory Economy.* Ithaca, N.Y.: Cornell University Press, 1971.

Wachtel, Howard M. *Workers' Management and Workers' Wages in Yugoslavia.* Ithaca, N.Y.: Cornell University Press, 1973.

Weisberg, Barry. *Beyond Repair: The Ecology of Capitalism.* Boston: Beacon Press, 1971.

Wilcox, Claire, et.al. *Economies of the World Today,* 3rd. ed. New York: Harcourt Brace Jovanovich, 1976.

Wilcynski, J. *Socialist Economic Development and Reforms.* London: Macmillan, 1972.

Wilensky, Harold L. *The Welfare State and Equality: Structural and Ideological Roots of Public Expenditure.* Berkeley, Ca.: University of California Press, 1975.

Wolfe, Alan. "Has Social Democracy a Future?" *Comparative Politics,* Vol. 11, no. 1 (October 1978).

—— *The Limits of Legitimacy.* New York: The Free Press, 1977.

Zaninovich, M. George. *The Development of Socialist Yugoslavia.* Baltimore: The Johns Hopkins Press, 1964.

FASCISM

The manner of conducting general affairs is the best criterion by which to judge of the morality and health of the body politic. In proportion to the degree of concord which reigns in the assemblies, that is, the nearer opinion approaches unanimity, the more the general will predominates; while tumults, dissensions, and long debates declare the ascendancy of private interests and the declining situation of the State....

At the other extremity of the circle, unanimity returns; the citizens are then so sunk in servitude that they have neither liberty nor will. Fear and flattery then make them change their votes into acclamations; instead of deliberating, they adore or they curse.[1]

No statement more succinctly captures the transformation of a well-ordered society into a fascist one. The retrogression is simply described. The healthy state is one in which a sense of public interest predominates and deliberations are undertaken in a spirit which tries to seek an outcome which is in the interest of the community as a whole. The intermediate society—the society of tumult, dissension and the ascendancy of private interests—is a regression into self-seeking; a society in which everyone seeks advantage and no one acknowledges a public purpose. There proceeds from this state of affairs a final regression. Rousseau, in his usual perceptive manner, describes in a few words that worst society:

...unanimity returns; the citizens are then so sunk in servitude

245

that they have neither liberty nor will. Fear and flattery then make them change their votes into acclamations....

This is a fascist society; a society where unity returns, where deliberation based on common values is replaced by cries for action motivated by irrational fears and desires or mere slavish habit. In contrast to such a society, even the rancorous divisions of modern pluralistic politics may give the appearance of a vital democracy.

As prescient as Rousseau may have been in describing the social psychology and retrogressive path of fascism, it remains for us to add that the contemporary or future fascist state was not really a possibility in the semifeudal era of the eighteenth century but requires the political environment of the twentieth century whose unique characteristics shape and direct the particular expression of fascism to make it different from any previous authoritarian rule. We wish to argue here that modern fascism is unique in that it is a phenomenon of mass politics and, second, that it incorporates class struggle. The particular characteristics of fascism are (1) that it is explicitly retrogressive and its retrograde characteristics are most noticeable in its backward-looking exclamations (or acclamations as the case may be) which accompany the degradation of political and social life; (2) that it is defensive—the attempt of a dominant class to retain its superior status in the face of a collapsing economy; and (3) that its catalyst is the growth of a mass political movement which threatens not only the superordinate status of the dominant political class but the power and control of the core of that class which owns and directs the economy through control of the productive modes of any given society.

In the twentieth century the dominant class in Europe and America has been the bourgeoisie, whose political rule has both shaped and responded to the prerequisites of liberalism, as outlined and discussed in Chapter 3. The "intermediate" nature of this political rule—its reliance on faction, pluralism, and the shifting consensus of "interest group politics," together with an emphasis on the provision of an "arena" of politics (in the form of constitutional and parliamentary structures of government) rather than a search for the public good or the unanimity of a general will, has overseen the development of a mass society. Social life in this century has remained largely atomistic and fractured. The strength of economic crisis has been the one catalyst which is capable of fundamental social and political cleavages and the one catalyst which is at the same time capable of coalescing large and disaggregated interests. Those interests are potentially class interests and the antagonisms which they embody are potentially class antagonisms. The growth of communist and socialist proletarian movements, due to the "massness" of the movements—that is, the sheer numbers which they command—and to the ideology of economic self-determination which they embody threaten not only the superordinate political status of the bourgeoisie but the power of the ruling capitalist class itself. When economic crisis occurs, the rebuttal power of these movements invokes a forceful and authoritarian political response on the part of the holders of power. The potential polarization of class struggle is anticipated and met by the capitalist class by measures which are, in turn, polarizing and militant. The alliance of power and mass is forged into an alliance of the capitalist class and the masses of the lower bourgeoisie.

Individuals are forced to choose, and the choice is a difficult one: whether to attempt to cling to a property status of varying security (depending on the extent of property holdings) and abandon their democratic and egalitarian values in the process or to join in a radical movement which risks both property and lives. Given the depoliticized nature of contemporary people, and the aculturation of self-interest norms, the choice to abandon democracy, even in its most superficial form as the rule of law, is a predictable one. The unanimity of defense ultimately replaces the unanimity of healthy political life, democracy. The retrogression is complete when a suitable rationale is found to legitimate the unity of defense. In this century, scapegoating has provided a large part of the rationale (Jews in Nazi Germany, blacks in comtemporary America), nationalism, the other part.

The unique characteristic of modern fascism, its "mass" quality, that alliance of numbers and power, distinguishes it from earlier tyrannies. But this mass quality should not be interpreted, as it has been by some,[2] as a kind of mystical mass psychology. The mass quality is a quality of power and alliance serving very specific political interests. It has less to do with the alienation of the common person than with the alienation of dominant political elites who respond to the erosion of their legitimacy and economic power base with a policy of manipulative alliance. Furthermore, the choice of the allied—the option of the protection of status and property over liberal democratic forms of rule—is a deliberate if ultimately destructive political choice. The "irrationality" of the choice is a function of its rationalization and expression—*not the function of a mystified "mass psychology."* Depoliticization and alienation *precede* fascism and provide a precondition for manipulation and alliance. They are neither the cause of fascism nor the condition inherent in mass publics.

The common element which runs through the writings of fascists, or those upon whom fascists rely to justify their creed, is a denial of the efficacy of reason, especially among the common people, and the glorification of leadership. The elevation of myth over the lessons of history is the chief mechanism of argumentation for these writers.

Fascist belief in the essential superiority of the leader is well documented, and one can recall the goose-stepping soldiers passing before Hitler with their upraised arms and brazen acclamations. Hitler, himself expresses very well the *Führer-prinzip*—the leadership principle—in the following passage:

Like the woman, whose psychic state is determined less by grounds of abstract reason than by indefinable emotional longing for a force which will complement her nature, and who, consequently, would rather bow to a strong man than dominate a weakling, likewise the masses love a commander more than a petitioner....[3]

Strong leadership and "control of the masses" is so much a characteristic of contemporary executive rule in virtually all the nations of the world that we tend to forget the lengths to which the logic of leadership can be pushed. Rather, it is the alienation of leadership and the insecurity of domination which we need monitor in checking the march of fascism.

Since Freud discovered the existence of the unconscious, the distrust of reason and our skepticism regarding the "thin veneer of civilization" has grown. We often fail to understand that Freud hoped to uncover the operation of unconscious motives in order to discover the means of reestablishing "normal" and healthy rational behavior. Theorists such as Gustave Le Bon (1841–1931)[4] went so far as to deny the possibility of rational action. Le Bon stressed that when persons acted in concert, the feelings of anonymity that being the member of a crowd gave them caused them to rely solely on their passions and instincts:

Moreover, by the mere fact that he forms part of an organized crowd, a man descends several rungs in the ladder of civilisation. Isolated, he may be a cultivated individual; in a crowd, he is a barbarian—that is, a creature acting by instinct. He possesses the spontaneity, the violence, the ferocity, and also the enthusiasm and heroism of primitive beings, whom he further tends to resemble by the facility with which he allows himself to be impressed by words and images—which would be entirely without action on each of the isolated individuals composing the crowd—and to be induced to commit acts contrary to his most obvious interests and his best-known habits. An individual in a crowd is a grain of sand amid other grains of sand, which the wind stirs up at will.[5]

A crowd may easily enact the part of an executioner, but not less easily that of a martyr. It is crowds that have furnished the torrents of blood requisite for the triumph of every belief.[6]

One might think that Le Bon is commenting on a lynch mob. But this is not the case. The irrational impulse is, according to Le Bon, true of any collectivity:

Electoral crowds—that is to say, collectivities invested with the

power of electing holders of certain functions—constitute het-
erogeneous crowds, but as their action is confined to a single,
clearly determined matter, namely, the choosing between different candidates, they present only a few of the characteristics previously described...they display in particular but slight aptitude
for reasoning, the absence of the critical spirit, irritability, cre-
dulity and simplicity. In their decision, moreover, is to be traced
the influence of the leaders of crowds and the part played by the
factors we have enumerated: affirmation, repetition, prestige, and
contagion.[7]

The Italian sociologist Vilfredo Pareto (1848–1923) is
even more forthright in his belief that deceit and force are
necessary tools of those who would rule, and that in all
societies government is circulated among elites whose rule
is either forceful, like a lion, or tricky, like a fox:

The use of force is indispensible to society; and when the higher
classes are averse to the use of force, which ordinarily happens
because the majority in those classes come to rely wholly on their
skill at chicanery, and the majority shrink from energetic acts now
through stupidity, now through cowardice, it becomes necessary,
if society is to subsist and prosper, that the governing class be
replaced by another which is willing and able to use force.[8]

Finally, Georges Sorel (1847–1922), the modern inter-
preter of the concept of "myth," adds another dimension
to the paradigm of the threat of the masses, which fascists
have found so congenial to their apology for elite rule and
the use of "defensive" force. Sorel asserts that it is primarily
through myth that people are motivated to act; and, as
myths are neither right nor wrong, subject neither to proof
nor disproof, they are invulnerable to criticism. In his best
known work, *Reflections on Violence*, Sorel, unlike the two
theorists discussed briefly above, defends the spontaneity
of action on the basis of its purgative and cathartic effects.
Paradoxically, while fascism relies for its authoritarian rule
upon the imputation of childlike, mindless, and passionate
motivation on the part of the undefined "masses," it at the
same time appeals to the pure spirit of the "people," the
race, or the nation for its legitimacy as an historical or trans-

formational force. Though fascists openly disdain and demean the common people, they at the same time present themselves as embodying the "spirit" of the people and the "times." Sorel's views on the purity of spontaneous and violent action, together with the historical and cathartic effect of such action on a mass level, become a rationalization for the strange irony of fascist ideology when used by Mussolini:

We have created our myth. The myth is a faith, it is a passion. It is not necessary that it shall be a reality. It is a reality by the fact that it is a goal, a hope, a faith, that it is courage. Our myth is the Nation! And to this myth, to this grandeur, that we wish to translate into a complete reality, we subordinate all the rest.[9]

Mussolini substituted the myth of the Nation for the myth of the General Strike, which was Sorel's cathartic myth. It is obviously a short step from the myth of the Nation to the myth of the Aryan race which legitimated the fascism of German nazism. Alfred Rosenberg, a leading Nazi propagandist, puts it this way:

Today a new faith is awakening: the myth of blood, the belief that it is by the blood that the divine mission of man is to be defended; the belief that, based on the clearest knowledge, Nordic blood represents that mystery which has overcome and replaced the ancient sacraments.
    The life of a race and of a people is not a philosophical creation which develops logically...it is rather the formation of a mystical synthesis, a manifestation of the soul....[10]

These myths are said to reside in the hearts and minds of the "masses," yet they are fashioned and articulated by elites or their apologists to substantiate the false universality of the alliance of power and the propertied classes, including the lower bourgeoisie in a time of economic crisis. They are explicitly antidemocratic and terroristic in the service of that alliance. The wholly nihilistic and destructive motives of the ideology of fascism, including the siege mentality of the beleaguered dominant class, imputes to the "masses" its own malevolence and fear of the loss of power. To relinquish power is to relinquish control over destiny. Rather than do that, the most retrograde of all political ideologies is used to justify retrenched political rule.

The contemporary world stands at a crossroads of our own which requires a choice between democracy or regression. The alternative of the recent past, that of muddling through, can no longer serve us as we face repeated and deep economic crises. Fascism is not simply an aberration of past historical experience. It is a developmental tendency. In contrast to the developmental tendency of progressive socialization of the benefits, burdens, and decisions of modern democratic life, fascism is a retrograde tendency, but one which is every bit as imminent. We can no longer simply take progress for granted, nor can we "suspend" democracy for the sake of economic efficiency in bad times and resurrect it again in good times. Incrementalism has never really been a mode of political choice, and it is fast becoming inadequate even as a type of managerial decision making. Authority must pass increasingly into the hands of people whose labor and common lives are the real substance of history, or into the hands of an elite who would repudiate popular government for the sake of shoring up a failing economic order. In America, with its history of racism and practice of ideological hegemony; with its traditional commitment to militarism, and its recent willingness to again "stand strong" against the communist threat (which it applies to every nation or group which seeks to avoid U.S. domination); with its recent turn away from concerns about human rights violations and its reassertion of "policeman of the world" status, we need be especially concerned about the suspension of democratic procedures and norms. Can we really accept the argument of one spokesman for the corporate elite speaking through a pronouncement of the Trilateral Commission?

Democracy...can very easily become a threat to itself in the United States. Political authority is never strong there, and it is particularly weak during a period of intense commitment to democratic and egalitarian ideals. In the United States the strength of the democratic ideal poses a problem for the governability of democracy in a way which is not the case elsewhere....

We have come to recognize that there are potentially desirable limits to economic growth. There are potentially desirable limits to the extension of political democracy.[11]

Do we dare accept this description of austerity as a description of contemporary American political life? Dare we accept this definition of the siege of democracy and in doing so accept the terms of an alliance against progress?

NOTES

1. Jean Jacques Rousseau, *The Social Contract* (1762) ed. Charles Frankell (New York: Hafner, 1947), p. 94.
2. William Kornhauser, *The Politics of Mass Society* (Glencoe, Ill.: Free Press, 1959), for example.
3. Adolf Hitler, *Mein Kampf* (1925–27), trans. Ralph Manheim (Boston: Houghton Mifflin Co., 1943), as quoted in William Ebenstein, *Modern Political Thought* (New York: Rinehart & Co., 1956), p. 328.
4. Le Bon's chief work is *The Crowd* (1895).
5. Gustave Le Bon, *The Crowd* (New York: Viking Press, 1960), p. 32.
6. Ibid., p. 37.
7. Ibid., p. 175.
8. Vilfredo Pareto, trans. Robert Josephy, *The Mind and Society*, ed. Arthur Livingston, (New York: Harcourt, Brace and Company, 1935), Vol. III, p. 1293.
9. Benito Mussolini (Naples, 24 October 1922), as quoted in Herman Finer, *Mussolini's Italy* (London: Victor Gollancz, 1935).
10. Alfred Rosenberg, *Selected Writings*, ed. Robert Pois (London: Jonathan Cape, 1970), p. 98.
11. Samuel Huntington, *The American Commonwealth*, ed. Nathan Glazer and Irving Kristol (New York: Basic Books, 1976), pp. 37–38.

BIBLIOGRAPHIC NOTE

The dominant view within the American social sciences has been that fascism is, by and large, a mass psychological reaction to crisis (historical dislocation or economic deprivation). This view includes the supposition that there exists a propensity within a mass population to accept fascism due to the inherent authoritarianism of so-called mass publics. The works that are particularly noteworthy in their focus on this psychological approach to the analysis of fascism include: T. W. Adorno, et. al., *The Authoritarian Personality* (1950); Wilhelm Reich, *The Mass Psychology of Fascism* (1946); Erich Fromm, *Escape From Freedom*; Emil Lederer, *The State of the Masses: The Threat of the Classless Society* (1940); and William Kornhauser, *The Politics of Mass Society* (1959). Our rejection of the approach is obvious in the foregone analysis as are, we hope, our reasons, both analytical and ethical. We believe the psychological approach of the texts mentioned above to be yet another example of blaming the victim. In our view it is the alienation of elites and not the masses which is the root cause of fascism.

A rather more sophisticated approach which one finds in the literature on fascism views fascism as a stage of development from feudalism to mature capitalism. For some particular reason relating to the historical specificity of a given nation's development toward capitalism (modernization), the accompanying liberalization of political institutions and cultural patterns did not occur. This may be something of a mutated development. The two most significant contributions to the "stages of mutant development" approach are A. E. Kenneth Organski's *The Stages of Political Development* (1965) and Barrington Moore Jr.'s *Social Origins of Dictatorship and Democracy* (1966). While these works deserve a close reading and have made a significant contribution to political theory, in our view they are fundamentally mistaken, for we see fascism not as the manifestation of mutant or aborted stages of development but rather as a retrograde position theoretically possible for *any* mature system. That is, we view all modern systems, socialist or capitalist, theoretically as vulnerable to a retrograde development expressing itself as fascism. While this theoretical development is, we believe, possible for all systems, it must be added that we view some systems as more vulnerable to a fascistic retrogression than others. Crisis, alone, will not precipitate such an extreme retrogression. Institutional, cultural, and *ideological* determinants of response, particularly those of elites, will determine the process. Furthermore, we view this process of fascistic retrogression as a *political* response which, while it involves to some extent the psychology of the elites (i.e., their alienation), is bound up primarily with the political and economic power which either elite classes or elite individuals possess.

For the present, in our judgement the best recent treatment on fascism is Rengo DeFelice's *Interpretations of Fascism* (1977). Particularly noteworthy are DeFelice's excerpts from and comments on *Der Fascismus* by Richard Lowenthal (pseud. Paul Sering). The following passage from Lowenthal is quoted by DeFelice (p. 53):

> Both before and after the Fascist upheaval, Capitalism dominates, but it is a Capitalism in which there are certain mutations: it is a Capitalism with restricted limits of accumulation, where economic dead weights abound, where the destruction of capital increases, and where there are more parasitic and reactionary strata. It is a Capitalism, moreover, with highly developed forces of production and organization, and where chaos prompts an increased need for planning the general result of these Capitalist transformations, particularly in their reactionary aspects, in the transformation of the state into a state which undertakes a policy of subsidizations.

BIBLIOGRAPHY

Adorno, Theodor W., et. al. *The Authoritarian Personality*. New York: Harper, 1960.

Arendt, Hannah. *The Origins of Totalitarianism*. New York: Meridian Books, 1958.

Bullock, Allan. *Hitler: A Study in Tyranny*. New York: Bantam Books, 1958.

Burnham, James. *The Managerial Revolution*. New York: John Day, 1941.

Cammett, J. M. "Communist Theories of Fascism," 1920–1935." *Science and Society*, No. 2 (1967).

DeFelice, Renzo. *Interpretations of Fascism*. Brenda Huff Everett, trans. Cambridge, Mass.: Harvard University Press, 1977. (Originally published Rome: Guis. Laterzo y Figli, 1969.)

Dobb, Maurice Herbert. *Political Economy and Capitalism: Some Essays in Economic Tradition*. London: Routledge, 1937.

Finer, Herman. *Mussolini's Italy*. London: Victor Gollancz, 1935.

Fromm, Erich. *Escape From Freedom*. New York: Holt, Rinehart, 1941.

Gentile, Giovani. *Genesis and Structure of Society*. H. S. Harris, trans. Urbana, Ill.: University of Illinois Press, 1960.

———— "The Philosophic Basis of Fascism." *Foreign Affairs*, Vol. 6 (January 1928).

deGovineur, Arthur. *The Inequality of the Human Races*. A. Collins, trans. New York: C. P. Putnam's Sons, 1915.

Gregor, A. James. *Interpretation of Fascism*. Morristown, N.J.: General Learning Press, 1974.

———— *The Fascist Persuasion in Radical Politics*. Princeton, N.J.: Princeton University Press, 1974.

———— *The Ideology of Fascism: The Rationale of Totalitarianism*. New York: The Free Press, 1969.

Hayes, Paul M. *Fascism*. London: Allen & Unwin, 1973.

Hitler, Adolf. *Mein Kampf*. Ralph Manheim, trans. Boston: Houghton Mifflin, 1962.

Hoffer, Eric. *The True Believer*. New York: Mentor Books, 1958.

Huntington, Samuel. "The Democratic Distemper" in Nathan Glazer and Irving Kristol, eds., *The American Commonwealth*. New York: Basic Books, 1976.

Kornhauser, William. *The Politics of Mass Society*. Glencoe, Ill.: Free Press, 1959.

Laqueur, Walter, ed., *Fascism: A Reader's Guide*. Berkeley, Ca.: University of California Press, 1976.

LeBon, Gustave. *The Crowd*. New York: Viking Press, 1960. (Originally published in 1895).

Lederer, Emil. *The State of the Masses: The Threat of the Classless Society*. New York: W. W. Norton, 1940.

Lipset, Seymour Martin. *Political Man: The Social Basics of Politics*. Garden City, N.Y.: Doubleday, 1960.

Michels, Robert. *Political Parties*. New York: Free Press, 1966. (Originally published in 1915.)

Moore, Barrington Jr. *Social Origins of Dictatorship and Democracy; Lord and Peasant in the Making of the Modern World*. Boston: Beacon, 1966.

Mosca, Gaetano. *The Ruling Class*. New York: McGraw-Hill Book Co., 1939. (Originally published in Italian, 1896.)

Mussolini, Benito. *Fascism: Doctrine and Institutions*. Rome: Ardita, 1935.

—— *Four Speeches on the Corporate State*. Rome: Laboremus, 1935.

—— *My Autobiography*. New York: Charles Scribner's Sons, 1928.

—— *The Corporate State*. Florence: Vallecchi, 1936.

Nolte, Ernst. *Three Faces of Fascism: Action Française, Italian Fascism, National Socialism*. Leila Vennewitz, trans. New York: Holt, Rinehart & Winston, 1966.

Organski, A. F. Kenneth. *The Stages of Political Development*. New York: Alfred A. Knopf, 1965.

Pareto, Vilfredo. *The Mind and Society*. Vol. III. Arthur Livingston, ed., and Roberto Josephy, trans. New York: Harcourt, Brace, 1935.

Reich, Wilhelm. *The Mass Psychology of Fascism*. Vincent R. Carfagno, trans. New York: Farrar, Straus and Giroux, 1970.

Rosco, Alberto. *The Political Doctrine of Fascism*. D. Bigongiari, trans. New York: International Conciliation Pamphlet, No. 223, Carnegie Endowment for International Peace, 1926.

Rosenberg, Alfred. *Selected Writings*. Robert Paris, ed. London: Jonathan Cape, 1970.

Rousseau, Jean Jacques. *The Social Contract* (1762). Charles Frankel, ed. New York: Hafner, 1947.

Samuels, Warren J. *Pareto and Policy*. The Hague: Elsevier, 1974.

Shirer, William L. *The Rise and Fall of the Third Reich*. Greenwich, Conn.: Crest Books, 1962.

Sorel, Georges. *Reflections on Violence*. T. E. Hulme and J. Roth, trans. New York: Collier Books, 1961. (Copyright by Free Press, 1950; first published in book form in French, 1908).

Speer, Albert. *Inside the Third Reich: Memoirs*. New York: Macmillan, 1970.

———— *Spandau, The Secret Diaries*. New York: Macmillan, 1976.

Sweezy, Paul M. *The Theory of Capitalist Development*. New York: Monthly Review Press, 1942.

Toland, John. *Adolf Hitler*. Garden City, N.Y.: Doubleday, 1976.

GLOSSARY

Alienation—a condition of existence whereby people have lost their naturally close relationship to their immediate environment. With Marx, this condition is underscored by a loss of the social character of life through class oppression.

Apathy, Political—an attitude of disinterestedness in politics. In the recent past, pluralist theory incorrectly assumed this to be a psychological attribute of the masses, and an element of contemporary life that facilitated political stability.

Aristocracy, Landed Gentry—a class whose position in society is determined by their ownership of the land, when such ownership was the primary form of wealth; today, the titled descendants of the great landholders of the past. In antiquity, aristocrats comprised a class noted for their ideas of honor, wisdom, and "correct" rule, in contrast to the oligarchic classes whose sole interest was the acquisition of wealth and power.

Balanced Budget—exists when expenditures and receipts of a unit of government (usually refers to the federal government) are equal. Considered a desirable state by economic conservatives.

Balance of Payments, International Finance—comprises a nation's aggregate international economic transactions over a period of time. Balance is established when transfers of money exiting the country equal its income from abroad. A favorable balance is said to exist when the flow of goods and services exiting the country exceeds that coming in; an unfavorable balance is the reverse.

Balance of Trade—the difference in value over a period of time between a country's imports and exports.

259

Bourgeoisie—"By bourgeoisie is meant the class of modern Capitalists, owners of social production and employers of wage labor."
(Karl Marx and Frederick Engels, *Manifesto of the Communist Party*, trans. and footnoted definition by Engels in the English Edition of 1888.)

Business Cycle—fluctuation in the vitality of business investment that leads to regular cycles of expansion and contraction of the economy. This may occur due to contingencies such as technological innovation, governmental economic policy, or natural disaster, etc. Marxist economists conceptualize a "long wave" decline of capitalist economic systems due to the rising organic composition of capital. (See also Constant Capital and Variable Capital.)

Capitalism—a system of production following feudalism in historical time and a progressive step in human history. During capitalism the forces of production (capital), consisting of tools, equipment, machinery, factories, information, organization, etc., are controlled by private individuals for the purpose of acquiring profit and accumulation based on the employment of wage-labor. Before history can progress beyond the increasingly stagnant state of capitalism (late or moribund capitalism) as an historical epoch, and move on to socialism, control over the means of production must be obtained by the mass of laborers for social ends rather than private profit.

Central Committee of the USSR—the executive branch of the Communist party. Its most significant committees are the Politburo and the Secretariat. A subject of dispute among students of the Soviet system is the degree of autonomy exercised by the Central Committee in relation to the powers of the Politburo.

Class—a term denoting the division of society into separate categories (capitalist, proletariat, and landowner) whose members are conscious of their discrete and separate interests vis-à-vis competing and antagonistic classes. Position within a class is determined by 1) the individual's relationship to the mode of production and 2) group consciousness. With Lenin, the articulation of class interests and control through an organization such as a political party further defines class.

Command Economy—a term used to distinguish a centrally planned and directed economy such as the Soviet Union's, from a market economy, where only loosely coordinated market forces are presumed to direct the quality and quantity of goods produced. (See Market Economy.)

Commodity Fetish—characteristic of a social relation of production where people who are alienated from their labor and from each other attribute "human" characteristics to things (possessions). John G. Gurley succinctly explains how this comes about:

> Labor and the means of production...are forces (factors) of production. But, in the capitalist mode, labor becomes wage-labor, a commodity, a material thing; means of production becomes capital, incarnated in a capitalist. Thus, living labor becomes a thing, and capital, which is dead (embodied) labor, becomes alive in the capitalist; an inversion of subject and object is accomplished.

> The acceptance, as the real thing, of the distortion that transfers social relations from people to their products, leads to a series of illusions and fantasies. *Commodities become fetishes in the same way that gods, the creations of humans, take on lives of their own*, fashioning social relations among themselves and the human world. In the religion of everyday life, objects are endowed with life, taking on the powers relinquished by their producers, who, as a consequence, diminish and deceive themselves; the objects come to rule over man. (John G. Gurley. *Challengers to Capitalism*, 2d ed. 1979, pp. 47–48.) (Emphasis added.)

Communism—a militant world-historical movement that seeks to abolish private property, class, and alienation:

> ...with the abolition of the basis of private property, with the communistic regulation of production (and implicit in this, the destruction of the alien relation between men and what they themselves produce), the power of the relation of supply and demand is dissolved into nothing, and men get exchange, production, the mode of their mutual relation under their own control again.

> Communism is for us not a *state of affairs* which is to be established, an *ideal* to which reality (will) have to adjust itself. We call communism the *real* movement which abolishes the present state of things. (Karl Marx and Frederick Engels. *The German Ideology*, 1845–46. Part I, International Publishers ed., pp. 25–26).

Computopia—a term referring to the view that the problems of a centrally planned economy may be solved by the development of ever more intricate and computerized mathematical models.

Constant Capital, "c"—a term used by Karl Marx to designate the value, measured in socially necessary labor time, of goods and raw materials used up in the production of a commodity. The term is used in distinction from variable capital, which is the wage paid in the production of commodities (the "Wage bill"). The formula c/v expresses the organic composition of capital and is the ratio of capital to labor costs.

Consumption—the proportion of one's income spent on goods. The gross national product is composed of personal consumption expenditures, gross private investment, government purchases of goods and services, and net foreign investment.

Counter-Cyclical Economic Measures—actions taken or policies formulated that are intended to have the effect of combating either recession or inflation. For example, a deliberate deficit of the federal government may be created to stimulate the economy and thereby overcome a recession; or an increase in taxes may be legislated in an effort to slow down inflation. Unemployment insurance and the income tax are considered automatic counter-cyclical devices.

Cybernetics—the study of artificial intelligence begun in the 1940s with the discovery of negative feedback as the hypothetical key to the working of the central nervous system and, thus, the beginning of thought. The development of computers and their simulation of cognitive processes has spurred research dealing with information processes and the post-industrial "production of intelligence."

Cynicism—a negative and denunciatory state of mind typified by a highly egoistic, antisocial, and ascetic posture of the individual toward society. So-called after the "dog-philosophers" of the Greek and Roman antiquity (3rd century B.C. to 2nd century A.D.) of whom Diogenes is well-celebrated.

Deficit Spending—a deliberate governmental policy to spend more than it receives back in revenues, with the purpose of stimulating the economy.

Democratic Centralism—a principle of the Communist party initiated by V. I. Lenin, that all party members, prior to a final decision being taken on a matter of policy, present their views in open and free discussion. Debate and opposition must cease and party discipline be adhered to after a decision is made and articulated.

Democratic Socialism—an ideology which maintains that socialism can and should be obtained through democratic (parliamentary) means as opposed to revolutionary means, and that the preservation of political and civil liberties such as freedom of speech and loyal opposition must be safeguarded.

Dialectical Materialism—with Karl Marx and Frederick Engels, an understanding of society and history based upon the material conditions of the lives of people; the social/political/economic interaction of people within those conditions; and the conscious efforts of people to change and determine the material conditions of their lives. This is in opposition to the "idealist" notion of Georg Hegel, for example, who would stress ideas and the Spirit as directing the development of the world. Matter and activity are conceived of as the fundamental impetus of human history, and change is considered the constant condition of that history.

Disposable Income—the money possesed by individuals after taxes.

Division of Labor—according to Adam Smith, the efficient division of production into simple tasks that enables increases in the volume and extent of industry. Taylorism, a "scientific management" movement of the late nineteenth and early twentieth century (named after its originator, Frederick Winslow Taylor), provided the twentieth century prototype of the organization of the labor process according to efficiency-of-production standards (only excluding the marginal concerns for the problem of a dehumanized workplace which even Smith had).

Egalitarianism—an ideology advocating equal division of income and/or wealth; in practice, generally a preference for greater relative equality of income than already exists, or a term used when comparing one society to another.

Elitism—an approach to decision-making theory in political science that places a defined and stable group of people at the center of the political process, in control of the outputs of a political system. As such, this group exerts power over non-decision-makers and repudiates the claim of pluralism that both decision-making and power are highly democratic in polyarchy.

Empiricism—the belief that all knowledge arises from experience; that understanding is an exclusively inductive process; and that the atomistic individual is the author of his or her own experience.

Equilibrium, Economic—a notion that there exists in the economy a natural tendency for the economy to seek a level at which there is full employment of labor and optimal employment of the factors of production. This notion is based on Say's Law (1767–1832) which states that "supply creates its own demand." Until John Maynard Keynes proved that the economy may reach equilibrium at any level of employment—certainly well below full employment—this notion of equilibrium was a cornerstone of classical economics.

Equilibrium, Political—a central concept of pluralist theory which holds that there exists a natural point of equilibrium in American society in which all groups have roughly the same access to political resources and power; that the latent ability of all groups, apparent and potential, to influence those who possess political resources is always in balance. This tendency toward balance is the measure of democracy. Elitist theory refutes these contentions.

Exchange Value/Use Value—as Adam Smith observed, goods are valued because they are intrinsically useful (possessing "use value"), and also because they may be exchanged for some other goods that the purchaser desired ("exchange value"). Both Adam Smith and Karl Marx believed that the ultimate value of a commodity was the amount of *socially* useful labor used to produce it.

Feudalism—the mode of production prevalent in the Middle Ages in which landed aristocracy, as the ruling class, oversaw the direct appropriation of agricultural surplus from the peasant/serf class. This manorial economy had as its political and juridical superstructure the absolutist state, whose function became ever more central to the feudal epoch as money rents replaced direct expropriation of the surplus.

Fiscal Crisis—the inability of government to continue to subsidize the profitability of business, while at the same time providing the social welfare requisites of a modern industrial state.

Fiscal Policy—a government policy of deliberately incurring a deficit or a surplus, in order to either stimulate or check the expansion of the economy; usually referred to in contrast to monetary policy, which is based upon the manipulation of the money supply through the interest rates.

Free Enterprise—a euphemism for capitalism.

Gini Index—a statistical measure of the degree of income equality that exists in a nation.

Gosplan—the central planning agency of the USSR; in charge of developing the five year plans that have shaped the development of the Soviet economy.

Gross National Product, GNP—a measure, in dollar amounts, of the value of the total goods and services produced in a given country.

Guild Socialism—an ideology which advocates that workers be represented politically, according to their craft or occupation—so-called "functional representation." As formulated by G. D. H. Cole, it is a forerunner of the "worker control" or "worker participation" movements of contemporary society.

Hegemony—a term referring to the domination and control of one nation or class over another; usually the extent of domination includes either an overt or insidious control of ideology, values, beliefs, and language beyond mere control of physical means (economic production or the State), but includes economic penetration.

Historical Dialectic—a concept of history that posits historical movement in terms of a progressive and dialectical pattern; the interaction of time (history) and matter (material) through human activity (praxis).

Historicism—a disparaging term leveled against those whose historical inquiry is considered by critics to be deterministic, that is, believing that the course of history is inevitable; a false charge used by Karl Popper against Plato, Hegel, and Marx.

Humanistic/Humanism—a philosophy which asserts that humans are the measure of all things; emphasizing the value of freedom in the provision of individual human development, and stressing the limitless nature of human potential.

Ideology—a logical system of beliefs that acts to structure reality; a belief system that serves to justify and rationalize an existing social order, e.g., liberalism is the ideology of capitalism; an elaborate misinterpretation of reality, supported *post hoc* by empirical "fact":

> Once upon a time an honest fellow had the idea that men were drowned in water only because they were possessed with the idea of gravity. If they were to knock this superstition out of their heads, say by stating it to be a superstition, a religious idea, they would be sublimely proof against any danger from water. His whole life long he fought against the illusion of gravity, of whose harmful results all statistics brought him new and manifold evidence. (Karl Marx and Frederick Engels, Preface to *The German Ideology*, 1846).

Inflation—a steady and persistent rise in prices.
> *Cost-push inflation* assumes the generator of high prices is the increase in the cost of production, especially increases in wages exceeding increases in the level of productivity.
> *Demand-pull inflation* assumes the generator of high prices to be too much money in the hands of consumers.
> *Profit-push inflation* assumes the cause of high inflation to be the ability of near-monopoly corporate enterprise to maintain and increase a profit margin beyond the requirements of the market.

Infrastructure—a term denoting the public facilities that enable the capitalist system to function beyond mere economic production, e.g.: law, courts and penal institutions, transport networks, educational systems, currency, etc.

Intelligentsia—those among the intellectuals who possess a consciousness of their membership in an "elite" class that sets them apart from others; sometimes, those involved in the "production of knowledge" in a post-industrial society.

International Monetary Fund—a concern of John Maynard Keynes; created by the Breton Woods Agreement among capitalist nations to function as a central fund to which member countries would subscribe for the purpose of promoting and stabilizing monetary transactions among countries.

Instrumentalism—the view held by critics of capitalism that the state exists primarily as an "instrument" of the ruling class and exercises little autonomy vis-à-vis that class. This view is held in contrast to the "structuralist" view which conceives of the state as a structured arrangement (through law and convention) and segmentation of power within the state. Both the structure of the state and of capitalism itself is thereby reified and, to some extent, autonomous from the direct or arbitrary control of individual capitalists. This autonomy is thought to provide an explanation for the phenomenon of discipline that may be enforced against individual firms or industries by the state (e.g., through regulatory legislation or legal prosecution).

Keynesian Economics—a contemporary economic approach that adheres to the view expressed in the writings of John Maynard Keynes, especially those views that contain a critique of traditional economic equilibrium theory (see Glossary), which accepts the necessity of state intervention in the regulation of the economy (particularly in the maintenance and stabilization of full employment).

Labor Theory of Value—a conceptualization of economic value based upon the quantity of socially useful labor that is expended in the production of the good; a view held by Adam Smith and Karl Marx, among others.

Laissez-Faire Economic Policy—the view that the state should not be involved in any incursion into natural market functioning of the economy, beyond the provision of an infrastructure such as law, order, and national defense; "the state which governs least, governs best."

Legitimation—a political system is considered legitimate when the monopoly of force exercised by the state is accepted by the people and considered by them to be justly exercised. Max Weber believed that people obeyed decisions for three main reasons: tradition, charisma (the magnetic and extraordinary appeal of the leader), and legality (the force of law). State and ideology promote legitimacy. The production and control of information and knowledge, and the orchestration of idea-formation (through the media or education) in contemporary society, are also important aspects of legitimation. The breakdown of legitimation is a prerequisite to revolution.

Liberalism—the ideology of capitalism that places great emphasis upon freedom and individualism. In contemporary times, conservativism is actually a variety of liberalism that particularly addresses the requirement for a laissez-faire posture of government toward the economy and society, while the positive version of liberalism advocates a measure of state intervention in the provision of opportunity to promote individual self-realization.

Lumpenproletariat—a term used by Marx to designate an intermediate, and to some extent, extraneous class comprised of the lowest elements of society; society's dropouts or victims—thieves, social degenerates, etc.,—who are important to a class analysis in terms of their potential support for and exploitation by demagogues.

Macroeconomics—a branch of the study of economics that takes as its focus aggregate functions in the economy; concerned, e.g., with aggregate demand, supply, investment, income, and the like, in contrast to disaggregated or microeconomics that focuses upon such activities as decision-making within the firm or particular industry-oriented movement.

Marginal Propensity to Consume—the proportion of an additional income unit that a person or an aggregation of individuals would spend; e.g., if my income is $30,000 and I receive an additional $1,000 and spend $800 of the money while saving $200, my propensity to consume expressed as a ratio would be .8; a concept which is central to understanding the Keynesian multiplier. See Multiplier (Keynesian).

Market Economy—an economy in which the quantity and quality of goods to be produced is determined by demand for the product as expressed in the marketplace. In a perfect competition economy, no producer or purchaser would be large enough to influence the market price. Such a pure market economy does not, in fact, exist and is rather a model developed by economists for heuristic purposes.

Market Socialism—a market economy that is regulated by a central agency such as the state or council of workers, for the purpose of controlling the quantity and quality of commodities produced while attempting to keep intact the demand-side of market forces; a response to the "anarchy of the marketplace" in the targeting and control of investment of surplus and production.

Materialism—the view that it is the material conditions of the immediate world that shape our thoughts, values, social relations—ourselves. Furthermore, both the subjective life of the individual and the social life that we all share become conscious activity and result in the "making of history" when the material basis and consequence of all human activity is comprehended.

Microeconomics—a branch of the study of economics that takes as its focus the study of the individual firm and the multitude of decisions and decision-making procedures operating at that level; in contrast to macroeconomics, which takes as its focus the aggregate economic system, and its functions.

Mode of Production—the manner in which the productive forces of an economy are organized, including the social relations surrounding such organization, during a given epoch in history; e.g., feudalism, capitalism, and socialism are discrete modes of production characterized by the particular manner in which surplus is extracted from the labor process and by the social relations and social/political/religious structures surrounding that process.

Monetary Policy—manipulation of the economy through manipulation of the money supply through interest rates.

Multiplier (Keynesian)—depending upon the marginal propensity to consume, an increase in one's income will have a multiplier effect and thereby increase total aggregate income. This occurs because any new unit of income spent becomes an additional new unit of income, for the seller a proportion of which is again spent by every successive seller.

Negative Freedom—the view that freedom depends upon the absence of external constraints. One is free, in Hobbes' words, "if you are not hindered from doing what you have the wit and will to do." (*Leviathan*, 1651.) This view fails to take into account, among other things, contingent and restricting factors such as poverty, lack of education, illness, and the continuous and *systemic* deprivation of classes or races of people; this is the dominant view of freedom within liberalism.

Neo-Marxism—contemporary theorists who accept, with various modifications, Karl Marx's basic theories regarding socialist organization, capitalist exploitation, dialectical materialism, history, and economics.

Nomenklatura—a system of clearances granted by the Communist party in the USSR that authorizes a person to hold a sensitive position such as a newspaper editor.

Oligopoly—a condition within the economy where a few firms produce most of the output in a given industry, e.g., cigarettes, automobiles, baby food, etc.

Phillips Curve—an inflation-unemployment relation is expressed schematically by the Phillips curve. This relation is believed to exist as an inverse relationship between inflation and unemployment; named after a British economist who, in a study of the British economy over a long period of time, provided empirical evidence to show that sustained periods of full employment are not possible without inflation.

Philosophical Radicalism—a term applied to early utilitarian thought, the chief proponents of which were James Mill and Jeremy Bentham.

Pluralism—an approach to the study of politics in the United States which assumes that political power is widely dispersed, that contending groups have roughly equal opportunity to the access of political resources, that electoral politics provide the most appropriate mechanisms for public accountability and representation, and that the stability and permeability of politics in the United States is highly exemplary as a model of liberal democracy; this approach has been repudiated by theories of elitism. (See Glossary)

Politburo—the policy-making agency of the Central Committee of the USSR Communist party; the most powerful organization in the Soviet Union; chaired by the Secretary of the Communist party.

Political Economy—a contemporary movement within academe to reunite the study of economics and politics in an effort to overcome the theoretical poverty that has been extant in both disciplines since their separation.

Positive Liberalism—a variety of contemporary liberalism which holds that the state can enhance freedom through direct action in the provision of opportunities for self-realization (education, job-training, medical care, etc.); based on the belief that guarantees of freedom without the provision of means to realize one's individual potential are meaningless; this is in contrast to the negative freedom variant of liberalism that continues to dominate contemporary liberalism.

Possessive Individualism—according to C. B. Macpherson (see Bibliography, Chapter Three), the underlying philosophical premise of the liberalism of Hobbes and Locke and, therefore, of liberalism generally; the belief that individuals have sole domain over their own being and are therefore exempt from obligation to society or anyone, as well as justified in an extremely acquisitive posture toward society and the natural world. This, according to Macpherson, is the Achilles heel of liberalism.

Praxis—the Marxian view that it is only through the combination of theory (reflective thinking) and practice that one can comprehend reality.

Profit—the share of surplus created by labor after the factors of production (labor, rent, interest,materials, depreciation) have been paid.

Proletariat—"By proletariat (is meant), the class of modern wage-labourers who, having no means of production of their own, are reduced to selling their labour-power in order to live."
(Karl Marx and Frederick Engels. *The Communist Manifesto.* trans. and footnoted by Engels in the English Edition of 1888).

Public Goods—those goods that are distinguished from market commodities by the fact that enjoyment of the benefits cannot be withheld from anyone in the public domain; if the good is to exist at all it must of necessity be shared. An example of a public good that is becoming less available is clean air.

Rate of Exploitation—a key concept of Marx which holds that in a capitalist economy the only reason that a laborer would be employed would be that he produced for the person who employed him more than he was paid. Marx almost always expressed this in terms of man hours, e.g., a laborer worked eight hours but received in wages the value of what he produced in six hours, the value of what he produced in the other two hours would be taken from him by his employer. This was expressed by Marx in the following formula $r = s/v$, (r is the rate of exploitation, s is surplus, and v is variable capital—the wage bill).

Rate of Profit—the percentage return on investment. Marx believed that there was a tendency for the rate of profit to fall and that this falling rate of profit gave rise to the recurring crisis in capitalism.

Reserve Army of the Unemployed—a position held by Marx that capitalism depended on the maintenance of a large body of unemployed workers whose existence kept pressure on wage rates and helped discipline workers who lived in fear of unemployment.

Say's Law—a French economist, J. B. Say (1767–1832), advanced the proposition that supply created its own demand and, therefore, there could not be overproduction or inadequate demand. Keynes has demonstrated that Say was incorrect.

Secretariat of the Communist Party—a party organ responsible for party organization, discipline, and ideological indoctrination.

Self-Realization—a position initially formulated by T. H. Green which holds that the end of man is the self-realization of his potential. Advocates of positive freedom also believe that people are free only to the extent that they are able to realize their human potential.

Socialism—a mode of production in which the productive forces are owned by the state or by the workers themselves. Private property exists only in the form of consumer goods and personal possessions, not in capital goods, i.e., those used in the production of other commodities. In the Soviet Union it is used to designate the current status of development, a transitory phase on the way to pure communism, at which time the state would atrophy.

Species-Being—the term used by Marx to refer to those qualities or conditions of people that are uniquely human, especially, those characterized by human labor.

Stagflation—a description of the economy in which there exists both recession and inflation, a condition that many economists only recently thought could not occur but one that has rather persistently plagued capitalist nations for the past decade.

Structuralism—a view held by some Marxists that while the state has a measure of autonomy from the ruling class, it does nevertheless operate to foster the long-run interest of capital. In doing so the state may, however, act against the short-run interests of even a majority of capitalists, if it were essential to do so for the ultimate survival of capitalism. Many Marxists see the "New Deal" as just that type of "systemic" response by the state.

Subsistence Wage—a Marxian principle that wages have a tendency to be at subsistence level in capitalism, subsistence being defined as the wages necessary to ensure a constant and adequate supply of labor, and sufficient to enable the laboring class to reproduce itself. It is defined in relative terms—a subsistence wage in the United States would be, of necessity, much higher than one in India.

Underconsumption—the lack of adequate aggregate demand, which is seen to be one of the major causes of recession.

Utilitarianism—a philosophy which holds that the motivating drive of man is to seek pleasure and avoid pain. Its chief proponent was Jeremy Bentham (see Bibliography, Chapter Three), who advocated "the greatest good for the greatest number."

Variable Capital—the term used by Marx for the direct labor costs used in the production process (the wage bill), in contrast to constant capital, which is a measure of the labor impounded in goods and raw materials used in the production of commodities.

Welfare State—a term frequently used to describe those societies in which the state provides a large amount of the social services, such as health care and economic security from unemployment.

World Bank—an international institution that, on the basis of subscription from the larger capitalist nations, makes loans to developing countries. It and the International Monetary Fund are institutions that enable the leading capitalist countries to exercise world hegemony, through finance.

INDEX